D0509090

what color is your smoothie?

From Red Berry Roundup to Super Smart Purple Tart—
300 Recipes for Vibrant Health

Britt Allen Brandon, CFNS, CPT

Author of *The Everything® Green Smoothies Book* with Nicole Cormier, RD, LDN

Aadamsmedia

Avon, Massachusetts

Published by Adams Media,
a division of F+W Media, Inc.
57 Littlefield Street, Avon, MA 02322. U.S.A.
www.adamsmedia.com

Contains material adapted and abridged from *The Everything® Green Smoothies Book* by Britt Brandon with Lorena Novak Bull, RD, copyright © 2011 by F+W Media, Inc., ISBN 10: 1-4405-2564-1, ISBN 13: 978-1-4405-2564-3.

ISBN 10: 1-4405-3616-3
ISBN 13: 978-1-4405-3616-8
eISBN 10: 1-4405-3627-9
eISBN 13: 978-1-4405-3627-4

Printed in the United States of America.

10   9   8   7   6   5   4   3   2   1

Library of Congress Cataloging-in-Publication Data
is available from the publisher.

This publication is designed to provide accurate and authoritative information with regard to the subject matter covered. It is sold with the understanding that the publisher is not engaged in rendering legal, accounting, or other professional advice. If legal advice or other expert assistance is required, the services of a competent professional person should be sought.

—From a *Declaration of Principles* jointly adopted by a Committee of the American Bar Association and a Committee of Publishers and Associations

Many of the designations used by manufacturers and sellers to distinguish their product are claimed as trademarks. Where those designations appear in this book and Adams Media was aware of a trademark claim, the designations have been printed with initial capital letters.

This book is intended as general information only, and should not be used to diagnose or treat any health condition. In light of the complex, individual, and specific nature of health problems, this book is not intended to replace professional medical advice. The ideas, procedures, and suggestions in this book are intended to supplement, not replace, the advice of a trained medical professional. Consult your physician before adopting any of the suggestions in this book, as well as about any condition that may require diagnosis or medical attention. The author and publisher disclaim any liability arising directly or indirectly from the use of this book.

This book is available at quantity discounts for bulk purchases. For information, please call 1-800-289-0963.

For my wonderful husband, Jimmy, and my beautiful children, Lilly, Lonni, and J.D.

Acknowledgments

I would like to say "thank you" to all of the amazing people who helped me turn the dream for this book into a reality!

To my amazing husband, Jimmy, who has been so wonderfully supportive in every step of this book's production. Thank you for always encouraging me to follow my dreams and for sharing in my excitement every step of the way! Thank you for creating an amazing life with me that only gets better each, and every, day! You are the best husband and the best friend anyone could ever ask for!

To my wonderful children, Lilly, Lonni, and JD: thank you for making my life absolutely amazing . . . and more than I ever dreamed it could be. Because of you, I always want to be better, yet try to appreciate what I have and what I am every day. I look at the three of you and hope to live a long, healthy life, to have the privilege of watching you grow and learn, to love you as beautiful children and amazing adults, and to know that I helped make this world a better place by bringing three of the most wonderful people into it. I love you more than you'll ever know!

To my dad: Thank you for everything! I love you so much, and I will be forever grateful to you for showing me the value of being a good person. Thank you for teaching me to follow my dreams and never give up! You're the best dad . . . and I love you!

To my brother, Neal: Your dedication to our never-ending sibling competitiveness inspires me that much more!

To my mom: I love you!

To the most sincere, supportive, positive, and loving best friend anyone could ever ask for: Jaimee, I can't tell you how thankful I am to have someone as wonderful as you in my life. Without your help, this book would never have been possible.

To the wonderful editors at Adams Media, namely Andrea Hakanson, for making this book possible.

Thank you! Thank you! Thank you!

Contents

Introduction

White. Red. Orange. Yellow. Green. Blue. Violet. Sound familiar? It should! These are the colors of the rainbow and today they represent a lot more than just a pretty optical illusion. Here, you'll learn how to "eat the rainbow"—to use brightly colored produce, each with its own high amounts of different concentrated nutrients—and reap the benefits of the wide variety of vitamins and minerals that your body needs to function at its best. You see, each distinct color, whether it be yellow or green or blue, has its own unique phytochemicals that indicate the powerful vitamins and minerals contained in those specifically colored foods. For example, a single cup of bright orange carrots provides almost *seven* times an entire day's worth of vitamin A in addition to a healthy helping of beta-carotene and potassium, while a cup of deep green spinach contains *eleven* times an entire day's worth of vitamin K boosted by its rich content of lutein and folate. And what better way to make sure that your body is getting the serious life-changing health benefits it deserves than through a healthy, delicious smoothie!

You may wonder why something as simple as a smoothie would be the "perfect" remedy for a less-than-nutritional diet. Well, getting into a new routine that focuses on better nutrition is a perfect place to start proactively changing your life for the better. Still, it can be difficult to find a quick, easy way to fit these nutrients into your busy schedule. Fortunately, a smoothie is something that's quickly prepared, easy to drink on the go, designed to your tastes, and packed with tons of valuable nutrients. It's honestly one of the healthiest meal or snack options available. With delicious produce that can satisfy your hunger with great taste and powerful health benefits, these tailor-made delights may just become your new favorite food!

You want to make sure to prepare your smoothies yourself, though. Almost everyone has taken note of the "smoothie movement," and these puréed fruit and vegetable sensations are popping up in the most unexpected places. Even popular fast-food chains have started introducing fruit smoothies on their menus as some of their "healthier" options. While these "fruit" concoctions may tote labels like "fresh fruit" and "fresh ingredients," these not-so-super smoothies are packed full of excessive amounts of sugar, fat, and calories, which far outweigh any benefits that they may bring to the table. While it may be tempting to opt for one of these quick-stop smoothies, keep in mind that *you* didn't create that smoothie, so *you* don't know what went into it. Instead, stay on the safe side and opt for a homemade, hand-selected, health-minded smoothie with benefits that will far outweigh those of any restaurant's smoothie every single time.

So, get ready to sip the rainbow! After all, the pot of gold that you'll find at the end is full of healthy, nutritious, delicious, and easy-to-make smoothies that will get you started on the path to looking good and feeling even better! Enjoy!

Part 1

Find Your Rainbow

The vibrantly colored fruits and vegetables found throughout this book work their magic in ways as unique as their shades. Each piece of produce is full of its own blend of vitamins, minerals, and phytochemicals that impacts different areas and functions of the body in different ways. In this part, you'll learn about the benefits each vitamin, mineral, and phytochemical provides as well as what nutrients are found in each fruit, veggie, and herb that you'll use to create your smoothies. The bottom line is this: You can take control of Your health and better your life by indulging in delicious, nutritious smoothie combinations that make drinking the rainbow easier than you ever thought possible!

Chapter 1

Nature's Formula for Better Health

Every day, millions of people around the world suffer from lack of energy, lack of focus, and restless sleep. But why settle for exhaustion when you can live a great life that's packed with days of energizing, long-lasting, productive satisfaction? Feeling great, looking great, and living your life to the fullest every day can become your new reality!

It sounds simplistic, but the truth is that you are what you eat and drink. And, while we all know that studies and research have shown the importance of consuming fruits and vegetables, few of us eat the five daily servings that are recommended by the USDA. But, by eating—and drinking!—an abundance of natural produce with as many colors as possible, you can deliver a wide spectrum of nutrients to your body. In this chapter, you'll learn how the vitamins, minerals, and macronutrients in the smoothies found in this book will turn your body into a clean, fuel-burning machine. Specifically, you'll learn the importance of phytochemicals and polyphenols, and you'll learn how sipping the rainbow will help you feel great, live a terrific life, and thoroughly enjoy every day just by improving your nutrition. So let's learn how you can make the most of the foods you choose!

Color Me Healthy

As you may know, each color group of fruit and vegetables has specific vitamins, minerals, and phytochemicals in levels that are higher than in other colored fruits. Because the actual colors of fruits and vegetables are byproducts of the naturally occurring chemicals and nutrients they contain, most of the produce belonging to each group contain many of the same elements. For example, strawberries and tomatoes both belong to the red group of produce, but while they share similar nutrients such as vitamin C, tomatoes have an abundant amount of lycopene and strawberries are packed full of manganese. A general list of the nutrients found in each color group appears below:

- **White:** While the paler colored fruits and vegetables may look like they contain less powerful nutrients, produce such as bananas and pears contain rich amounts of B vitamins and minerals such as calcium and magnesium. The high content of beta-glucans and lignans that are unique to white fruits and vegetables make their delicious addition to your daily diet that much more beneficial.
- **Red:** Red fruits and vegetables, such as tomatoes and watermelon, are typically high in vitamins A (beta-carotene) and C, as well as minerals such as manganese and zinc. Surprisingly, many red fruits and vegetables

(especially watermelon) contribute essential protein in addition to their abundant vitamins and minerals. The ellagic acid and hesperidin in the bright red varieties of fruits and veggies make for delicious disease-fighters with loads of vitamins and minerals that perform a variety of health-promoting tasks.

- **Orange:** Bright orange fruits and vegetables are packed with vitamin A (especially cantaloupe and mango) and B vitamins, in addition to important potassium and selenium. These rich sources of beta-carotene and lycopene add major health benefits to every fruit and vegetable in this vibrant group of produce.
- **Yellow:** Yellow produce contains high amounts of A, Bs, and C vitamins, and powerful minerals such as manganese and magnesium. Fighting cancers and high cholesterol is easy with these yellow tasty fruits and veggies because they contain abundant amounts of flavonoids and zeaxanthin that help to build immunity, protect cells, and promote overall health.
- **Green:** All of the deep green fruits and veggies used in this book contain unique combinations of powerful vitamins such as A, K, and Bs, as well as essential minerals such as calcium, zinc, and iron. The chlorophyll, zeaxanthin, and quercetin in deep green fruits and vegetables work to enhance the health-boosting properties of their already powerful vitamins and minerals.
- **Blue:** Blue fruits and vegetables are rich in B vitamins and vitamin C, and they are also packed full of important minerals, including calcium and iron. In addition, the anthocyanins and anthocyanadins that join forces for amazing health protection are found in high amounts in all types of blue produce.
- **Violet:** Fruits and vegetables that have the vibrant violet coloring are rich in vitamins A and K, and they also contain anthocyanins, which give these fruits their beautiful purple hue. Minerals such as copper and iron (found especially in raisins) are also plentiful in these fruits and veggies. The powerful health-promoting properties of violet produce are even more plentiful when you consider the benefits from the rich amounts of flavonoids and betalains found in each scrumptious bite.

Now that you know some of the vitamins and minerals that are included with each color, let's take a look at what this really means from a nutritional standpoint.

Meet Your Vitamins

Vitamins play a major role in every aspect of how your body and brain function—ranging from nerve impulses to muscle contractions to clarity of mind to lasting energy, and even the quality of your sleep. In fact, the Food and Drug Administration (FDA) and the United States Department of Agriculture (USDA) have identified the following thirteen specific vitamins as imperative for optimal health.

- Vitamin A (Carotenoids)
- Vitamin B1 (Thiamine)
- Vitamin B2 (Riboflavin)
- Vitamin B3 (Niacin)
- Vitamin B5 (Pantothenic acid)
- Vitamin B6 (Pyridoxine)
- Vitamin B7 (Biotin)
- Vitamin B9 (Folic Acid)
- Vitamin B12 (Cobalamin)
- Vitamin C
- Vitamin D
- Vitamin E
- Vitamin K

Luckily, all of these vitamins (which are discussed in depth next) can be found easily in the fruits and vegetables you eat—and drink—every day.

Too Much of a Good Thing

There's a rule of thumb that for every vitamin's extreme necessity and benefit, there is an equally consequential dysfunction that can result from a lack of it. For example, vitamin B is well known to help with metabolic functioning and energy production and maintenance. With regular consumption of nutritious foods that contain vitamin B, people feel the benefits in their energy levels and metabolism; on the contrary, a deficiency of vitamin B results in a slower or irregular metabolism and a negative fluctuation in energy levels.

But before you learn how each vitamin will affect your body, it's important for you to know that there are two classifications of vitamins: water-soluble and fat-soluble.

Water-soluble vitamins—which include all of the B vitamins and vitamin C—are easily dissolved in water and in your bloodstream. Because their excesses are flushed out on a regular basis in your urine, you need a consistent renewal of these vitamins daily.

Fat-soluble vitamins—which include vitamins A, D, E, and K—are first absorbed by your body's fat stores before entering the bloodstream to perform their functions. Each of these vitamins serves a different purpose in your body's functioning, so it is of the utmost importance that you get a certain amount of each on a regular basis. However, because the excesses of these vitamins are stored in the liver, it is important not to exceed the recommended amount.

The suggested daily values of some of the vitamins discussed in this chapter can vary depending on the specific needs of each individual. For example, pregnant women have very different needs than elderly males. As well, they may fluctuate depending upon certain individual conditions, such as weight, lifestyle, and age. However, the imperative need for them remains for every body and every life.

Vitamin A (Carotenoids)

Fat-soluble vitamins that start as out carotenoids (the orange pigments of plants) are transformed into vitamin A when your body needs it. Important to the immune system and to the development of red blood cells, vitamin A is an essential element, especially for pregnant women (it helps in the healthy development of a fetus). Vitamin A also aids in the synthesis of your body's proteins and helps your eyes by preventing premature aging, free radical damage, and diseases specific to the eyes. This vitamin can be found in a wide variety of deep orange, yellow, green, and red fruits and vegetables, as well as in certain milks and milk products such as almond milk, cow's milk, and yogurts. Some great sources of vitamin A include:

- Bell peppers
- Carrots
- Green leafy vegetables
- Mangoes
- Melons
- Milk (all kinds)
- Pumpkins
- Squashes
- Sweet potatoes
- Tomatoes
- Yogurt

Vitamin B1 (Thiamine)

A water-soluble vitamin that serves as a heavy-duty body system multitasker, vitamin B1 aids in everything from digestion to proper nerve impulse functioning, from muscle functioning to carbohydrate metabolism, and even the synthesis of DNA and RNA. Consuming adequate amounts of this vitamin is imperative to getting the most out of your body every day. Some great sources of vitamin B1 include:

- Brussels sprouts
- Eggplants
- Lettuces
- Mushrooms
- Peas
- Spinach
- Tomatoes

Vitamin B2 (Riboflavin)

A water-soluble vitamin with a major focus on the health of the body's cells, vitamin B2 is most widely recognized as an aid in all of the major processes of a cell's functioning and in promoting healthy cell growth. Also known as riboflavin, B2 helps the body produce red blood cells and metabolize the blood-healthy mineral, iron. Credited with supporting good vision and healthy skin, this is a vitamin that helps everything in the body from the inside out. Some great sources of vitamin B2 include:

- Almonds
- Asparagus
- Lettuces
- Mushrooms
- Spinach
- Yogurt

Vitamin B3 (Niacin)

A water-soluble vitamin that helps with the production, processing, and maintenance of various hormones including sex hormones, hormones related to stress, and hormones that affect insulin levels, vitamin B3 also raises the levels of "good cholesterol" (HDL) and reduces the levels of "bad cholesterol" (LDL). This vitamin, also known as niacin, is best consumed through nutritious foods because its supplements may cause skin irritation and discomfort. Some great sources of vitamin B3 include:

- Asparagus
- Mushrooms
- Sea plants
- Whole grains

Vitamin B5 (Pantothenic Acid)

A water-soluble vitamin that aids with hormone production, fat metabolism, and the production of cortisol (a steroid hormone that is released in response to low blood sugar and stress), vitamin B5 (also known as pantothenic acid) also helps the body process ingested carbohydrates, proteins, and fats. Heavily involved in the energy-producing process that follows food consumption, pantothenic acid is extremely important in regulating and optimizing daily energy levels, natural weight management, and the optimal metabolic functioning many people desire. Great sources of vitamin B5 include:

- Avocados
- Berries
- Broccoli
- Cauliflower
- Corn
- Green leafy vegetables
- Lentils

- Mushrooms
- Squashes
- Sweet potatoes
- Tomatoes
- Whole grains
- Yogurt

Vitamin B6 (Pyridoxine)

A water-soluble vitamin, B6 (also known as pyridoxine) aids in everything from the optimal functioning of the nerves and the proper manufacturing of blood cells to strengthening the body's immune system and helping it absorb and process macronutrients. Optimum vitamin B6 levels are a necessity for total body health, and it can be easily consumed from a wide variety of natural foods. Some great sources of vitamin B6 include:

- Avocados
- Bananas
- Oats
- Peanut Butter
- Potatoes
- Spinach
- Walnuts

Vitamin B7 (Biotin)

Vitamin B7 (also known as biotin) is a water-soluble vitamin that helps promote an efficient metabolism by helping your body process carbohydrates and fat. Whether you're looking to engage in regular physical activity, enhance your physical abilities, maintain an optimal body composition, or work toward a more efficient metabolism, you can benefit from this vitamin, which can be absorbed from some very tasty fruits, veggies, nuts, and grains. Some great sources of vitamin B7 include:

- Almonds
- Avocados
- Berries
- Cabbage
- Carrots
- Cauliflower
- Cucumbers
- Lettuces
- Oats
- Onions
- Spinach
- Tomatoes
- Walnuts
- Whole grains

Vitamin B9 (Folic Acid)

A water-soluble vitamin that helps optimize blood functions like production and circulation, vitamin B9 (also known as folic acid or folate) is an important vitamin that you need to include in your daily diet. This vitamin is especially important for people suffering from iron deficiencies and women who are nursing, pregnant, or may become pregnant because it works to improve the absorption of iron and to ensure the proper development of a growing fetus. Some great sources of vitamin B9 include:

• Asparagus
• Beans
• Beets
• Cauliflower
• Citrus fruits
• Lettuces
• Spinach
• Whole grains

Vitamin B12 (Cobalamin)

Vitamin B12 (also known as cobalamin) is a water-soluble vitamin that is most well-known for its promotion of energy and metabolic maintenance. In addition to optimizing the body's metabolic processes, vitamin B12 is also absolutely necessary in red blood cell production and in the formation and maintenance of healthy nerve cells. Many people opt for a B12 supplement (which is most often recommended in a sublingual liquid form or a shot), but this vitamin can easily be absorbed through natural sources. A great source of vitamin B12 includes:

• Yogurt

You'll notice there's only one source of vitamin B12 on this list. Why? This vitamin is primarily found in meat and dairy products, so you can add it to your diet by adding yogurt to your smoothies (see recipes in Part 2).

Vitamin C

A water-soluble vitamin that is highly regarded as a protector of the immune system, vitamin C works as a multitasking agent for your body's overall health. Aside from boosting the body's defenses by acting as a strong antioxidant—a disease-fighting property found in plants, fruits, and vegetables—that fights damaging free radicals, vitamin C plays a crucial part in the absorption of iron, the regeneration of vitamin E, and the development and regeneration of the body's collagen. While many people reach for citrus sources to replenish their vitamin C stores, it can also easily be obtained from a wide array of other natural foods, including:

- Asparagus
- Bell peppers
- Broccoli
- Cauliflower
- Citrus fruits
- Green leafy vegetables
- Kiwis
- Mangoes
- Papayas
- Peas
- Potatoes
- Strawberries

Vitamin D

A fat-soluble vitamin that helps the body absorb other nutrients, vitamin D regulates almost all of your body systems' functions. This vitamin also helps your immune system function by improving the absorption of essential nutrients that help your body to thrive and perform optimally. As well, it regulates your blood pressure, helps your body absorb and utilize calcium, and regulates your body's glucose tolerance by aiding in the digestion, absorption, and maintenance of nutrients, which minimizes the risk and effects of diabetes. Some great sources of vitamin D include:

- Milk
- Mushrooms
- Vitamin D–fortified grains and cereals
- Yogurt

Vitamin E

Vitamin E is a fat-soluble vitamin that is highly regarded as a strong antioxidant capable of correcting the damage done by free radicals, which are damaging chemicals that can alter the growth of healthy cells. In addition to the way it works to correct the damage to the body's cells, vitamin E plays an important role in the communication between the body's cells by keeping fluid levels and cell environments clear and healthy. All of these disease-fighting abilities help your body maintain healthy blood quality, bone structure, and muscle tissue. Some great sources of vitamin E include:

- Apples
- Avocados
- Carrots
- Green leafy vegetables
- Nuts
- Tomatoes
- Vegetable oils
- Whole grains

Vitamin K

Fat-soluble vitamins in the K class are classified into three types:

1. K1 (phylloquinone)
2. K2 (menaquinone)
3. K3 (menadione)

Most commonly recognized in the form of a shot given to infants at birth, vitamin K prevents bleeding in infants by promoting clotting properties in the body. In adults, vitamin K promotes the same function of proper blood clotting. But the benefits don't end there. Vitamin K also aids in the metabolism of essential amino acids that optimize the body's overall metabolism as well as the utilization of important nutrients. Some great sources of vitamin K include:

- Green leafy vegetables
- Lentils
- Parsley
- Peas
- Sea plants
- Vegetable oils

Meet Your Minerals

Minerals are another major support network that betters the body's functioning. By contributing and assisting in almost every process from developing and strengthening teeth and bones to optimizing the quality and volume of our blood, minerals are just another necessary nutrient we have to get from outside sources. Aside from carrying out their own individual tasks, most minerals actually support the roles of other minerals and promote health through a symbiotic relationship that improves the quality of each. For example, calcium is absolutely necessary for strong teeth and bones, and fluorine acts as a support system for calcium's hard work by providing the teeth with added protection against tooth decay. Hand in hand, each of the following ten minerals recognized by the Food and Drug Administration (FDA) and the United States Department of Agriculture (USDA) as being needed on a daily basis plays an important role in ensuring that your body runs at its best each and every day.

- Calcium
- Copper
- Iron
- Magnesium
- Manganese
- Phosphorous
- Potassium
- Selenium

- Sodium
- Zinc

While there are many supplements available that can offer up the synthetic forms of many minerals, getting those same minerals from natural food sources is always the better (and safer) alternative. By consuming the fresh and frozen produce, nuts, and whole grains that are rich in the minerals your body needs, you can be sure that you're supplying your body with adequate amounts of naturally produced minerals that will keep your body and mind running at their best!

Calcium

This important mineral is most often associated with (a) healthy teeth and bones, and (b) dairy products. These correlations aren't too far off base, but the functions and sources of calcium aren't that limited. With adequate calcium intake, your body promotes proper hormone release and regulation. By making sure you take the correct amount for your needs, areas of your body that are in need of calcium have adequate amounts more readily available and are able to absorb and utilize it easily. Also improving the quality of nerve impulses in all of the body's systems, calcium helps the brain and body which need these smooth nerve impulses to communicate with one another efficiently; without them

functioning at their best, your reflexes, muscle contractions, and thought processes would all suffer. Some great sources of calcium include:

- Almonds
- Beans/lentils
- Broccoli
- Dairy products
- Green leafy vegetables
- Rhubarb
- Turnips
- Tofu

Keep It Coming

The body needs regular amounts of calcium on a regular basis in order to maintain the body's proper functioning, so if there is not enough of a supply consumed in foods and liquids, it taps into the calcium stores of the bones. If this continues for years, the bones' strength weakens, and they can become susceptible to breaking very easily, a disease know as osteoporosis.

Copper

Copper has so much to do with its fellow mineral, iron, that the symptoms of copper deficiency are actually the same as iron deficiency (anemia). This mineral is of utmost importance to the quality of the blood and all of its functions; without copper, red blood cell production and the cells' quality would be severely impaired. Because copper is so involved in the quality of our blood, it also plays a major role in absorbing and supplying oxygen to the bloodstream. The ever-important blood-supporting iron consumed in foods would not be adequately absorbed, stored, or metabolized by the body without the necessary amounts of copper available. In addition to all of the support copper gives to our blood functions, it also acts as a strong antioxidant that can fight off free radical damage in healthy cells. Some great sources of copper include:

• Almonds
• Barley
• Cashews
• Garbanzo beans
• Lentils
• Mushrooms
• Navy beans
• Peanut butter
• Soybeans
• Tempeh
• Whole grains

Iodine

Iodine plays an important role in all of the body's hormonal functioning, the metabolism, and the maintenance of a healthy body weight. Iodine content in foods is dependent on the quality of the environment; because of the high levels of iodine found in natural waters, marine life is able to store high amounts of it and is a great source for the natural variety. However, because of the poor quality of soils in which animals and plants are raised, some forms of protein and plant foods can be lacking in iodine; iodine deficiencies are seen at a high rate in underdeveloped countries where soil quality is extremely poor, resulting in severe cases of thyroid disease such as hypothyroidism and goiters. Iodine-fortified salt used by most people around the world ensures an adequate intake of this mineral, but here you're relying on a synthetic form of this mineral. Natural options are available, and choosing organic fruits and vegetables can ensure that your produce is of the highest quality. Some great sources of iodine include:

• Milk
• Navy beans
• Potatoes
• Seafood
• Sea plants
• Strawberries
• Yogurt

Iron

Iron is one mineral that plays a vital role in improving the quality of life, regardless of your age, gender, or health conditions. There are two different classifications of iron: iron obtained from meat sources is called *heme iron*, and iron obtained from plant sources is called *non-heme iron*. But no matter where your iron comes from, this mineral is a major contributor and overseer to the quality of your blood. Iron's roles include forming the body's red blood cells by regulating the quality of their production and monitoring the enzymatic activities that control the production of red blood cells and blood vessels. The resulting symptoms if one becomes iron deficient can be minimal, including easy bruising and dark circles under the eyes, to severe, including dizziness and fatigue. If you are experiencing these symptoms or suffering from iron-deficiency anemia, it is important to take note that an inadequate intake of vitamin A can also increase iron-deficiency anemia and its symptoms. Some great sources of iron include:

FOR HEME IRON
- Beef
- Tuna
- Venison

FOR NON-HEME IRON
- Cashews
- Garbanzo beans
- Kidney beans
- Lentils
- Molasses
- Potatoes
- Prunes
- Soybeans
- Spinach

Optimized Minerals

As another mineral that is greatly impacted by the presence or absence of other minerals, iron absorption is impacted by, and can affect, the effectiveness and levels of other minerals in the body. For optimal iron absorption, adequate copper levels need to be maintained. Vitamin C ingested at the same time improves the absorption of iron, while calcium ingested at the same time impairs the absorption of iron. In addition, when iron and zinc are consumed in the same meal, iron impairs the effectiveness of zinc.

Magnesium

Magnesium plays an important part in almost every body function, from insulin production and utilization to the generation of healthy cells, and from bone strength to proper blood clotting. It even affects the quality of the processing of B vitamins! Like so many other minerals, magnesium has a huge impact on the absorption of other minerals; by ensuring that your body has adequate levels of magnesium, you can ensure the quality absorption of potassium and calcium as well. Athletes and those who strive to gain better control of their body composition can also greatly benefit from increased attention to their intake of this essential mineral because, among other important tasks, magnesium makes the body's metabolism of carbohydrates and fats its main priority. In addition, this mineral supports the body's use and regeneration of DNA and RNA. Some great sources of magnesium include:

- Almonds
- Apples
- Apricots
- Bananas
- Black beans
- Cashews
- Green leafy vegetables
- Lima beans
- Molasses
- Navy beans
- Peanuts

Manganese

Although the full extent of manganese's effects on the body is still not as fully understood as some of the other minerals, its role in optimizing metabolic functions is an important one. By consuming adequate amounts of manganese, you ensure that the metabolic processes of absorbing, processing, storing, and utilizing all of the macronutrients (including carbohydrates, proteins, fats, and cholesterols) is top-notch. Playing an important part in the enzyme reactions related to the macronutrients not only helps the body function at its best, it also makes for more regular blood sugar levels that can help everything from energy levels to brain functioning. While most people know little about manganese, its sources, and its benefits, it is important to note that this is a very important mineral that is a must in your diet. Some great sources of manganese include:

- Almonds
- Beans/lentils
- Cloves
- Oats
- Peanuts
- Pecans
- Pineapples
- Raspberries
- Spinach
- Sweet potatoes
- Tempeh

Phosphorous

Phosphorous is another mineral that is inte-
gral to many of your body's processes. It helps
form strong teeth and bones, and it positively
affects proper nerve cell functioning, the regulation of hormone production, and the maintenance of optimal enzyme production. Luckily,
phosphorous is one mineral that is present in
exceptionally high amounts in plant foods, so
you can rejoice in the fact that practically every
smoothie's delicious natural ingredients contain this health-promoting mineral. Some great
sources of phosphorous include:

• Almonds
• Bananas
• Berries
• Garbanzo beans
• Lentils
• Milk
• Tomatoes
• Yogurt

Potassium

Potassium's main priority is to maintain
proper fluid balance within your body by keeping the fluid balance within all cells of the body
at optimal levels. Adequate hydration is vital to
survival, and without adequate levels of potassium to safeguard the body's hydration and cell
functioning, all of your body's systems would
be severely impaired. The symptoms of inadequate potassium levels can range from a slight
tingling in the hands and feet to muscle weak-
ness to even severe vomiting and diarrhea. Some
great sources of potassium include:

• Artichokes
• Bananas
• Green leafy vegetables
• Prunes
• Raisins
• Spinach
• Squashes
• Tomatoes
• Yams and sweet potatoes

Selenium

Selenium works to maintain healthy cells by protecting them from free radical damage. When free radicals interact with healthy cells, transformations take place that cause the originally healthy cells to mutate into unhealthy cells; with enough unhealthy cells in the body, certain illnesses, such as cancers, can result. While selenium also aids in enzymatic activities throughout the body, its main role is to serve as an antioxidant that works hand in hand with vitamin E to protect your body's sensitive cells from harmful changes that could possibly turn normal cells into cancerous ones. Some great sources of selenium include:

- Milk
- Mushrooms
- Walnuts
- Whole grains
- Yogurt

Sodium

Heavily involved with maintaining proper fluid levels in the body, sodium regulates your body's blood volume and blood pressure. In addition, adequate levels of sodium ensure for optimal absorption and use of the essential amino acids, other important minerals, and, of course, water! The good news is that by consuming adequate amounts of sodium through fruits, vegetables, nuts, and whole grains, you can ensure that your body will be supplied with the right amounts *and* of the natural variety. But don't overdo it; many people suffer from sodium sensitivity, which can show itself with the uncomfortable symptoms of water retention and swelling in the hands, feet, and lower legs. Some great sources of sodium include:

- Fruits
- Nuts
- Vegetables
- Whole grains

Zinc

While zinc offers up major benefits in bettering the functioning of almost all of the body's systems, you may be surprised to hear that this mineral has to be present in order for *all* chemical reactions to take place; that means enzyme reactions, cell functioning, and everything from digestion to thought processes require zinc for optimal results. Getting adequate amounts of zinc can ensure that your body's processes are happening when, where, and how they're intended. Some great sources of zinc include:

- Almonds
- Beans

- Cashews
- Garbanzo beans
- Mushrooms
- Peas
- Yogurt

Potent Potential

Like many other vitamins and minerals whose effectiveness is affected by the supplementation or high intake of other minerals, zinc's potency is undermined by taking increased amounts of (or combining it with) folic acid, calcium, and iron.

Meet Your Macronutrients

Micronutrients are the vitamins and minerals found within foods, while the *macronutrients* that are used for our body's basic functioning are the carbohydrates, proteins, and fats. It is essential to pay attention to the *sources* of these nutrients, not just to their presence and quantity. While there are many supplements available that can increase your intake, the purest and most beneficial varieties of these nutrients are those found in natural foods. After all, the complex carbohydrates available in an apple are very different from the refined carbohydrates of a slice of white bread; the protein ingested from a serving of broccoli is accompanied by very different nutrients than a serving of protein from a slice of cheese; and the fats found in olive oil are not only different from the fats in a serving of steak, but they are also processed and stored by the body very differently. Gaining nutrition from fruits, vegetables, and natural plant sources such as whole grains can be far more beneficial to your body, so, when given the choice, always opt for the natural vibrant fruits and veggies: nature's nutrition powerhouses!

The bottom line is this: When you "eat the colors of the rainbow" through a variety of natural sources like fruits, vegetables, and whole grains, your body receives a wide array of all of the necessary nutrients it needs—and then some! Read on to learn more about the important macronutrients and how they affect your body.

Carbohydrates

The body requires carbohydrates in order to function . . . period! Because the body metabolizes carbohydrates into *glucose* (blood sugar) to be used as energy by all of your body's systems, the types of carbohydrates you consume have a great impact on the quality of that energy. The rate at which carbohydrates raise glucose levels in the blood (you've heard the terms "sugar rush" and "crash") is measured by the glycemic index. Because foods that rank lower on the glycemic index—like fruits and vegetables—impact blood glucose slowly and steadily, you feel more satisfied for longer, experience longer-lasting energy, and avoid the inevitable "crash" associated with higher glycemic foods that cause blood sugar to spike quickly and drop quickly. Eating and drinking a rainbow of fruits and vegetables as the main sources of your carbohydrate portion of your daily diet helps the body and brain maintain a healthy balance and work the way they're intended. The impressive benefits include better controlled blood sugar (which, in turn, lowers the risks and effects of diabetes), a more easily maintained lean body mass and ideal weight, and better overall energy levels. So, forget the refined breads and pastas and reach for a natural smoothie instead!

Proteins

When most people think of protein sources, the most common example that comes to mind is meat. But while animal products are great sources of this necessary nutrient, buckwheat, quinoa, and hempseed—found in many of the recipes in Part 2—also help supply our bodies with all of the essential and nonessential amino acids, which help almost every part of your body function at its highest level. And the good news is that if you're eating plant foods (i.e., fruits and veggies) that don't contain all of the complete proteins in themselves it's easy to add in other complementary plant sources to round out those proteins to meet your needs. In addition, there are a number of protein supplements that can be combined with the fruits and vegetables in a smoothie to increase the amount of protein (and, specifically, amino acids) in your diet. Simply and easily, everyone can get adequate amounts of quality protein in their diet through the natural foods available, and in combination with delicious supplements.

Fats

Of all of the macronutrients, fat gets a bad rap. Most of the diets people try out recommend lowering fat intake, but the truth is that there are many kinds of fats, and while some have been identified as being harmful to your health in high amounts, others are actually very beneficial for both your brain and body. By excluding fats from your diet completely, you can actually diminish the quality of your health. Fish oils, nuts, and plant sources (avocados, olive oil, etc.) provide the body and the brain with rich fats that help your cells communicate, react faster, and function better overall. While saturated fats from animal sources and trans fats from hydrogenized food products have been shown to negatively impact the brain, blood, and heart, unsaturated fats have all exhibited the powers to improve health and well-being by reducing inflammation, promoting better brain activity, lowering "bad" cholesterol (LDL) and raising "good" cholesterol (HDL), maintaining quality blood health, and optimizing metabolic functioning. If you're worried about the fats you're consuming, simply choose fruits, vegetables, and whole grains that can supply your body with all it needs naturally—without any of the unnatural or unhealthy dangers that could raise concerns.

Phytochemicals and Fiber

In addition to attaining all the amazing vitamins, minerals, and macronutrients that sipping the rainbow can bring, having a smoothie once a day can ensure that your body is getting all the fiber and phytochemicals it needs to thrive. These two substances are found in every single smoothie in Part 2. How can they benefit you? Read on . . .

Phytochemicals

Adding a rainbow of plant foods in your smoothies ensures that every serving will include an abundance of phytochemicals, chemical substances only found in plants, which are responsible for proactive health protection throughout the body. Surprisingly, phytochemicals are not classified as actual nutrients like vitamins and minerals, but these strong antioxidants offer up extremely important health benefits that are virtually unmatched. The classes of phytochemicals are short and simple, but each serves an individually powerful purpose. Each class works to make your body healthier by improving everything from memory to eye health, detoxifying the body's organs and improving the immune system's strength, and even acting as strong antioxidants that fight common germs and bacteria. The classes and benefits are as follows:

- *Phenols*: chemical compounds found in plants that have been studied for their protective properties against free radical damage to cells
- *Isoflavones*: plant hormones that are similar to human estrogen and work to accelerate metabolism, strengthen bones, and increase absorption of good cholesterol; found in most soy products
- *Phytosterols and saponins*: plant-derived substances shown to positively affect cholesterol levels
- *Sulfur compounds*: amino acids found in plants, which work to optimize metabolism and ensure healthy muscle

By enjoying an abundance of brightly colored fruits and vegetables, you can provide your body with these powerful health protectors easily and deliciously.

Fiber

Found in natural plant sources like fruits, vegetables, legumes, and grains, fiber is the element in foods that is not able to be digested by the human body. While this sounds like it wouldn't contribute to the body's health, fiber acts as the important "scrub-brush" of your digestive system by moving food along through the colon, picking up foods and bacteria left behind, and speeding up the transit time of digested food. There are two forms of fiber: *soluble fiber*, which dissolves in liquid and forms a gel-like substance in the intestinal tract before passing through, and *insoluble fiber*, which does not dissolve and passes through the digestive tract in close to its original form. Both help your body digest foods—which contributes to a sustained feeling of fullness—and prevent dangerous health conditions like colon cancer, unhealthy levels of fat in the blood, and unhealthy cholesterol levels. Eating a fiber-filled diet also results in reduced body fat deposits in the stomach area, fewer bouts of indigestion, and improved regularity.

When taking the importance of diet into consideration, it's important to note that each of the elements that make up "sound" nutrition contribute to your body's optimal functioning in very unique ways. Each food's color signifies the content of specific organic compounds that can promote certain health factors, protect against disease, and help the body to maintain optimum functioning of its systems. By choosing a variety of these colorful natural foods, you can easily consume a wide array of essential vitamins, minerals, carbohydrates, proteins, healthy fats, fiber, and protective phytochemicals that can improve your health and the quality of your life easily—and tastily!

Chapter 2

Blending for a Better Life:
All You Need to Know

Now that you know about the important vitamins, minerals, phytochemicals, and macronutrients that bright, vibrant fruits and vegetables contain, it's time to take a look at how you can most easily get these nutrients into a delicious smoothie that will be perfect for *you*. In this chapter, you'll learn how to prepare a smoothie and how to actually choose ingredients that are tailored to your specific tastes, wants, and needs—and you'll find info that details the vitamins, minerals, and quality nutrition of each, with quick tips of their availability and whether a particular ingredient is best used fresh, frozen, or canned.

You'll also learn about some amazing ingredients and some healthy additions that you may have never tried. Trying out new things or new tastes can be intimidating, so the information about these products should help simplify picking and choosing what appeals to you. Every single ingredient that goes into your smoothies should be beneficial, so knowing about the "Optional Additions" is almost as important as knowing about the produce! Not only do these mix-ins improve the quality and taste of your smoothies, they also add amazing benefits that may fit your specific needs.

As you become more and more comfortable with making smoothies—and with the flavors, textures, and tastes that you can add into them—take the time to go through this chapter and highlight the ingredients you find most interesting. Whether you know you like a certain fruit or veggie, are tempted to try something new, or are attracted to the health benefits and qualities of an ingredient, simply highlight it and make a point to add those ingredients to your shopping list. To ensure that making your smoothie ingredient list is as easy as possible, you'll find an appendix of all the fruits and vegetables in this chapter with their main vitamins, minerals, or antioxidants and the corresponding benefits of each at the back of the book. Soon you'll have a list of ingredients that will help you choose the smoothie recipes that tailor your smoothies specifically to you. Keep in mind that not every fruit, veggie, and herb is listed, but the ones you'll find here are healthy, delicious, and will get you off on the right foot!

Meet Your Fruits

Every fruit used in the recipes in Part 2 is detailed in the following list. Broken down by their vibrant color group, here you'll find information about each fruit's nutritional content, health benefits, and what serving size equals a fruit serving to make the selection of your smoothie ingredients that much easier! Whether you're looking for specific vitamins, minerals, phytochemicals, or health benefits, here you'll learn which fruits will contribute the best sources of nutrients to fit your needs.

White

APPLES

1 medium apple = 1 fruit serving

To prepare: Core and cube

"An apple a day keeps the doctor away" is a cliché that actually couldn't be more accurate. While these delicious, convenient, hand-held fruits come in a wide variety of colors and flavors, their main health benefits come from the strong health-protecting polyphenols (chemical compounds that give fruits and vegetables their unique hues), vitamin C, and multitasking fiber that come packed into each and every variety. The polyphenols do double duty as powerful antioxidants that have been shown to protect the cardiovascular system and respiratory system, regulate the blood sugar, and ward off many types of cancer. Apples have also been strongly associated with a decreased susceptibility to lung cancer and a lower risk of asthma. Beyond the antioxidant health benefits of apples, the fiber of the skin and flesh can keep your body regular, act to reduce "bad" cholesterol (LDL) levels in the blood, and help you feel full for longer.

An Apple a Day

Apples lend a lightly sweet taste to any smoothie, so to aim for "an apple a day" isn't so far out of reach. Consider it as a background flavor in any of your smoothies.

BANANAS

1 banana = 1 fruit serving

To prepare: Peel and chop

Bananas are most well-known for their high levels of potassium, but they're also packed with tons of additional vitamins, minerals, and phytochemicals, including B6 and C, that can prevent uncomfortable and dangerous conditions like water retention and irregularity, while also promoting a healthy balance within the body. The abundant potassium helps to maintain a normal blood pressure, which translates to a reduced risk of heart diseases and conditions, and the antioxidants that complement the potassium promote everything from eye health to bone strength. This delicious ingredient adds a smooth, almost creamy texture to any smoothie and is worth its weight in the health benefits that can change your life for the better!

COCONUTS

½ cup coconut meat cut up = 1 fruit serving

To prepare: Remove outer layers and break the coconut's shell. Peel the remaining skin from the white flesh until no brown bits remain.

Coconut meat is a smoothie ingredient that is absolutely brimming with B vitamins and vitamin C as well as a wide variety of phytochemicals, that work to provide some major health benefits! Fighting off everything from the common cold to the flu, preventing cancer and premature aging, and contributing to stable blood sugar levels and consistent energy levels, coconuts have been used for health-promoting purposes for centuries. While this tropical fruit can be hard to find in common stores, most grocery stores and produce stands offer them in natural form or in an organic, no additives added form (in the dried fruit area)—and they're well worth the hunt!

PEARS

1 medium pear = 1 fruit serving

To prepare: Core and cube

If you're looking for a powerful, health-protecting, cancer-fighting fruit, the pear is the answer to your prayers! The vitamin C in pears works to promote immunity and help the body to regenerate vitamin E, while the copper in this delicious fruit helps to prevent and reverse damage done to the cells by dangerous free radicals. In addition to these vitamins and minerals, the fiber contained in the pear's skin and flesh helps the body ward off a variety of cancers, including colon cancer.

Red

CHERRIES

½ cup = 1 fruit serving

To prepare: Remove stems and pits

Packed with vitamin C, cherries offer up more than just immunity-building benefits. Also charged with a number of powerful phytochemicals and antioxidants that give them their deep red coloring, cherries can work wonders in protecting the heart against disease, promoting the quality of the blood, and promoting healthy functioning of the cells by preventing free radical damage. So, if your goal is to maintain a youthful glow, control your blood pressure, or prevent cancers and dangerous diseases, these beautiful and delicious berries contain the essential vitamins and phytochemicals that will make drinking the red spectrum of the rainbow work for you!

CRANBERRIES

½ cup = 1 fruit serving

To prepare: Wash

With a sweet, tart flavor and deep red color, these gems can turn any smoothie into a pleasure for the palate and the eyes. As well, the anti-bacterial and free radical–fighting properties of the anthocyanins, flavonols, vitamins C and K, and manganese in cranberries make them an amazingly powerful fruit for fighting off bacteria. Cancer protection is just one more benefit in the long list of reasons to consume cranberries, so maximize your life-changing smoothies with tasty additions of this beautiful fruit!

GRAPEFRUIT

½ large or ½ cup = 1 fruit serving

To prepare: Remove skin and seeds

While these beautiful fruits may make you pucker up, their sweet and tart flavors are a unique addition to smoothie recipes that can pack up a wide array of additional health benefits. Being a citrus fruit, the grapefruit is packed with vitamin C, lycopene, and liminoids (the powerful antioxidant specific to citrus), which all work together to combat illness and disease while promoting healthy cell production and function. By enjoying this delicious fruit and the antioxidants and vitamins it contains, you can also reap the benefits of reduced risk for serious illnesses such as heart disease and rheumatoid arthritis, as well as harmful cell damage that can negatively affect DNA and contribute to certain cancers. Even health of the blood and blood pressure can be optimized by increasing your intake of grapefruit, so add some beneficial sweet tartness to your next smoothie by blending in this rich fruit in bulk!

POMEGRANATES

1 medium pomegranate = 1 fruit serving

To prepare: Cut in half and tap hard bottom until jewels release

Rich in vitamins C, K, and many of the Bs, this delicious fruit is packed with jewels of healthy goodness that work hard to promote blood quality and keep the organs free of toxins and foreign invaders. Although it's well-known that pomegranates are packed with sweet flavored "seeds" (also known as the pomegranate's "jewels") of health-promoting nutrition, only recently has this wonder fruit caught the attention of the masses. You'll love the tangy taste it brings to your smoothie.

RASPBERRIES

½ cup = 1 fruit serving

To prepare: Wash

Known for their sweet, yet tart, unique flavor, raspberries have a special texture to accompany the rich nutrients like vitamin C, folate, and fiber that they contribute to any smoothie. Rich in vitamin C, which boosts immunity and protects cells from damage, these delicious berries are renowned for containing powerful antioxidants that can prevent and reverse cell damage, along with anthocyanins (the chemicals that give red, purple, and blue foods their vibrant colors) that can ward off infections and prevent undesirable bacteria growth in the body.

STRAWBERRIES

½ cup = 1 fruit serving

To prepare: Wash and remove tops

These deep red fruits are sweet, have a distinct flavor, and are packed with tons of nutrients, including vitamin C, manganese, and fiber, that all boost the quality of any smoothie. Brimming with powerful antioxidants, anti-inflammatory nutrients, and vitamin C, strawberries are known to help with cancer prevention, cardiovascular protection, and stable regulation of blood sugar, which contributes to a lower risk of diabetes.

WATERMELON

½ cup diced = 1 fruit serving

To prepare: Remove rind and cut

Bright red, juicy watermelon is hard to beat on a hot summer's day, but it also adds great-tasting flavor and loads of health benefits to any smoothie. This beta-carotene–rich food is packed with vitamins C, A, and D, which act to protect all of your body's systems and cells. Whether you'd like to enhance the quality of your skin or protect the health of your heart, watermelon is the perfect fruit for you. In addition to the strong antioxidant properties in watermelon, there's also a surprising protein content that you may not expect!

Orange
APRICOTS

¼ cup dried or 1 whole = 1 fruit serving

To prepare: Remove stem and seeds

While most people think of the dried variety of apricots when this fruit comes to mind, the natural, fresh fruit is recommended for daily smoothie making because of the regular tendency of food manufacturers to add sugar to their dried fruits. Apricots contain rich amounts of beta-carotene that come from their vitamin A and C servings and color them their delightful orange hue. They provide a load of benefits that can effect everything from your eyes to your digestion. In addition, the fiber in these fruits can help combat certain cancers, promote healthy cholesterol levels, and provide a feeling of fullness that will last longer than comparable servings of other foods.

CANTALOUPE

½ cup diced = 1 fruit serving

To prepare: Remove rind and seeds

When it comes to life-altering vitamins, cantaloupe provides some hefty servings that can promote optimal functioning of everything from your vision to your respiratory system. While combating a number of health issues like common colds, and even stopping dangerous damage to cells from free radical exposure, cantaloupe's doses of vitamins A and C coupled with its high content of beta-carotene make this fruit a powerful ally in optimizing health. Sweet and smooth, this melon makes for a delicious addition to any smoothie.

ORANGES

1 medium/large orange = 1 fruit serving

To prepare: Remove rind and seeds

Well-known for being one of the best fruit sources of vitamin C, oranges also provide a variety of other vitamins, minerals, and phytochemicals like folate, potassium, fiber, and vitamin A that can improve the quality of your health. Getting their bright orange coloring from phytonutrients specific to the citrus group, oranges provide a double dose of strong antioxidant power to help in maintaining a strong immune system. Not only is a daily dose of oranges great for your immunity, this fruit can also contribute some major health benefits to your regularity, your heart, your blood, your digestive system, and cancers that can attack your mouth, colon, and lungs—pretty impressive for a fruit that's available in every grocery store and produce market for an even more impressive low price.

PAPAYA

½ cup cut up = 1 fruit serving

To prepare: Remove rind and seeds

The number of vitamins and minerals found in papayas is astounding! Plentiful vitamins, potassium, and calcium all join forces with powerful antioxidants in this fiber-rich fruit that will turn any smoothie into an orange delight packed with tons of health benefits. Improving the health of the eyes and the skin with vitamin A, boosting brain functioning and blood quality with vitamin E, and promoting the immune system while also combating serious diseases that stem from cell damage by free radicals with its rich amounts of vitamin C, papaya is as beneficial as it is beautiful!

Yellow
LEMONS AND LIMES

1 large lemon or lime = 1 fruit serving

To prepare: Remove rind and seeds

Rich in vitamin C, which acts to protect against illness while promoting proper functioning of the body's systems, these small fruits pack a sour-pucker punch! Adding a tart flavor to any smoothie blend, the health benefits of lemons and limes make it well worth acquiring a taste for them. Rich in anti-inflammatory elements, including vitamin C and unique phytochemical limonins, which can fight free radicals and protect the body from cancerous invasions, these fruits are able to help alleviate painful conditions such as arthritis, cardiovascular disease, and the daily common aches and pains from joint stiffness. And you can achieve these benefits with just a few additions to your daily routine.

MANGOES

½ cup = 1 fruit serving

To prepare: Remove rind and seeds and chop

Packed with an overly abundant amount of vitamin A, this tasty fruit can cover more than an entire day's needs of vitamin A that helps everything from brain functioning to eye health, all in just one serving. In addition, mangoes are also high in B vitamins and vitamin C, which add a multitude of health benefits such as metabolism improvement and immune system strength to smoothies in which they're used. Smooth and sweet, this deep yellow fruit gets its rich coloring from the beta-carotenes that also add tons of antioxidants that can prevent illness and promote healthy functioning of all of the body's systems.

PEACHES AND NECTARINES

1 medium peach or nectarine = 1 fruit serving

To prepare: Remove pit

These deep yellow fruits make for a sweet smoothie with delicious flavor and lots of health benefits. These rich sources of vitamin A and powerful antioxidants serve as a helpful combination in promoting better eyesight, preventing premature aging, and warding off illnesses that could otherwise harm the balance of the body's cells and system functioning. Peaches are best when fresh, but if you're craving a peach smoothie in the off season, frozen will suffice.

PINEAPPLE

½ cup chopped = 1 fruit serving

To prepare: Remove skin and core

This deliciously sweet tropical fruit is as tasty as it is beautiful. Pineapple protects and serves your body in many wonderful ways with its loads of manganese, vitamin C, and copper. The vitamin C content of pineapple gets the most attention for helping to promote the body's immune system's defenses while also acting as a strong antioxidant that can aid in preventing infections and damage to normally healthy cells. A phytochemical called bromelain also ensures that the pineapple acts as a strong anti-inflammatory agent.

Green
AVOCADOS

½ cup chopped = 1 fruit serving

To prepare: Remove skin and seed

While the avocado does contain higher amounts of fats than other fruits, the types of fats found here are the "good" fats that we're supposed to consume naturally in nature. Like those found in olive oils, the fats found in avocados promote the healthy functioning of blood cells and cancer-fighting antibodies, which affect all organs and systems in the body from the brain to the heart. Due to the high content of rich carotenoid antioxidants like alpha-carotene, beta-carotene, and zeaxanthin, smoothies containing these vibrant fruits also have anti-inflammatory benefits in every sip! This fruit also helps your body absorb the powerful phytochemicals like beta-carotenes and *lycopene* that come from other foods. So, reaping the benefits of this fruit means reaping the benefits of many others, too!

HONEYDEW MELON

½ cup cubed = 1 fruit serving

To prepare: Remove skin and seeds and cube

With a pale to deep green coloring, the extremely sweet honeydew melon can turn any plain smoothie into a light green, sweet treat packed with immunity-defending nutrients. The vitamin C, metabolism-boosting vitamin Bs, as well as the essential mineral potassium serve as great promoters of blood health by controlling cholesterol levels, regulating blood sugar levels, and maintaining optimal blood pressure. The powerful antioxidants and potassium work hand in hand to make this a beneficial, delicious, nutritious powerhouse of a fruit that can add it all to any smoothie!

KIWIFRUIT

1 kiwifruit = 1 fruit serving

To prepare: Remove skin

Even though oranges pack a ton of vitamin C, the kiwifruit takes the vitamin C prize! This tropical fruit, which is known for its slick, smooth texture and black specks of seeds, utilizes its powerful nutritional content for the greater good. The vitamin C boosts immunity, the fiber promotes regularity, and the phytochemicals combat cancer in many major organ systems and reverse damage to cells and DNA molecules. Kiwifruit also plays a major role in fighting cancers, controlling diabetes, reducing the effects of all types of arthritis, and even calming conditions such as asthma through its anti-inflammatory properties.

Blue
BLUEBERRIES

½ cup = 1 fruit serving

To prepare: Wash

These delicious berries are scrumptious, sweet, and can boost the power of any smoothie with their rich content of vitamin C, manganese, and dietary fiber. Also rich in powerful antioxidants, the anthocyanins that give blueberries their deep blue coloring, these berries can provide their healing power to almost every aspect of the body's functioning. With more than a dozen phytochemicals that all blast immune-system invaders and healthy cell assailants, blueberries also have positive effects on the blood, blood sugar levels, the brain, cancer prevention, reduction of "bad" cholesterols and raising of "good" cholesterols, memory, and even the eyes!

Violet

BLACKBERRIES

½ cup = 1 fruit serving

To prepare: Wash

While most people are accustomed to seeing blackberries used in products like jams and teas, these beautiful, deep purple fruits make for amazingly powerful and delicious smoothie ingredients. The vitamin C helps improve your body's immune system by acting as an antibacterial element that helps fight off infections, while the colorful antioxidants reduce aches and pains by providing anti-inflammatory benefits, and those same two elements work hand in hand to help ward off cancers by acting as powerful fighters against free radical damage to healthy cells.

FIGS

½ cup = 1 fruit serving

To prepare: Remove stems and bottoms

With a deliciously sweet flavor and smooth texture, this fruit makes for a perfect smoothie ingredient. The potassium found in figs helps your body to regulate your blood pressure, and their high calcium content promotes bone and teeth quality. As a low-glycemic food that packs tons of fiber into each and every sip, this fruit will also help you maintain a healthy weight by controlling blood sugar levels and providing a feeling of fullness. The added benefit of the ultra-important fiber content of these fruits makes them a healthy helper in the area of colon health and regularity, too.

GRAPES

½ cup = 1 fruit serving

To prepare: Wash

Concord grapes are one of the more convenient sweet treats that make being healthier a delicious endeavor. Containing a strong antioxidant responsible for their vibrant violet shade, these bite-sized fruits help to ward off infections and serious diseases. Containing vitamin C and phytochemicals, grapes not only protect cells from free radical damage, but they also have the capabilities to halt and reverse any damage done to healthy cells—including brain cells—before further transitioning can take place. In addition, grapes provide anti-inflammatory benefits and loads of fiber, which help reduce common discomforts and promote blood health, increase regularity, and maintain heart health.

PLUMS AND PRUNES

1 plum or 1 prune = 1 fruit serving

To prepare: Remove pit (and peel, optional)

Excellent sources of vitamin C, which works hard to protect your immune system, these delicious fruits come in not just one delicious version, but two! Plums are the fresh version and prunes are the dried alternative, and either way you choose to indulge in these delicious fruits, they make for excellent, sweet-tasting, nutrition-packed smoothie ingredients. Plums and prunes contain unique phytonutrients like anthocyanins that act as strong antioxidants and prevent damage to the cells of the blood, brain, heart, and even to the fats that allow cell membranes to function and communicate properly. Little known phenols like the chlorogenic acid and neochlorogenic acid that brim in every sip contribute the added benefits of super-antioxidants that specifically protect the fats that form our brain and blood cells from free radical damage. Delicious and nutritious, plums and prunes can dramatically improve your health and well-being in just a few sips!

Meet Your Veggies

Every vegetable that you'll find in the recipes in Part 2 adds its own unique taste, bountiful nutrition, and specific health benefits to the smoothie you create. Here you'll find detailed information about the vitamins, minerals, and phytochemicals found in each vegetable, along with the positive effects that can take place in the body as a result of including these vegetables in your diet. Take a look and begin to make easy and educated choices about what to include in your smoothies. You'll start reaping those incredible benefits right away!

Please note that while, without a doubt, blue is a beautiful color that is full of rich phytochemical and nutrient content, unique blue-colored foods are limited to the fruit section. Indulging in the violet selection of veggies will provide an immense amount of nutrition that closely compares to those of the blue category, though.

White
CAULIFLOWER
½ cup = 1 veggie serving
To prepare: Wash head and cut florets into chunks

A cruciferous vegetable that pales in color comparisons to other vibrant veggies, cauliflower can hold its own when it comes to nutritional content. High contents of vitamin C make this veggie a great immune-fighting element in the diet, but the fiber-rich contributions to the body's total health are what make this vegetable a star to take note of. The fiber content of cauliflower is what brings out the most recognized benefits, including reduced rates of cancer, improved digestion, reduced indigestion, and improved blood quality. Despite having a very mild flavor, cauliflower makes for a nutritious addition to any type of smoothie.

GARLIC
1 ounce = 1 veggie serving
To prepare: Peel

With vitamins and minerals like vitamin B to promote healthy blood, and manganese and vitamin C, which act as health protectors against illness and inflammation, garlic is most notably recognized in the health community for its sulfur compound, *allicin*, which acts as a strong supporter of cardiovascular health, as well as an anti-inflammatory, antibacterial, and antiviral agent. By promoting blood quality in terms of the levels of triglycerides and cholesterols, preventing inflammation within blood cells and muscle cells, and fending off the growth of unhealthy bacteria and the invasion of viral illnesses, this is an amazing vegetable that definitely deserves credit for its amazing power and its amazing taste.

MUSHROOMS

1 cup whole/ ½ cup chopped = 1 veggie serving

To prepare: Remove dirt with a towel (DO NOT WASH)

With the button mushroom surpassing its mushroom relatives in terms of health benefits and health-promoting nutrients, the white button mushroom is the one recommended for use in smoothie recipes. Surprisingly, these mushrooms pack tons of B vitamins that protect the cardiovascular system against disease, as well as the minerals selenium, copper, and potassium, which work together to maintain the health and optimal environment for healthy growth in cells.

By utilizing the vitamins, minerals, and phytochemicals for health, these little white veggies aid in the prevention of serious diseases—including cardiovascular disease, diabetes, and certain cancers—by providing support in the form of antioxidants and anti-inflammatory agents.

POTATOES

1 small or ½ cup = 1 veggie serving

To prepare: Wash thoroughly (and peel, optional)

While noted for their starchiness, potatoes add B vitamins that optimize the blood and metabolism, vitamin C for improved immunity, and a good amount of potent potassium to add hydrating benefits to every sip of your savory smoothie. While blending potatoes in a smoothie may sound odd, these vegetables can add a smooth texture, light flavor, and immense health benefit to any thick smoothie variety. Highly recommended to be blended with similar white fruits and vegetables, or even with other vegetables that can easily overpower their color and flavor, potatoes remain an important element of any diet.

YELLOW ONIONS

1 medium or ½ cup = 1 veggie serving

To prepare: Peel and remove stem and bottom

With a sweet, spicy flavor, yellow onions are not an overpowering ingredient, and they make for a complementary taste sensation in predominately vegetable smoothies. Containing vitamin C, chromium, and fiber, these tasty veggies make for a delicious and nutritious addition to savory smoothies in need of a zippy boost. With the high content of vitamin C and chromium working together to promote the health and proper functioning of the body's cells, cardiovascular system, and immune system, these veggies also strengthen and support healthy bone growth. They also help control the blood sugar and blood pressure with their healthy doses of fiber, manganese, and copper. With all of these amazing health benefits, yellow onions can contribute a lot more than just "zing!" to your smoothies!

Red

RED PEPPERS

½ large or ½ cup = 1 veggie serving

To prepare: Wash and remove stem, core, and seeds

With almost 300 percent of your daily recommendation of vitamin C to improve immune-system defenses (which makes red peppers a great addition to any daily diet), and more than 100 percent of vitamin A for eye and skin health in a single cup, red bell peppers are an amazing source of great nutrition. With rich additions of phytochemicals like lycopene and beta-carotene, which act as powerful health-protecting antioxidants, red bell peppers make for delicious

smoothie ingredients that can promote immunity, prevent serious illness, and protect the systems, organs, and functioning of the body.

TOMATOES

1 medium or ½ cup diced = 1 veggie serving
To prepare: Rinse thoroughly

While tomatoes contain healthy amounts of vitamin C and potassium that promote immunity and healthy cell formation respectively, it's the joining of these two nutrients with the powerful well-known lycopene that makes this a wonder veggie well suited for any smoothie. When combined, these three nutrients fight off illness, prevent certain cancers, maintain a toxin-free environment in your organs and blood, and promote healthy circulation and blood pressure. Mild in flavor, deep in color, and rich in nutrients, tomatoes are a smart addition to any smoothie-maker's diet.

Orange

CARROTS

1 large or ½ cup = 1 veggie serving
To prepare: Wash (and peel, optional)

One of the most vitamin- and mineral-rich vegetables available, the simple carrot lends a sweet flavor and an amazing color to any smoothie. The vibrant orange carrot contains immense amounts of vitamins A, Bs, C, D, E, and K in addition to the essential minerals calcium, phosphorous, potassium, and sodium. These nutrients do a lot of amazing things. In particular, the fiber promotes optimal digestion, the vitamins A and C fend off infections, and the rich minerals like potassium and manganese even promote and improve the quality of hair, skin, and nails. Carrots truly are a delightfully flavorful vegetable that can work wonders on the health of every part of the body, head to toe.

PUMPKIN

½ cup fresh/cooked cubed or puréed = 1 veggie serving

To prepare: Remove stem, skin, and seeds or buy canned pumpkin purée as discussed below

Not just for pumpkin pie anymore, pumpkin purée can make for a healthy element of any diet. Rich in vitamins A and C that work together to promote cell health in the eyes and skin, as well as a variety of minerals and a wide array of antioxidants that contribute to the healthy functioning of those same cells, pumpkin purée can be a deliciously sweet addition to your smoothies with loads of health benefits. Playing an important role in preventing inflammatory diseases, providing rich antioxidant benefits such as improved immune-system functioning, and offering a double whammy of rich vitamin A and beta-carotene that acts to protect the health of the eyes, pumpkin is worth considering the next time you're craving a sweet, healthy smoothie. If you don't want to go to all the work of puréeing your own pumpkin, please feel free to use canned. Rather than being stringy or gritty (and requiring a ton of prep time), canned pumpkin purée is as nutritious, more convenient, and more tasty than the fresh alternative. Be sure to purchase pumpkin purée and not pumpkin pie filling.

YAMS AND SWEET POTATOES

½ large = 1 veggie serving

To prepare: Wash thoroughly (and peel, optional)

Yams and sweet potatoes can add plentiful amounts of vitamins, minerals, and anthocyanins. Vitamins A, Bs, and C, minerals like calcium and potassium, and deep orange *beta-carotene* come together in these smooth, starchy vegetables that add loads of sweetness to any delicious smoothie. By including these beautiful gems in your diet, you can reap the benefits of improved eye health from the vitamin A, better blood quality from the Bs, and a stronger immune system from the vitamin C. No need to add sweeteners—these nutritious vegetables are sweet enough!

Yellow
ACORN SQUASH

½ cup chopped/mashed = 1 veggie serving

To prepare: Remove skin and seeds

Related to the pumpkin, everything from the flesh to the seeds of this delightfully sweet veggie can add loads of wonderful benefits to any daily diet. Simple to cook and soften, acorn squash makes the perfect ingredient in any healthy smoothie, adding powerful antioxidants like beta-carotene, vision-protecting elements like vitamins A and C, and rich fiber that can "clean out" the colon while preventing certain cancers.

CORN

½ cup fresh/frozen = 1 veggie serving

To prepare: Stand cob's flat end on a flat surface. Run knife along cob from top to bottom, collect kernels, and discard cob

Natural corn kernels (fresh or frozen) can add a ton of essential vitamins, including B1 and folate for better blood health and improved iron absorption. With disease-fighting and anti-inflammatory antioxidants like zeaxanthin, and regularity-promoting and disease-fighting fiber, corn is a plus for any recipe.

YELLOW SQUASH

½ cup cut or sliced, cooked/raw = 1 veggie serving

To prepare: Wash and cut

A relative of the zucchini, this summer squash is rich in vitamin B, calcium, and potassium. Helping to maintain healthy eyesight and promoting stable blood sugar levels with vitamin A, contributing to strong bones with calcium, and providing a positive metabolic regulation with the B vitamins and potassium, yellow squash is as nutritious as it is delicious. Just slightly sweet with little other flavor, yellow squash can be blended into any smoothie for a slight flavor addition with loads of nutritional benefit.

Green

ASPARAGUS

½ cup = 1 veggie serving

To prepare: Wash and remove the bottom 1–2" portion of the spears

Contributing a unique flavor to any dish, asparagus makes any smoothie recipe special. Packed with vitamins, minerals, and antioxidants, asparagus's star elements are the anti-inflammatory saponins that can promote and protect the health of the cells, digestive system, the blood, and the heart, all the while preventing serious diseases like diabetes, heart disease, and certain cancers. Also including impressive amounts of B vitamins like folate, biotin, choline, and pantothenic acid, this health star of a veggie can be an important addition to any pregnant woman's diet for promoting and protecting the health of both mom and baby.

BROCCOLI

½ cup cooked/raw = 1 veggie serving

To prepare: Wash and remove florets from stalk

Loaded with vitamins like B6, C, and E, and the important mineral calcium, broccoli is one of the cruciferous vegetables that can add tons of taste and nutrition to any smoothie. Because of its high content of fiber and rich antioxidants, broccoli can provide the body with protective benefits that aid in fighting off cancers, cell malformation, and immunity assailants while improving regularity and the health of the digestive system. Also containing a healthy dose of protein, broccoli is a vegetable that can provide many benefits along with its delicious flavor and beautiful color.

CELERY

½ cup chopped or 1 whole = 1 veggie serving

To prepare: Separate stalks and wash thoroughly; chop

Deliciously crisp and slightly spicy, celery has a taste all its own—and since it's easily blended into most vegetable smoothies, celery's zippy taste can also add a delightful background flavor to many of the fruit varieties. Containing remarkable amounts of vitamin C and potassium, which act to protect the body's cells and systems while regulating the blood and body's water content, celery is more highly regarded for its natural sodium content, which acts as a natural regulator of water retention in the body, as well as the pH of the blood.

CUCUMBERS

½ cup cut up or chopped = 1 veggie serving

To prepare: Peel skin and chop

Rich in vitamins C and A for improved immune system, manganese for preventing inflammation, and the well-known antioxidant beta-carotene, cucumbers protect the body and its systems from diseases, infections, and inflammatory conditions, while also promoting skin, hair, nail, and eye health. Clearly, they make for a healthy and refreshing addition to any diet. Unless using an English cucumber that can be eaten with the skin intact, remove the waxy skin with a peeler before blending.

LEEKS AND SCALLIONS

½ cup chopped or 1 whole = 1 veggie serving

To prepare: Separate and wash thoroughly

Contributing a slightly pungent flavor, leeks and scallions are some of the more mild-tasting varieties of the onion family. Being rich sources of potent antioxidants, these delightful smoothie additions can boost your immunity with the added benefits of antibacterial properties that can fend off common infections, as well as serious diseases.

PEAS

½ cup = 1 veggie serving

To prepare: Wash thoroughly

Starchy and sweet, peas add a unique texture, flavor, and loads of nutritional benefits to your smoothies. Packed with strong antioxidants that aid in anti-inflammatory processes, while also building immunity, peas are health-promoting morsels in "pea-sized" packages. Helpful in regulating blood sugar through their low glycemic index rating, peas also contain loads of fiber that can contribute to smooth digestion and regularity, while preventing certain cancers, too! Contributing a creamy green color to any smoothie, peas are a nutritional vegetable that adds a splendid, unexpected sweetness.

ROMAINE LETTUCE

1 cup leaves = 1 veggie serving

To prepare: Separate leaves and wash thoroughly

Vitamin C, potassium, and beta-carotene are the triple threat of vitamins, minerals, and phytochemicals that charge up this crisp, slightly sweet vegetable. Protecting the heart and blood with its potassium and beta-carotene, and the immune system with the vitamin C, romaine is a great-tasting ingredient with tons of nutrition and helpful health benefits that improve the power of any smoothie immensely.

SPINACH

1 cup leaves or ½ cup cooked = 1 veggie serving

To prepare: Wash thoroughly

Given this deep green veggie's popularity and recognition for its ability to promote muscle strength and immunity protection, Popeye's obsession with this leafy green wasn't that far off base. Packed with calcium, iron, fiber, and folate (a B vitamin), spinach is loaded with benefits that can promote bone health, stimulate the digestive system, and improve both the blood's quality and the heart's overall functioning. The combination of folate, iron, and calcium makes spinach an absolute necessity in any pregnant woman's diet for immense benefits to the developing fetus, as well as the expectant mom.

SPIRULINA

With more protein than even meat and soy, spirulina is actually a type of algae. Brimming with valuable minerals like calcium, magnesium, and iron, this fresh green addition works great in green smoothies, and it can boost the nutrition content of many fruit and vegetable smoothies, too. Available in powder, liquid, or its natural form, spirulina is packed with antioxidants that can provide tons of health benefits.

WHEATGRASS

A wonderful addition to smoothies that boosts the nutritional content exponentially, this green is packed with vitamins A for optimal mineral absorption, B for improved metabolism, and C for better immunity, along with a host of minerals—including calcium and iron, which act to ensure both bone and blood health. Packed with fiber, this green also contains enzymes and antioxidants that can promote health in any number of ways.

ZUCCHINI

½ cup raw/cooked = 1 veggie serving

To prepare: Wash thoroughly and chop

With B vitamins, and minerals like calcium and potassium, zucchini is a "blank canvas" vegetable that adds little flavor but provides nutritional benefits to the body, including stronger bones and teeth, improved metabolism function, and increased water content—making it a nutritious addition to predominately fruit smoothies that already pack some flavorful elements.

Violet

BEETS

1 large or ½ cup cut up = 1 veggie serving

To prepare: Wash, peel, and boil until tender, approximately 15 minutes

Containing a unique phytonutrient called betalin, beets provide and protect your body's total health by acting as powerful antioxidants that fight off infections and cell mutations, as anti-toxin combatants by detoxifying the body's major organs and blood, and as anti-inflammatory agents that can promote a healthy body free

of diseases and aches and pains. Slap on some gloves to prevent staining on hands and clothes, boil some beets until tender (roughly 15 minutes), and start adding these delicious and nutritious morsels to your power smoothies for even more power!

EGGPLANT

½ cup cubed = 1 veggie serving

To prepare: Wash thoroughly, remove stem, and chop

With a beautiful deep purple skin that looks as though it was sprayed with a glossy sheen, eggplants are as eye-catching as they are nutritious. Packed with tons of nutrients, this vegetable is most highly noted as containing rich amounts of powerful anthocyanins that serve as defending antioxidants that ensure proper functioning of the brain, the skin, the heart, and all of the elements of the blood. Because it has only a slight taste, eggplant can be a delicious background flavor that also serves to boost the nutritional value in many smoothies.

RED CABBAGE

½ cup chopped = 1 veggie serving

To prepare: Separate leaves and wash thoroughly

Rich in vitamins A and C that both serve to protect skin and eye health, red cabbage is brimming with health benefits. The abundant purple anthocyanins that lend this cabbage its beautiful hue also make it one of the best sources of cancer-combating, inflammation-fighting foods you can get. Crisp and unique in flavor, this delicious ingredient is a perfect star or addition to any smoothie, adding color, flavor, and amazing health benefits.

Meet Your Herbs and Spices

Many people think of herbs and spices as the dried varieties that add intense flavors to entrees, soups, and baked goods, but many of those aromatic additions can act in their fresh state as perfect smoothie ingredients that improve the nutritional content while also boosting the flavor. Even in very small amounts, fresh herbs from basil and rosemary to vanilla and cloves can be packed with important vitamins, minerals, phytochemicals, and fiber that add these essential nutrients to healthy smoothies—and all with the added benefits of unique taste sensations.

Basil

To prepare: Wash thoroughly and remove stems

A potent, uniquely flavored herb rich in vitamins A and C plus beta-carotene, basil is one herb that can help your eyes, your heart, and your immunity while tingling your taste buds. Basil also adds a deep green coloring and equally bright taste sensation to any smoothie.

Cardamom

To prepare: Ground cardamom is preferred

Most well-known for creating the delightfully unique flavor of chai tea, cardamom contains an important chemical makeup of rich antioxidants that has the ability to improve the quality of one's overall health while also targeting specific conditions. Used in western medicine's treatment for soothing irritable digestive issues, cardamom is as respected as ginger by many who have used it to calm indigestion, nausea, and even headaches.

Cilantro

To prepare: Wash thoroughly and remove stems

Very powerful in taste, cilantro is just as powerful in its nutritional benefits, too. With minerals like iron and manganese for improved blood quality, cilantro also contains a long list of strong antioxidants that protect and promote overall health. These antioxidants join forces to fight off unhealthy levels of "bad" cholesterol while improving the "good," to promote healthy blood sugar levels, and to reduce inflammation throughout the body. Cilantro thus helps in the prevention of heart disease, diabetes, and other dangerous and debilitating conditions.

Cinnamon

To prepare: Use whole sticks or grate with a fine grater

Delicious, aromatic, and with a very distinct flavor, cinnamon provides an immense amount of health benefits, including blood sugar regulation, which can reduce the chances and effects of diabetes. Cinnamon's antimicrobial qualities can aid the immune system in fending off illness from bacterial invaders. As well, the rich content of iron and manganese can promote proper blood clotting. Abundant in nutrition and taste, cinnamon is a quality addition to any smoothie combination.

Cloves

To prepare: Crush or purchase ground

In addition to being the perfect ingredient for pumpkin pie and gingerbread, cloves are the perfect herbs to add to smoothies that need a little extra "kick." Packed with vitamin C for improved immunity and ultra-important calcium for bone and hormone health, this spice contains omega-3 fatty acids for better brain functioning, which may be the most enticing aspect of adding this to your diet. Contributing to reduced inflammation, better blood quality, and an improved immune system, cloves go far beyond being just another tasty spice.

Dill

To prepare: Wash thoroughly

Tiny, yet powerful, dill is surprisingly rich in iron, manganese, and calcium. This mineral-rich herb also contributes important antioxidants and fiber that offer major health benefits and give a light flavor to any smoothie. By promoting healthy functioning of all of the body's systems and protecting the blood, brain, and organs from immunity offenders, dill is a delightful herb that's as pretty as it is powerful.

Ginger

To prepare: Peel

Long renowned for its ability to settle stomachaches, ginger's natural healing properties can help with much, much more! Adding a sweet, yet slightly spicy, flavor to any smoothie as well as essential minerals like potassium, magnesium, and copper, ginger is a delicious and nutritious ingredient you'll enjoy having on hand. In addition to being able to calm nausea (especially in pregnant women experiencing morning sickness), ginger can act as a strong anti-inflammatory while also preventing certain cancers and debilitating diseases.

Mint

To prepare: Wash thoroughly and remove stems

By improving the quality of your blood and promoting better blood and cardiovascular functioning with all of its antioxidant power, mint adds quality health benefits to your fruit or vegetable smoothies. With the mint family containing varieties like peppermint and spearmint, your choices of mint additions allow for more experimentation while reaping major health benefits.

Rosemary

To prepare: Remove stems

Not just for sprinkling on roasted potatoes, this brain-healthy herb adds a rich, earthy flavor to your smoothies. But rosemary packs even more of a punch on the nutritional side. With its powerful antioxidant, carnosic acid, which has been shown to improve brain functioning, protect the important organ from free radical damage, and reduce the risk of strokes and other neurodegenerative diseases, rosemary is one herb that can really feed your brain.

Sage

To prepare: Remove stems

Rich in strong phenol compounds like *rosmarinic acid*, which benefit everything from the brain to the blood, this deep green herb can add a sweet, yet savory, flavor to your smoothie while boosting its health-helping properties. With strong antioxidants that promote well-being while preventing inflammation, sage is a simple herbal addition with powerful nutritional contributions.

Thyme

To prepare: Remove stems

Even adding a tablespoon of this vitamin K–filled herb to your daily diet can help promote optimal brain functioning by protecting the fatty tissues necessary for neuron firing. With the added benefits of thyme's content of iron on the blood, calcium on bones and teeth, and fiber on digestion, this delicious herb is paired best with vegetables and can make for a nutrition-boosting addition to your favorite smoothies.

Turmeric

To prepare: Ground turmeric is preferred

This delightfully deep orange-brown herb can turn any smoothie into one that has many health benefits. From cancer prevention to improved liver functioning, this antioxidant-rich ingredient can protect the body's cells from dangerous free radical damage while also promoting the functioning of essential processes throughout the body. Flushing toxins, combating cancer, and calming inflammation, turmeric's manganese, iron, and vitamin B6 content make this spice worth its weight in gold in terms of bettering your health!

Vanilla

To prepare: Slice bean lengthwise and remove the pulp

Vitamins of the B complex for improved metabolism, minerals like copper and manganese for better system functioning, and a specific phytochemical called *vanillin* that promotes quality overall health with its antioxidant properties all come together in this aromatic spice's nutritional makeup. Delicious and nutritious, the unique flavors and health benefits of vanilla make this spice a must-have for any smoothie that needs a little nutritional enhancement. Keep in mind though that vanilla extract is not the same as the actual pulp from the bean, so steer clear of the extracts and stick to the potent pulp.

Optional Additions

Simplicity is best, but sometimes you just need to add a little something extra. Whether you're looking for ingredients that will improve the amount of a specific nutrient, add texture, or enhance the flavor of your smoothie, there are many optional additions available. Here, you'll find suggestions for smoothie additions that simplify your smoothie making by breaking down each ingredient by its flavor, nutrition, health benefits, and overall contribution to you smoothies. Please note that any changes to a prescribed diet should be made only after you consult with your physician.

Agave Nectar and Honeys

Being natural sweeteners, honey and agave nectars add a lot of sweetness with loads of nutrition and health benefits. Acting as a strong source of antibacterial, antimicrobial, and antifungal agents, the powerful antioxidants of honey and agave make for a much more beneficial alternative to other (not-so-natural) sweeteners available.

Almonds

Rich in vitamin E, manganese, and magnesium, these delicious nuts lend a mild nutty flavor and tons of health benefits to any smoothie. Helpful in controlling blood sugar levels, controlling the amount of "bad" cholesterol (LDL) in the blood, and contributing a clean source of protein, almonds are a delicious way to serve and protect your body!

Flaxseeds

High in omega-3 content, which benefits the brain and all of the body's cells, ground flaxseed is a simple way to boost the brain-healthy quality of any smoothie. Also contributing lecithin, an antioxidant that can facilitate digestion, flaxseeds are a mild, nutty-flavored, healthy ingredient to add.

Hazelnuts

Containing vitamin E and many B vitamins, along with important minerals like calcium, magnesium, and potassium, hazelnuts add more than just delicious taste to your smoothies. Protecting the eyes, the heart, the blood, and the digestive system, hazelnuts put their nutrients to good use.

Maple Syrup

High concentrations of zinc and manganese in maple syrup work to promote cell functioning and nutrient processing and absorption. As well, antioxidants that promote total health add nutritional benefits to your smoothies, with the sweetness that can come only from maple syrup. With fewer calories and more minerals than honey, maple syrup is a delicious and nutritious alternative to other natural sweeteners.

Oats

Steel-cut oats boost the energy-promoting carbohydrate content of any smoothie while adding tons of delicious flavor and heart-healthy vitamins and minerals. Also a great aid in regulating blood sugar levels and preventing serious diseases like cardiovascular disease and diabetes, oats are a delicious and nutritious thickening agent for any smoothie.

Protein Powder

Available in whey or soy varieties, there are more protein powders available on the market than you can possibly imagine. These supplemental protein sources boost the protein content and Branch Chain Amino Acids (BCAAs)—both of which work to improve muscle function. Lending a variety of base flavors, including vanilla, chocolate, and strawberry, protein powders can boost the nutrition of your smoothie with just one scoop.

Walnuts

Whole walnuts are miniature nutrition powerhouses packed with vitamin E, monounsaturated fats (the healthy kind!), and omega-3 fatty acids. These healthy nutrients help this nut work as an anti-inflammatory, act as a strong antioxidant, and provide healthy fats essential for brain functioning.

Wheat Germ

Boosting vitamin E and vitamin B content in your favorite smoothies for improved blood health and metabolic functioning, this delightfully crunchy addition can add loads of the important mineral copper, which will help everything from nerve impulses to blood quality.

Optional Base Liquids

If you think you have to start your smoothie with
a splash of milk, you couldn't be more wrong!
With a variety of liquids available to use as a base
for your smoothies, you can customize however
you want. From hydrating water with no colors, flavors, or calories to flavored kefir, which
is packed with probiotics (micro-organisms
that boost your immune system and neutralize
bad bacteria; you'll find probiotic powder added
into various smoothies throughout) and protein,
there are quality liquid additions available that
can boost the taste and the nutritional value of
your smoothies. Rather than opting for cow's
milk which can be packed with unwanted hormones and antibiotics, these milk alternatives
offer sound nutrition without the unwanted
additives. Which ones will be your favorites?

Almond Milk

Almond milk is packed with all of the benefits that come from a delicious and nutritious top
nut: the almond. Brimming with vitamin E and
loads of minerals, including copper, magnesium,
and calcium, which fight free radical damage and
protect the heart, hair, eyes, and bones, almond
milk is a low-calorie, healthy fat–containing
ingredient perfect for any smoothie, whether it's
veggie or fruit. You can make almond milk from
scratch at home or buy it at a grocery or health
food store.

┌─ *Easy, Homemade Almond Milk* ─────

If you find yourself fresh out of your favorite
store-bought almond milk or are interested in
creating your very own homemade version,
the process is easy. Simply combine 1 cup
of natural almonds with 2 cups of water in a
blender and emulsify completely until all bits
are blended. This creation can be stored for
up to three or four days in your fridge . . . if it
even lasts that long!

Coconut Milk

Boasting an impressive amount of calcium that far surpasses the calcium content of
2% dairy milk, new varieties of lactose-free,
dairy-free coconut milks are becoming more
readily available. Low in calories and containing Medium Chain Amino Acids (MCAAs)—a

healthy fat found in coconuts—this slightly sweet and very tasty liquid addition can help load any smoothie with ever-important nutrition and very few calories. Keep in mind that the coconut milk included in these recipes is not the canned variety that is packed with sweeteners and additives.

Coffee

You may not have even thought about adding coffee to your smoothie, but regular coffee is actually surprisingly high in antioxidants that aid in combating free radical damage to cells. Lending a strong, unique taste to smoothie blends, coffee can give a "kick" to your favorite recipes while also counting as important daily recommended water servings.

Greek-Style Yogurts

Adding an average of 20 grams of muscle health–promoting protein (which is considerably higher than the average 10 grams delivered in traditional yogurts), Greek-style yogurt also contributes fewer carbohydrates in each healthy dose. Creating a thick, creamy texture in your favorite smoothies, this yogurt is a healthy addition that can turn any plain old smoothie into a protein-packed power smoothie in just one whirl.

Juices

Most smoothie recipes recommend using water as the base liquid because it doesn't have any additives and because it's the most natural source of hydration, but some recipes use not-from-concentrate, organic apple juice for an added sweetness that is still in a natural form. Because many juices are from concentrate, packed with sugars, or have been altered with added coloring, flavoring, and various additives, it's a good idea to use only juices that are labeled "all natural, organic, not from concentrate." Those juices don't contain any added sugars and have an ingredient list made up of only fruit and water. Luckily, because smoothies contain so many flavorful ingredients, flavored juices aren't really necessary.

Kefir

Kefir, a smooth, yogurtlike milk alternative, will give your smoothie a creamy depth with loads of flavor. Easily digested because of its high content of probiotics, along with B vitamins, vitamin K, and biotin, kefir works well with both fruit- and vegetable-based smoothies—and, since variety is the spice of life, kefir is available in its natural flavor as well as blueberry and strawberry.

Rice Milk

Another alternative to traditional dairy milk, rice milk offers up amazing nutrition in a light, waterlike, lightly flavored liquid. Processed from brown rice, this "milk" is packed with important B vitamins that benefit everything from the metabolism to skin, hair, and nails. In addition, rice milk also contains a healthy dose of vitamin E, which aids your body in vitamin and mineral absorption.

Soymilk

The FDA, American Heart Association, and the American Cancer Society all approve and promote soymilk as a healthy, nutritious liquid addition to any daily diet. While its taste is mild and its texture feels like a thinner version of common dairy milks, soymilk contains vitamin B and added calcium and minerals, which are able to fend off certain cancers, fight "bad" cholesterols, reverse the bone loss associated with osteoporosis, and regulate blood sugar.

Buyer Beware

While there are many organizations and researchers that promote the use of soymilk in the diet, there are numerous studies that have been performed and are still ongoing concerning the amount of estrogen in soy and soy products. While the effects soy's estrogen can have on consumers may be minimal, it is important to note that soy has been suspected to contribute to early development in young children and possibly to act as a contributing factor in certain cancers.

Teas

Green, white, black, red raspberry tea leaf, and many other organic, natural varieties of tea contain rich amounts of antioxidants that can fight free radicals that damage the body's cells. Lending light flavors, but rich colors, tea is a delightful, nutrient-rich addition to any smoothie. Just remember to use tea that's been given time to cool rather than tea that's piping hot.

Water

The standard recommendation for daily water intake is eight 8-ounce portions, but many people don't reach those hydrating goals. Free of added colors, flavors, and sugars, water is a total-body conditioning tool that is absolutely necessary for optimal brain and body functioning. By "sneaking" water into your smoothies, you can quickly and easily take care of water requirements in a delightfully delicious way!

Time to Make a Smoothie

Now that you know what ingredients you need to put into your smoothies, it's time to see what supplies you'll need. The following items are necessary to keep your smoothie-making fast, easy, and fun!

Designated Area

Wherever you're planning to prepare your smoothies, you want to set aside a clean, designated area that will keep your preparation, creation, and cleanup as quick and efficient as possible. By simplifying the smoothie-making process, you may find it easier to stick to the new lifestyle . . . and enjoy the benefits every day for the rest of your days! A smoothie station doesn't require much space, but you'll need room to keep the essential tools (described next) until needed, when being used, and after cleanup.

Blender

If you're going to be drinking a lot of smoothies, you'll want to have a blender on hand. Whether you use a top-of-the-line smoothie emulsifier or rely on a blender that you've had for years is your choice. The speed or intensity of the setting you use shouldn't make a difference

in the smoothie's taste; as long as you're able to blend the ingredients thoroughly, your blender is perfect! Loud or quiet, new or old, expensive or cheap, as long as it works, you're good to go.

Cutting Board

Because produce has juices, and the colors of those juices are as vibrant as the fruits that produce them, a cutting board will save you from stains, drips, or just messes that can be easily avoided. For maximum efficiency, simplify the process and speed up your cleanup with a trusty little stowaway cutting board.

Cutting Tools

A sharp knife that can remove rinds, cut through cores, or separate skin is a very useful tool in any smoothie station. Being able to remove the unnecessary parts of the produce in a safe and timely manner will make your smoothie-creation experience that much more enjoyable. You won't have to struggle with a knife that's not sharp enough or a corer that's missing. You may also want to invest in a peeler; this speedy tool can come in handy when even a sharp knife seems to make a job just a little too tedious.

Storage for Whole Foods

Because fruits and veggies start to lose their nutrients soon after being harvested (unless flash frozen), you will benefit from more plentiful and powerful vitamins, minerals, and phytochemicals if you use your produce at its freshest! Try to use your fruit and vegetables as soon as possible after their purchase to ensure you're getting the most by sipping the rainbow. Until you're able to use them, though, you'll want to store them in cool, dark places to prevent them from going bad quickly. Refrigerating fresh produce is a great option as well, but may cause foods to expire more quickly.

Storage Containers for Liquids

After you've prepared your smoothie, you have the option of consuming the entire heaping helping, or storing it for later. (Note that 1 cup = 1 serving throughout.) Because smoothies contain all-natural fruits, vegetables, and ingredients, unfortunately they won't stay fresh for very long. Unless you freeze the remaining smoothie in a glass container appropriate to the smoothie's amount, only refrigerate your smoothie for a few hours. Otherwise, it may not be appetizing (or healthy) to consume.

Making Your Perfect Smoothie: Decisions, Decisions

Now that you know all about the important ingredients you can choose from, any possible additions, and the basic smoothie station tools, it's time to take a look at some helpful tips that can make mastering smoothie-making as fast, easy, and enjoyable as possible. Because this is a new approach to bettering your health, it's important that it fits into your lifestyle, that you enjoy it enough to stick with it, and that you reap the benefits by including all of the colors of the rainbow in your smoothies.

Typically, people who quit new routines do so out of frustration, because they feel overwhelmed, or because they're trying to change too much too quickly. But smoothie-making can become the best part of your day if you think things through ahead of time, and just try to keep the process simple. Remember, the goal is to have fun, feel great, and better your life! As you begin, simply keep the following advice in mind.

Celebrate the Four Seasons

With every season, you can create delicious smoothies with amazingly fresh fruits and veggies that just seem to personify that time of year. Amazing citrus in the summer and delicious apples and pumpkins in the fall make for a nutrition-packed treat that matches the weather outside. Also, choosing smoothie recipes that use fruits and veggies at their seasonal peak allows you to make fresh-tasting, nutrient-rich smoothies to die for! So mix and match all different kinds of ingredients with your favorite in-season produce to create even more great-tasting smoothies you'll enjoy. For example, if you love peaches, there's nothing that will beat the sensational taste of fresh, juicy peaches in their prime, and the same goes for vibrant, ripe strawberries. Just keep it fresh, keep it fun, and have a great time experimenting with all of the many ways you can use smoothies as your delicious way to better health!

Decide on Savory or Sweet

By adding distinct flavors—as well as plentiful vitamins and minerals—each fruit and vegetable brings something unique to the table, and that distinction is what will help you create amazingly delicious smoothie recipes. If you prefer sweeter smoothies, fruits like berries and tropical fruits, and veggies like sweet carrots and squashes, may be more in touch with your tastes. If savory smoothies are your thing, delicious concoctions of vibrant vegetables and herbs may turn into a smoothie suited to your savory sensations.

What to Avoid

Canned fruits and vegetables are best to avoid when you consider ingredients designed for optimal health benefits. Because canned varieties normally contain high levels of sugars and sodium, preservatives, syrups, or added ingredients, they should be saved for different dishes. Keep your smoothies natural, whole, and healthy. Aside from certain canned varieties that specify the ingredients as organic, natural, no preservatives, no additives, and no added sugars, steer clear of canned alternatives.

Keep Your Goals in Mind

Because fruits and vegetables vary so extremely in terms of their color, nutrition, and health benefits, keep the nutritional payoffs of the fruits and veggies discussed earlier in this chapter in mind as you choose what to put into your smoothie. For example, if you're looking for the perfect smoothie recipe that packs a punch of repairing protein, a recipe rich in fruits or vegetables that support protein synthesis, with the added benefits of a protein powder addition, may be just what the doctor ordered. Trying different taste combinations, using the best ingredients, and making the best smoothies possible with the healthiest goals in mind will keep your diet on track for better health and the best life ever!

Part 2

Smoothies

Now that you know what to use to create beautiful, rainbow smoothies, it's time to learn exactly *how* you can create them. In this part, each color is introduced with a detailed explanation of the unique vitamins, minerals, and phytochemicals that can be found in the fruits and vegetables of that particular shade. And along with a convenient list of specific nutrients, you'll learn about the variety of health improvements you can benefit from just by including these colorful fruits and vegetables in your diet.

Sweet or savory, the smoothies that follow appeal to any taste or craving imaginable. And by combining delicious fruits and vegetables to create completely different taste sensations—and provide unique health benefits as a result—you can enjoy a smoothie creation that not only appeals to your taste buds, but also contains the perfect combination of nutrients that will fit your health needs and help you reach your goals for better health. Enjoy!

Chapter 3

White

Apples • *Bananas* • *Cauliflower* • *Coconuts* • *Garlic* •
Ginger • *Mushrooms* • *Onions* • *Pears* • *Potatoes*

When looking for fruits and vegetables to use in your smoothies, don't overlook the pale or white produce that's used in the recipes in this chapter. Their pale coloring doesn't mean that these fruits and veggies are missing any nutrients; rather, they hold rich varieties of phytochemicals and are packed full of additional vitamins and minerals.

White fruits and veggies contain allicin, a phytochemical that promotes heart health and protects the body's immunity while promoting enzyme activity, as well as lignans, powerful antioxidants that may reduce the risks of breast, colon, and ovarian cancers. *Epigallocatechin gallate* (EGCG), a powerful antioxidant that has been researched for its benefits in fighting deadly autoimmune diseases and cancers is also found in white foods. Powerful and mighty, this combination of strong crusaders in the fight against cancers and disease is reason enough to include them in your diet on a regular basis.

In addition, white foods contain a high amount of vitamins, which play an important role in the body by targeting specific areas in which they can help promote the best possible functioning. The white group of produce is plentiful in vitamins like Bs (namely folate), C, and K, which take total body health to a whole new level. Consuming these vitamins promotes a healthy metabolism, aids in digestion, and betters nutrient processing and absorption, which means better use of carbohydrates for energy, better protein synthesis and use for repair, and optimal delivery of essential nutrients to the heart, muscles, and nervous system. In addition, these vitamins improve energy levels that are maintained for longer periods of time, aid in the production of red blood cells, maintain healthy blood cholesterol by increasing the amount of "good" (HDL) while reducing the amount of "bad" (LDL), regulate the formation and levels of hormones, promote healthy immunity, and protect cells from damage by acting as a strong antioxidant. They even reduce the risk for serious illnesses and diseases, including cardiovascular disease, stroke, and cancers. White fruits and veggies also provide a beneficial list of minerals, including calcium, magnesium, manganese, potassium, selenium, and zinc, which all contribute to the body's overall health by improving the quality of nutrient absorption and production, as well as the effectiveness of the nutrition delivered to teeth and bones, cells, major organs, the blood, the nervous system, the heart, the brain, and even the skin. Deficiencies of these vitamins and minerals can result in symptoms that range from slight, like insomnia, to severe, like bone loss and chronic fatigue. Your best bet for total health is to include the whites in your colored smoothies.

In addition to experiencing the health benefits of white smoothies, you'll also find that white produce is incredibly versatile. Because the produce available in the paler color spectrum include sweet and spicy, these sweet and savory foods are delicious and nutritious ingredients that can be combined with other colors to "vamp up" vibrantly colored recipes or act alone for their very own white tasty treats. So, the next time you're perusing the grocery store, produce stand, or farmers' market for some great produce that will pack a punch in tasty nutrition, keep these white foods in mind.

Basic Banana Blend

There's nothing easier than a simple recipe of just a few ingredients. And the potassium in the bananas here works to fight any water weight that may have occurred from eating high-sodium foods. This basic concoction of smooth, beautiful bananas needs nothing but water and ice to be an enticing smoothie that packs tons of flavor and nutrition, with just a quick whirl of the blender.

YIELDS: 2 CUPS

Ingredients

2 bananas, peeled
1 cup water
1 cup ice

1. In a blender, combine the bananas and water with ½ cup ice, and blend until thoroughly combined.

2. Add remaining ice as needed and blend until desired consistency is achieved.

PER 1 CUP SERVING Calories: 105 | Fat: 0.4 g | Protein: 1 g | Sodium: 1 mg | Fiber: 3 g | Carbohydrates: 27 g

Blissful Bananas

Even though this delicious smoothie packs tons of vitamins and minerals, its benefits don't stop there. The carbohydrate- and fiber-rich combination of bananas and oats in this delightful blend make for a satisfying snack or meal that will fuel your body, keep you focused, and satisfy your hunger.

YIELDS: 3 CUPS

Ingredients

2 bananas, peeled
¼ cup rolled oats
2 cups water
1 cup ice

1. In a blender, combine the bananas, oats, and 1 cup water with ½ cup ice, and blend until thoroughly combined.

2. While blending, add remaining water and ice until desired consistency is achieved.

PER 1 CUP SERVING Calories: 143 | Fat: 1 g | Protein: 3 g | Sodium: 2 mg | Fiber: 4 g | Carbohydrates: 34 g

Bananas with Bs

Bananas are packed with rich amounts of the vitamins B5 and B6, which makes them a delicious way to ensure that you're getting enough of these ultra-important vitamins, which promote energy and a healthy metabolism. Combined with creamy kefir, bananas ensure that the health benefits and the taste of this smoothie provide a scrumptious way to healthy living.

YIELDS: 3 CUPS

Ingredients

2 bananas, peeled
1 cup plain kefir
1 cup water
1 cup ice

1. In a blender, combine the bananas, kefir, and ½ cup water with ½ cup ice, and blend until thoroughly combined.

2. While blending, add remaining water and ice until desired consistency is achieved.

PER 1 CUP SERVING Calories: 115 | Fat: 0.5 g | Protein: 5.5 g | Sodium: 64 mg | Fiber: 2 g | Carbohydrates: 24 g

Banana Banger

If you're a peanut butter lover, this recipe is for you. Replacing common peanut butter, which may be packed with sodium, sugar, and trans fats, with all-natural almond butter, which packs protein, healthy fat, and great taste, this smoothie ensures that you'll provide your metabolism with the clean fuel it needs to function at its best.

YIELDS: 3 CUPS

Ingredients

2 bananas, peeled
2 tablespoons natural almond butter
1 cup plain kefir
1 cup water
1 cup ice

1. In a blender, combine the bananas, almond butter, kefir, and ½ cup water with ½ cup ice, and blend until thoroughly combined.

2. While blending, add remaining water and ice until desired consistency is achieved.

PER 1 CUP SERVING Calories: 140 | Fat: 3 g | Protein: 6 g | Sodium: 64 mg | Fiber: 2 g | Carbohydrates: 25 g

Banana Split

If you're like most people, banana splits bring back memories of carefree childhood bliss. Here, instead of using processed ice cream and additives, this smoothie uses all-natural ingredients that are packed full of B vitamins and vitamin C, minerals like potassium and calcium, and powerful phyto-chemicals, which work together to improve immunity and cell health. This puts a healthy spin on a not-so-healthy timeless classic.

YIELDS: 3 CUPS

Ingredients

2 bananas, peeled
½ cup coconut meat
¼ cup cherries, pitted
1 cup plain kefir
1 cup water
1 cup ice

1. In a blender, combine the bananas, coconut meat, cherries, kefir, and ½ cup water with ½ cup ice, and blend until thoroughly combined.

2. While blending, add remaining water and ice until desired consistency is achieved.

PER 1 CUP SERVING Calories: 127 | Fat: 1 g | Protein: 6 g | Sodium: 64 mg | Fiber: 2 g | Carbohydrates: 26 g

Vanilla Chiller

The simple flavor of vanilla is satisfying all on its own, but this smoothie combines it with aromatic cloves, sweet maple syrup, and the creaminess of kefir that make this smoothie deliciously light, bright, and flavorful. And if that's not exciting enough, vanilla is full of vanillin, an antioxidant that provides all of the body's systems' cells with protection against free radical damage.

YIELDS: 2 CUPS

Ingredients

2 vanilla beans' pulp
1 teaspoon ground cloves
1 teaspoon all-natural, organic maple syrup
2 cups plain kefir
1 cup ice

1. In a blender, combine the vanilla beans' pulp, cloves, maple syrup, and kefir with ½ cup ice, and blend until thoroughly combined.

2. While blending, add remaining ice until desired consistency is achieved.

PER 1 CUP SERVING Calories: 163 | Fat: 4 g | Protein: 14 g | Sodium: 194 mg | Fiber: 0.4 g | Carbohydrates: 23 g

Crazy for Coconuts

The simplicity of combining uniquely-flavored, vitamin B–packed coconut meat and coconut milk with the light flavor of pure vanilla bean makes for one delicious smoothie that also provides health benefits galore, including better blood quality and improved mood.

YIELDS: 3 CUPS

Ingredients

1 cup coconut meat
1 vanilla bean's pulp
2 cups coconut milk
1 cup ice

1. In a blender, combine the coconut meat, vanilla bean's pulp, and coconut milk with ½ cup ice, and blend until thoroughly combined.

2. While blending, add remaining ice until desired consistency is achieved.

PER 1 CUP SERVING Calories: 173 | Fat: 16 g | Protein: 1 g | Sodium: 25 mg | Fiber: 2 g | Carbohydrates: 6 g

Easy Island Time

Coconut meat, banana, and pineapple each lend their own unique flavor and texture to this delicious smoothie. But this combo provides more than just beauty and taste; the vitamin C and phytochemicals like bromelain improve immunity, better system functioning, and make this smoothie an all-around winner!

YIELDS: 4 CUPS

Ingredients

1 cup coconut meat
1 banana, peeled
½ cup pineapple
2 cups coconut milk
1 cup ice

1. In a blender, combine coconut meat, banana, pineapple, and coconut milk with ½ cup ice, and blend until thoroughly combined.

2. While blending, add remaining ice until desired consistency is achieved.

PER 1 CUP SERVING Calories: 163 | Fat: 12 g | Protein: 1 g | Sodium: 19 mg | Fiber: 3 g | Carbohydrates: 14 g

Heaven Scent

Heavenly: the word that best describes the aroma and taste of this deliciously sweet smoothie, which combines the flavors of coconut, banana, vanilla, aromatic spices, sweet maple syrup, and almonds. But while the smoothie may be heavenly—and heaven sent—the combination of nutrients like B vitamins and rich minerals packed in each sip will help keep you away from heaven's gates by protecting your blood, brain, and heart.

YIELDS: 3 CUPS

Ingredients

1 cup coconut meat
1 banana, peeled
1 vanilla bean's pulp
1 teaspoon ground cloves
1 teaspoon ground ginger
1 teaspoon all-natural, organic maple syrup
2 cups vanilla almond milk
2 cups ice

1. In a blender, combine the coconut meat, banana, vanilla bean's pulp, cloves, ginger, maple syrup, and almond milk with 1 cup ice, and blend until thoroughly combined.

2. While blending, add remaining ice until desired consistency is achieved.

PER 1 CUP SERVING Calories: 232 | Fat: 12 g | Protein: 7 g | Sodium: 92 mg | Fiber: 5 g | Carbohydrates: 26 g

Hydrating Honey

When you combine the nutrients found in bananas with the antioxidants found in honey, you get a very simple cocktail of health benefits. Packed with potassium from the bananas, this smoothie helps to maintain a healthy fluid balance of the body. And the amazingly rich honey brings some extra antioxidants—which help to keep cells healthy and protected from catastrophic cancerous mutations—with a unique sweetness that will really get your taste buds buzzing.

YIELDS: 2 CUPS

Ingredients

2 bananas, peeled
1 cup water
1 tablespoon all-natural, organic honey
1 cup ice

1. In a blender, combine the bananas, water, and honey with ½ cup ice, and blend until thoroughly combined.

2. While blending, add remaining ice until desired consistency is achieved.

PER 1 CUP SERVING Calories: 138 | Fat: 0.4 g | Protein: 1 g | Sodium: 2 mg | Fiber: 3 g | Carbohydrates: 36 g

The Bee's Knees

Sweet honey swirls in each sip of this delicious smoothie blend, which is packed with nutritious ingredients like banana, oats, wheat germ, and kefir. A thick, creamy treat, this will boost your energy levels and keep you moving all day long.

YIELDS: 3 CUPS

Ingredients

1 banana, peeled
¼ cup rolled oats
⅛ cup honey wheat germ
2 tablespoons all-natural, organic honey
2 cups plain kefir
1 cup ice

1. In a blender, combine the banana, oats, wheat germ, honey, and kefir with ½ cup ice, and blend until thoroughly combined.

2. While blending, add remaining ice until desired consistency is achieved.

PER 1 CUP SERVING Calories: 212 | Fat: 1 g | Protein: 12 g | Sodium: 128 mg | Fiber: 2 g | Carbohydrates: 40 g

Spicy Pear Surprise

The sweet and unique flavor of delicious pears is combined with the aromatic blend of spicy ginger, cloves, and cardamom for a heightened sensual experience all swirled up in a nutritious smoothie. And if that wasn't enough, this smoothie is also packed to the brim with plentiful magnesium, which acts as the fuel that will start your metabolic fire!

YIELDS: 3 CUPS

Ingredients

2 pears, cored
1 teaspoon ground ginger
1 teaspoon ground cloves
1 teaspoon ground cardamom
2 cups water
1 cup ice

1. In a blender, combine the pears, ginger, cloves, cardamom, and 1 cup water with ½ cup ice, and blend until thoroughly combined.

2. While blending, add remaining water and ice until desired consistency is achieved.

PER 1 CUP SERVING Calories: 28 | Fat: 0 g | Protein: 0 g | Sodium: 2 mg | Fiber: 2 g | Carbohydrates: 7 g

Cauliflower-Garlic

Maybe you wouldn't think that a cauliflower and garlic smoothie would be delicious, but you'd be wrong. In addition to its bold taste, this smoothie also provides the antibacterial, antiviral antioxidant allicin found in garlic, which works diligently to protect your body from illness and disease. Quick, easy, and tasty, this savory smoothie satisfies your appetite *and* your daily veggie servings all at the same time.

YIELDS: 2 CUPS

Ingredients

2 cups cauliflower florets
2 garlic cloves
1 cup Greek-style yogurt
1 cup water
1 cup ice

1. In a blender, combine the cauliflower, garlic, yogurt, and ½ cup water with ½ cup ice, and blend until thoroughly combined.

2. While blending, add remaining water and ice until desired consistency is achieved.

PER 1 CUP SERVING Calories: 96 | Fat: 0 g | Protein: 14 g | Sodium: 77 mg | Fiber: 2 g | Carbohydrates: 11 g

Apple-nana

Simple and sweet, this smoothie takes the flavors of apples and bananas that you know and love, and blends them together in a cool, icy treat. The addition of pure apple juice gives this already sweet concoction a kick of apple deliciousness that helps blend everything together for a taste that's just right!

YIELDS: 2 CUPS

Ingredients

1 banana, peeled
1 yellow apple, cored
1 cup all-natural, organic apple juice (not from concentrate)
1 cup ice

1. In a blender, combine the banana, apple, and apple juice with ½ cup ice, and blend until thoroughly combined.

2. While blending, add remaining ice until desired consistency is achieved.

PER 1 CUP SERVING Calories: 91 | Fat: 0 g | Protein: 1 g | Sodium: 1 mg | Fiber: 3 g | Carbohydrates: 24 g

Coo-Coo for Coconuts

If you're a coconut lover, this smoothie will make you coo-coo! Combining only coconut meat and coconut milk with frosty ice for a delicious frothy treat, this is a smoothie that will make your taste buds sing! To make this smoothie even better, consider that fact that the B vitamins in every sip work hard to keep your brain and metabolism functioning at peak performance—making for a happier, fitter you!

YIELDS: 3 CUPS

Ingredients
2 cups coconut meat
2 cups coconut milk
1 cup ice

1. In a blender, combine the coconut meat and coconut milk with ½ cup ice, and blend until thoroughly combined.

2. While blending, add remaining ice until desired consistency is achieved.

PER 1 CUP SERVING Calories: 728 | Fat: 75 g | Protein: 7 g | Sodium: 45 mg | Fiber: 7 g | Carbohydrates: 19 g

Perfect Pears

Pears are practically perfect on their own, but when paired with pure apple juice, which adds an extra boost of flavor and a perfected texture, this pear smoothie becomes a sweet, simple, and delicious jolt of energy-promoting nutrition from its rich concentration of vitamin C and plentiful B vitamins.

YIELDS: 2 CUPS

Ingredients
2 pears, cored
1 cup all-natural, organic apple juice (not from concentrate)
1 cup ice

1. In a blender, combine the pears and apple juice with ½ cup ice, and blend until thoroughly combined.

2. While blending, add remaining ice until desired consistency is achieved.

PER 1 CUP SERVING Calories: 92 | Fat: 0 g | Protein: 1 g | Sodium: 5 mg | Fiber: 3 g | Carbohydrates: 23 g

Iced Apples and Spice

This frosty smoothie, which is packed with apples and delicious spices, will likely make you think of a delicious apple pie. Even though it's packed with bounds of nutrition from the rich vitamin C and *quercetin* in the apples and minerals in the spices, the smoothie tastes so great you may forget to focus on its powerful health benefits.

YIELDS: 2 CUPS

Ingredients
2 yellow apples, cored
1 teaspoon ground cinnamon
1 teaspoon ground cloves
1 teaspoon ground ginger
1 cup all-natural, organic apple juice (not from concentrate)
1 cup ice

1. In a blender, combine the apples, cinnamon, cloves, ginger, and apple juice with ½ cup ice, and blend until thoroughly combined.

2. While blending, add remaining ice until desired consistency is achieved.

PER 1 CUP SERVING Calories: 140 | Fat: 1 g | Protein: 1 g | Sodium: 8 mg | Fiber: 3 g | Carbohydrates: 36 g

Tasty Trio

Combining the sweet tastes of apple, banana, and pear in a smoothie blended with even sweeter apple juice adds an incredible amount of extra taste and texture! In addition, this Tasty Trio gives you a deliciously powerful treat packed with more nutrition than you'd probably every imagine! The B vitamins, potassium, and vitamin C all combine for a better-looking, better-feeling you!

YIELDS: 2½ CUPS

Ingredients
1 yellow apple, cored
1 banana, peeled
1 pear, cored
1 cup all-natural, organic apple juice (not from concentrate)
1 cup ice

1. In a blender, combine the apple, banana, pear, and apple juice with ½ cup ice, and blend until thoroughly combined.

2. While blending, add remaining ice until desired consistency is achieved.

PER 1 CUP SERVING Calories: 111 | Fat: 0 g | Protein: 1 g | Sodium: 4 mg | Fiber: 3 g | Carbohydrates: 28 g

Banana Nut

Forget about the banana bread packed with excess fat, calories, and who-knows-what-else, and opt for this delicious smoothie recipe instead! Using great ingredients that contribute to a wonderful taste, this smoothie goes above and beyond and gives your body protein, clean carbohydrates, and omega-3 and omega-6 fatty acids—all with the delicious taste of your favorite comfort bread!

YIELDS: 2 CUPS

Ingredients

1 cup vanilla almond milk
½ cup almonds
½ cup walnuts
2 bananas, peeled
1 cup ice

1. In a blender, combine the almond milk with the almonds and walnuts and blend until nuts are completely emulsified.

2. Add the bananas and ½ cup ice, and blend until thoroughly combined.

3. While blending, add remaining ice until desired consistency is achieved.

PER 1 CUP SERVING Calories: 486 | Fat: 32 g | Protein: 14 g | Sodium: 62 mg | Fiber: 8 g | Carbohydrates: 40 g

Pear and Banana Passion Smoothie

Loaded up with tons of protein for muscle repair, probiotics for immune-system support, and antioxidants for cell protection simply by adding protein powder, kefir, and aromatic spices, this smoothie gives pears an even more powerful presence in the long list of foods you should consume daily.

YIELDS: 3 CUPS

Ingredients

2 pears, cored
1 cup plain kefir
1 scoop vanilla protein powder
1 teaspoon cinnamon
1 cup water
1 cup ice

1. In a blender, combine the pears, kefir, protein powder, cinnamon, and water with ½ cup ice, and blend until thoroughly combined.

2. While blending, add remaining ice until desired consistency is achieved.

PER 1 CUP SERVING Calories: 107 | Fat: 1 g | Protein: 13 g | Sodium: 63 mg | Fiber: 2 g | Carbohydrates: 13 g

Calming Coconut Cooler

If you're out of ideas for bedtime treats that contribute more than sugar, fat, and calories, you're looking at the right recipe! Here smooth chamomile tea meets with the natural, unique sweetness of coconut and ginger for a nutritious, sensational-tasting smoothie that will set your mind at ease and gently rock you off to sleep.

YIELDS: 2 CUPS

Ingredients

1½ cups coconut meat
1½ cups cooled chamomile tea
1 tablespoon grated ginger
1 cup ice

1. In a blender, combine the coconut meat, chamomile tea, and grated ginger with ½ cup ice, and blend until thoroughly combined.

2. While blending, add remaining ice until desired consistency is achieved.

PER 1 CUP SERVING Calories: 215 | Fat: 20 g | Protein: 2 g | Sodium: 12 mg | Fiber: 5 g | Carbohydrates: 10 g

Button Mushroom Bliss

If you thought mushrooms were great only in entrees and soups, think again! This smoothie makes for a savory treat when you're not really craving something sweet. Combining mushrooms, garlic, and creamy kefir, this smooth, savory concoction will hit the spot and provide rich nutrients like iron, magnesium, and probiotics for improved immunity, too.

YIELDS: 2 CUPS

Ingredients

1 cup white button mushrooms
2 cloves garlic
1 cup plain kefir
½ cup water
1 cup ice

1. In a blender, combine the mushrooms, garlic, and kefir with ½ cup ice, and blend until thoroughly combined.

2. While blending, add water and remaining ice until desired consistency is achieved.

PER 1 CUP SERVING Calories: 80 | Fat: 0 g | Protein: 8 g | Sodium: 97 mg | Fiber: 0 g | Carbohydrates: 12 g

Cool Cauliflower Blend

When you use lightly flavored cauliflower as your smoothie's star, the possibilities are infinite! This pleasant-tasting, smooth base allows you to add eye-opening, sweet yellow onions and pungent garlic for a rich smoothie that's out of this world! Here the rich phytochemicals found in garlic and onions combine to fend off illnesses by promoting immunity wrapped in deliciousness. What could be better than that?

YIELDS: 2 CUPS

Ingredients
1 cup cauliflower florets
½ yellow onion
2 cloves garlic
1 cup plain kefir
½ cup water
1 cup ice

1. In a blender, combine the cauliflower, onion, garlic, and kefir with ½ cup ice, and blend until thoroughly combined.

2. While blending, add the water and remaining ice until desired consistency is achieved.

PER 1 CUP SERVING Calories: 96 | Fat: 0 g | Protein: 8 g | Sodium: 111 mg | Fiber: 2 g | Carbohydrates: 15 g

Mega Mashed Potato

Your favorite side dish just got a delicious makeover. Packed with B vitamins, minerals such as copper and magnesium, and complex carbohydrates that all work together to supply long-lasting energy, this smoothie takes potatoes to a portable convenience in a delicious treat packed with valuable nutrition.

YIELDS: 2 CUPS

Ingredients
1 cup potatoes, softened and removed from skin
2 cloves garlic
½ cup yellow onion
1 cup plain kefir
1 cup water
1 cup ice

1. In a blender, combine the potatoes, garlic, onion, kefir, and ½ cup water with ½ cup ice, and blend until thoroughly combined.

2. While blending, add remaining water and ice until desired consistency is achieved.

PER 1 CUP SERVING Calories: 140 | Fat: 0 g | Protein: 9 g | Sodium: 101 mg | Fiber: 3 g | Carbohydrates: 26 g

Potassium-Packed Protein Smoothie

As if bananas weren't nutritious enough on their own, this smoothie includes protein powder and kefir. This delicious combination adds protein and probiotics to the already important potassium-rich fruits, which work together to fuel muscles with nutrition while keeping an optimum fluid balance.

YIELDS: 3 CUPS

Ingredients

2 bananas, peeled
1 scoop vanilla protein powder
1 cup plain kefir
1 cup water
1 cup ice

1. In a blender, combine the bananas, protein powder, kefir, and ½ cup water with ½ cup ice, and blend until thoroughly combined.

2. While blending, add remaining water and ice until desired consistency is achieved.

PER 1 CUP SERVING Calories: 152 | Fat: 1 g | Protein: 14 g | Sodium: 64 mg | Fiber: 2 g | Carbohydrates: 25 g

Simple Apple Smoothie

You've heard the saying, "an apple a day keeps the doctor away," so get your apple in at breakfast, lunch, dinner, dessert, or snack time. With tons of flavor and a sweet, refreshing hit of nutrition from all of the immunity-building vitamin C, this recipe makes for a delectable treat that's quick, easy, and simply sweet.

YIELDS: 2 CUPS

Ingredients

2 yellow apples, cored
1 cup all-natural, organic apple juice (not from concentrate)
1 cup ice

1. In a blender, combine the apples and apple juice with ½ cup ice, and blend until thoroughly combined.

2. While blending, add remaining ice until desired consistency is achieved.

PER 1 CUP SERVING Calories: 134 | Fat: 0 g | Protein: 1 g | Sodium: 5 mg | Fiber: 2 g | Carbohydrates: 35 g

Sweet and Spicy Apple-Pear

The zing of ginger adds a powerful antioxidant-packed kick to the apple-pear splendor in this delicious smoothie. Protecting everything from the skin to the heart with the anti-inflammatory benefits of the antioxidants, all of the fruits and spice in this recipe combine for a sweet, spicy way to consume those fruit servings without any trouble at all!

YIELDS: 2 CUPS

Ingredients

1 yellow apple, cored
1 pear, cored
1 cup all-natural, organic apple juice (not from concentrate)
1 tablespoon grated ginger
1 cup ice

1. In a blender, combine the apple, pear, juice, and ginger with ½ cup ice, and blend until thoroughly combined.

2. While blending, add remaining ice until desired consistency is achieved.

PER 1 CUP SERVING Calories: 115 | Fat: 0 g | Protein: 1 g | Sodium: 5 mg | Fiber: 3 g | Carbohydrates: 29 g

Smooth Chai Chiller

While chai lattes and teas can be found in almost any street corner's coffee shop, this natural alternative is full of powerful antioxidant-rich ingredients like banana, coconut, ginger, spices, and creamy almond milk, which combine to create a delightfully great-tasting recipe that also helps your body fight disease! Let's see your favorite coffeehouse do that!

YIELDS: 4 CUPS

Ingredients

1 banana, peeled
½ cup coconut meat
1 teaspoon ground ginger
1 teaspoon cinnamon
1 teaspoon ground cloves
1 teaspoon ground cardamom
2 cups vanilla almond milk
1 cup ice

1. In a blender, combine the banana, coconut meat, ginger, cinnamon, cloves, cardamom, and almond milk with ½ cup ice, and blend until thoroughly combined.

2. While blending, add remaining ice until desired consistency is achieved.

PER 1 CUP SERVING Calories: 100 | Fat: 5 g | Protein: 4 g | Sodium: 63 mg | Fiber: 3 g | Carbohydrates: 13 g

Snow White

The tropical flavors of coconut and pineapple are whirled into creamy coconut milk for a delicious treat that's amped up with the sweet addition of vanilla and the spicy kick of ginger. Packed with tons of nutritious vitamins and minerals like B vitamins and vitamin C that help build up immunity, this smoothie takes out any ice cream or frozen yogurt option!

YIELDS: 2 CUPS

Ingredients

1 cup coconut meat
¼ cup pineapple
1 tablespoon grated ginger
1 vanilla bean's pulp
1½ cups coconut milk
1 cup ice

1. In a blender, combine the coconut meat, pineapple, ginger, vanilla bean's pulp, and coconut milk with ½ cup ice, and blend until thoroughly combined.

2. While blending, add remaining ice until desired consistency is achieved.

PER 1 CUP SERVING Calories: 492 | Fat: 50 g | Protein: 5 g | Sodium: 30 mg | Fiber: 4 g | Carbohydrates: 13 g

Creamy Pear Perfection

Pears and protein powder that provide your muscles with all of the necessary nutrition for repair make for a creamy spin on "healthy" drink options. Delicious and unique, this smoothie gets even better with the addition of probiotic-rich kefir for immunity-protecting power. Helping out with all aspects of your health, this powerful, tasty smoothie will do your body good!

YIELDS: 2 CUPS

Ingredients

2 pears, cored
1 scoop vanilla protein powder
1 cup plain kefir
1 cup ice

1. In a blender, combine the pears, protein powder, and kefir with ½ cup ice, and blend until thoroughly combined.

2. While blending, add remaining ice until desired consistency is achieved.

PER 1 CUP SERVING Calories: 158 | Fat: 1 g | Protein: 19 g | Sodium: 94 mg | Fiber: 3 g | Carbohydrates: 19 g

Slightly Spicy Celery-Apple

When you combine the unique, crisp flavors of celery and apple, you get a sweet blend of deliciousness with a slightly spicy kick. Brimming with important vitamins and minerals like vitamin C and sodium, which can aid in everything from digestion to "beating the bloat," these ingredients make for an amazing smoothie that tastes great and does a body better!

YIELDS: 2½ CUPS

Ingredients
2 celery stalks
2 yellow apples, cored
1 cup coconut milk
1 cup ice

1. In a blender, combine the celery, apples, and coconut milk with ½ cup ice, and blend until thoroughly combined.

2. While blending, add remaining ice until desired consistency is achieved.

PER 1 CUP SERVING Calories: 204 | Fat: 16 g | Protein: 2 g | Sodium: 31 mg | Fiber: 2 g | Carbohydrates: 16 g

White Tea Wonder

Fresh fruit and aromatic spice give white tea a delicious and nutritious spin that tastes amazing! Antioxidants, quercetin, and vitamin C, which are needed to maintain a healthy functioning of all of your body's systems, are packed into every sip of this sinful smoothie. It sure beats plain old tea and is way more appealing than an everyday piece of fruit.

YIELDS: 2 CUPS

Ingredients
1 yellow apple, cored
1 pear, cored
1 teaspoon ground cardamom
1½ cups white tea, cooled
1 cup ice

1. In a blender, combine the apple, pear, cardamom, and white tea with ½ cup ice, and blend until thoroughly combined.

2. While blending, add remaining ice until desired consistency is achieved.

PER 1 CUP SERVING Calories: 58 | Fat: 0 g | Protein: 0 g | Sodium: 2 mg | Fiber: 3 g | Carbohydrates: 15 g

Winter Wonderland

Rather than opting for a coffeehouse's calorie- and sugar-packed version of a spiced tea, this smoothie has amazing taste, tons of nutrition, and no unnatural ingredients. Its creaminess comes from the potassium-rich banana, its aromatic appeal from the fragrant variety of spice, and its plentiful, powerful antioxidants from the white tea. Raise your glass and drink up, because this smoothie is one delicious wonder!

YIELDS: 2 CUPS

Ingredients

2 cups white tea
1 teaspoon ground cinnamon
1 teaspoon ground nutmeg
1 teaspoon ground cloves
1 teaspoon ground cardamom
1 banana, peeled
1 cup ice

1. In a blender, combine the white tea, cinnamon, nutmeg, cloves, cardamom, and banana with ½ cup ice, and blend until thoroughly combined.

2. While blending, add remaining ice until desired consistency is achieved.

PER 1 CUP SERVING Calories: 64 | Fat: 2 g | Protein: 1 g | Sodium: 6 mg | Fiber: 2 g | Carbohydrates: 15 g

Summertime Splendor

When the tropical tastes of summer meet up in this smoothie, you'll want to savor every scrumptious sip! Filled with vitamin C, calcium, potassium, antioxidants, and fiber for amazing immunity protection, bone strength, and regularity, the creaminess and great-tasting tropical fruits combine in this recipe to make for one heck of a healthy treat!

YIELDS: 2 CUPS

Ingredients

1 cup pineapple
1 orange, peeled and deseeded
1 banana, peeled
1 cup coconut milk
1 cup ice

1. In a blender, combine the pineapple, orange, banana, and coconut milk with ½ cup ice, and blend until thoroughly combined.

2. While blending, add remaining ice until desired consistency is achieved.

PER 1 CUP SERVING Calories: 294 | Fat: 24 g | Protein: 3 g | Sodium: 15 mg | Fiber: 3 g | Carbohydrates: 22 g

Vanilla-Pear Perfection

Although pears taste delicious on their own, adding the naturally aromatic vanilla bean's pulp raises its deliciousness level just a bit. Tasting great isn't the only perk of this smoothie, when you take into consideration the disease-fighting antioxidant benefits that you get from the vanillin in each and every sip. Rich, creamy, and flavorful, this smoothie blends together an amazing fruit, a delicious spice, and smooth vanilla almond milk for a cool creation that's sure to amaze.

YIELDS: 2 CUPS

Ingredients
2 pears, cored
1 vanilla bean's pulp
1 cup vanilla almond milk
1 cup ice

1. In a blender, combine the pears, vanilla bean's pulp, and almond milk with ½ cup ice, and blend until thoroughly combined.

2. While blending, add remaining ice until desired consistency is achieved.

PER 1 CUP SERVING Calories: 77 | Fat: 1 g | Protein: 3 g | Sodium: 60 mg | Fiber: 4 g | Carbohydrates: 13 g

Squirrel-y Smoothie

Taking nuttiness to the next level, this healthy smoothie is packed with flavors that can only come from uniquely delicious nuts. The muscle-assisting protein, omega-3s and omega-6s, and healthy fats that all combine for better brain health and overall body functioning make this smoothie even better! Wonderful walnuts, amazing almonds, unique flaxseeds, and creamy almond milk combine with a sweet, smooth banana for a crazy creation that would make any squirrel nutty!

YIELDS: 2 CUPS

Ingredients
½ cup walnuts
½ cup almonds
⅛ cup ground flaxseed
1 banana, peeled
1 cup almond milk
1 cup ice

1. In a blender, combine the walnuts, almonds, flaxseed, banana, and almond milk with ½ cup ice, and blend until thoroughly combined.

2. While blending, add remaining ice until desired consistency is achieved.

PER 1 CUP SERVING Calories: 450 | Fat: 35 g | Protein: 15 g | Sodium: 61 mg | Fiber: 9 g | Carbohydrates: 29 g

Natural Fruit Sea Breeze

Savor the sensation of a brisk sea breeze in every amazing sip of this tropical concoction. Combining the tart flavors of citrus with sweet smooth banana, sweet pineapple, and coconut—and the high nutritional content of all the B vitamins found here—this smoothie will take your body to its metabolic peak performance and your mind to the beach with every dreamy, creamy sip!

YIELDS: 4 CUPS

Ingredients
1 whole white grapefruit, peeled and deseeded
1 banana, peeled
½ cup coconut meat
½ cup pineapple
1 cup coconut milk
1 cup ice

1. In a blender, combine the grapefruit, banana, coconut meat, pineapple, and coconut milk with ½ cup ice, and blend until thoroughly combined.

2. While blending, add remaining ice until desired consistency is achieved.

PER 1 CUP SERVING Calories: 204 | Fat: 16 g | Protein: 2 g | Sodium: 10 mg | Fiber: 3 g | Carbohydrates: 18 g

Maple-Cinnamon Oatmeal

When a steaming hot bowl of oatmeal doesn't do the trick, maybe the exact opposite is exactly what you need! Cool, creamy, and sweet, this smoothie takes the delicious flavors of rolled oats, aromatic cinnamon, and sweet maple syrup and combines them in an out-of-this-world oatmeal concoction that will take the place of hot oatmeal in anyone's heart!

YIELDS: 2 CUPS

Ingredients
1 banana, peeled
½ cup rolled oats
1 teaspoon organic, pure maple syrup
1 teaspoon ground cinnamon
1 cup vanilla almond milk
1 cup ice

1. In a blender, combine the banana, oats, maple syrup, cinnamon, and almond milk with ½ cup ice, and blend until thoroughly combined.

2. While blending, add remaining ice until desired consistency is achieved.

PER 1 CUP SERVING Calories: 175 | Fat: 3 g | Protein: 6 g | Sodium: 64 mg | Fiber: 4 g | Carbohydrates: 34 g

Garlicky Mushroom

Creamy, spicy, and filled with flavor, this mushroom smoothie does amazing things. The protein-packed Greek-style yogurt adds tons of creaminess to the smoothie and support for the muscles of every body system, as well as all enzymatic reactions within the body. And the spicy antioxidant and anti-inflammatory garlic brings the simple taste of mushrooms to a whole new realm. Savory and delicious, this is a healthy combination to savor for a snack, lunch, or dinner.

YIELDS: 2 CUPS

Ingredients
1½ cups white button mushrooms
2 cloves garlic
½ cup Greek-style yogurt
1 cup rice milk
1 cup ice

1. In a blender, combine the mushrooms, garlic, yogurt, and ½ cup rice milk with ½ cup ice, and blend until thoroughly combined.

2. While blending, add remaining rice milk and ice until desired consistency is achieved.

PER 1 CUP SERVING Calories: 85 | Fat: 5 g | Protein: 11 g | Sodium: 86 mg | Fiber: 1 g | Carbohydrates: 9 g

Mushroom-Cauliflower

Mushrooms and cauliflower join forces in this amazing smoothie that is packed with tons of nutrition and delicious flavor. Filled with vitamin C, calcium, and magnesium, it acts as a powerful antioxidant and anti-inflammatory agent—and, in addition, it's loaded up with tons of antibacterial benefits that make it easy to sip the rainbow.

YIELDS: 3 CUPS

Ingredients
1 cup white button mushrooms
1 cup cauliflower
1 clove garlic
1 cup rice milk
1 cup ice

1. In a blender, combine the mushrooms, cauliflower, garlic, and rice milk with ½ cup ice, and blend until thoroughly combined.

2. While blending, add remaining ice until desired consistency is achieved.

PER 1 CUP SERVING Calories: 48 | Fat: 1 g | Protein: 2 g | Sodium: 41 mg | Fiber: 1 g | Carbohydrates: 12 g

Ginger-Apple Tea

Sweet apples and spicy ginger pair up in this delightful smoothie that makes being healthy easy. Every delicious sip of this bright white dream brims with strong antioxidants that will keep your body moving, your mind clear, and your life right on track!

YIELDS: 2 CUPS

Ingredients
2 yellow apples, cored
1 tablespoon grated ginger
1 teaspoon ground ginger
1½ cups white tea
1 cup ice

1. In a blender, combine the apples, gingers, and white tea with ½ cup ice, and blend until thoroughly combined.

2. While blending, add remaining ice until desired consistency is achieved.

PER 1 CUP SERVING Calories: 83 | Fat: 0 g | Protein: 1 g | Sodium: 2 mg | Fiber: 2 g | Carbohydrates: 22 g

Thick and Creamy Banana Tea

While tea and bananas may not seem complementary, there is something to be said for this delicious combination of sweet spices and syrup, creamy banana, protein-packed yogurt, and antioxidant-rich tea. Not only does each magical ingredient work wonders for your body by protecting your healthy cells, promoting healthy cell production, and even regenerating and repairing damaged cells, but also, the taste combination works so well, you'll wish you'd thought of it long ago!

YIELDS: 3 CUPS

Ingredients
2 bananas, peeled
½ cup Greek-style yogurt
1 teaspoon ground nutmeg
1 teaspoon ground cinnamon
1 teaspoon pure, organic maple syrup
1½ cups white tea
1 cup ice

1. In a blender, combine the bananas, yogurt, nutmeg, cinnamon, maple syrup, and 1 cup white tea with ½ cup ice, and blend until thoroughly combined.

2. While blending, add remaining white tea and ice until desired consistency is achieved.

PER 1 CUP SERVING Calories: 106 | Fat: 0 g | Protein: 5 g | Sodium: 19 mg | Fiber: 3 g | Carbohydrates: 23 g

Tropical Tea Twist

By adding a tropical twist to the already delicious flavor of white tea, this recipe makes for a smoothie that is bright, powerful, and insanely tasty! When only tropical ingredients seem to sound appealing, whirl them up in this delightful, vitamin C–filled drink that acts to protect your immune system with every single sip.

YIELDS: 3 CUPS

Ingredients
1 cup pineapple
1 orange, peeled and deseeded
½ white grapefruit, peeled and deseeded
½ cup coconut meat
1 cup white tea
1 cup ice

1. In a blender, combine the pineapple, orange, grapefruit, coconut meat, and white tea with ½ cup ice, and blend until thoroughly combined.

2. While blending, add remaining ice until desired consistency is achieved.

PER 1 CUP SERVING Calories: 111 | Fat: 5 g | Protein: 2 g | Sodium: 4 mg | Fiber: 3 g | Carbohydrates: 18 g

Whirl of White Grapefruit

While white grapefruit is the tartest of the grapefruit varieties, combining it with sweet, smooth banana makes for a cool creation that is slightly sweet, slightly tart, and slightly creamy, but overall absolutely delicious!

YIELDS: 3 CUPS

Ingredients
2 white grapefruits, peeled and deseeded
1 banana, peeled
1 cup water
1 cup ice

1. In a blender, combine the grapefruits, banana, and ½ cup water with ½ cup ice, and blend until thoroughly combined.

2. While blending, add remaining water and ice until desired consistency is achieved.

PER 1 CUP SERVING Calories: 90 | Fat: 0 g | Protein: 2 g | Sodium: 0 mg | Fiber: 3 g | Carbohydrates: 23 g

Chapter 4

Red

Cherries • Cranberries • Grapefruit •
Pomegranates • Raspberries • Red Peppers •
Strawberries • Tomatoes • Watermelon

Known for its sweet berries and refreshing, uniquely flavored fruits and vegetables, the red group of natural foods is not only nutritious, but tasty, too! With a wide range of flavors, textures, appearances, and astounding benefits, the red assortment of produce is quite an impressive one. The most surprising aspect of this vibrantly colored category is that, unlike other color groups that keep the sweet focus on fruits and the savory on vegetables, here you'll find both: sweet and savory fruits and sweet and savory vegetables. Even the most produce-opposed critics can find something they love in this delicious variety of scrumptious foods.

But red produce does more than just taste good. The powerful phytochemicals that paint red produce its luscious color—including *flavonols, anthocyanins, anthocyanadins, phenolic acids, lycopene,* and *lutein*—are also incredibly powerful in terms of halting cell damage, reversing its effects, and promoting healthy growth instead. From the hair on your head to the circulation in your feet, these antioxidants and anti-inflammatory agents make life better by helping your body be all that it can be—and nothing less.

Adding to the appeal, red produce is rich in valuable nutrients that contain the power to change your life dramatically. The vitamins A, B1, B2, B5, B6, B9, C, E, and K are all bursting out of every single crimson fruit and vegetable. Promoting the health and well-being of almost every aspect of the body, these vitamins work together to protect the body's cells from dangerous free radicals that can cause disastrous mutations that lead to serious diseases like cancer. In addition to the protection of the body's cells, these vitamins work diligently to promote the quality of the skeletal, endocrine, cardiovascular, digestive, and nervous systems. Maintaining healthy blood quality, proper hormone balance, optimal metabolic functioning, and proper nutrient absorption are all important roles of the scarlet foods that are rich in these vitamins. With healing powers that can be unleashed from their valuable mineral content too, deep red fruits and vegetables contain calcium, copper, iron, magnesium, manganese, phosphorous, potassium, selenium, and zinc that join forces to maintain the quality of the blood, the cells, the brain, the heart, all of the major organs, and the body's physical appearance.

It's true: Red fruits and veggies make for some delicious smoothie stars and supporters. Craving a protein-packed, creamy, sweet treat? A lusciously tart combo that will liven your senses? How about a beautiful, bright red berry that will brighten your day? In each case, red foods provide delicious, nutritious options that will satisfy your needs. Blending well with other varieties of fruits and veggies that can greatly increase the nutrition content of your smoothie— or even better, the ability of another nutrient to be absorbed—these health-promoting foods are easy to find, easy to use, and delicious to spin into any smoothie!

Red Berry Roundup

Packed with four different varieties of vibrant red berries, this is a delicious, creamy smoothie that packs rich phytochemicals and vitamins A and C for top-notch immunity-building defenses. Along with great nutrition from the berries, you'll benefit from the good bacteria in the probiotic-rich kefir.

YIELDS: 3 CUPS

Ingredients
½ cup strawberries
½ cup raspberries
½ cup cranberries
½ cup cherries, pitted
1 cup strawberry kefir
½ cup water
1 cup ice

1. In a blender, combine the strawberries, raspberries, cranberries, cherries, kefir, and water with ½ cup ice, and blend until thoroughly combined.

2. While blending, add remaining ice until desired consistency is achieved.

PER 1 CUP SERVING Calories: 88 | Fat: 0 g | Protein: 5 g | Sodium: 64 mg | Fiber: 3 g | Carbohydrates: 17 g

Red Apple Dapple

Simple and sweet, this smoothie needs only the tartness of cherries and the unique deliciousness of apples to make it zing! Tons of rich antioxidants, like the quercetin in apples, fill every sip of this delicious smoothie treat that can do double duty as breakfast or dessert. You'll promote overall health while fending off colds and allergies.

YIELDS: 3 CUPS

Ingredients
2 red apples, cored
1 cup cherries, pitted
1½ cups all-natural, organic apple juice (not from concentrate)
1 cup ice

1. In a blender, combine the apples, cherries, and 1 cup apple juice with ½ cup ice, and blend until thoroughly combined.

2. While blending, add remaining apple juice and ice until desired consistency is achieved.

PER 1 CUP SERVING Calories: 141 | Fat: 0 g | Protein: 1 g | Sodium: 5 mg | Fiber: 3 g | Carbohydrates: 36 g

Sweet Strawberry Start

Sweet strawberries are a delicious food to kick off your morning routine. Blended with sweet bananas and creamy kefir, this recipe makes for a nutritious, complex carbohydrate–rich jumpstart that will give you long-lasting energy.

YIELDS: 4 CUPS

Ingredients

2 cups strawberries
1 banana, peeled
1 cup strawberry kefir
½ cup coconut milk
1 cup ice

1. In a blender, combine the strawberries, banana, kefir, and coconut milk with ½ cup ice, and blend until thoroughly combined.

2. While blending, add remaining ice until desired consistency is achieved.

PER 1 CUP SERVING Calories: 140 | Fat: 6 g | Protein: 5 g | Sodium: 52 mg | Fiber: 2 g | Carbohydrates: 18 g

Ridiculous Raspberries 'n' Cream

The delightful tastes of strawberry kefir and coconut milk get all jazzed up with the splendid addition of raspberries in this delicious, nutritious smoothie. The rich red ingredients deliver an antioxidant blast that will keep your body healthy and moving in the right direction!

YIELDS: 2 CUPS

Ingredients

2 cups raspberries
1 cup strawberry kefir
1 cup coconut milk
1 cup ice

1. In a blender, combine the raspberries, kefir, and ½ cup coconut milk with ½ cup ice, and blend until thoroughly combined.

2. While blending, add remaining coconut milk and ice until desired consistency is achieved.

PER 1 CUP SERVING Calories: 355 | Fat: 25 g | Protein: 11 g | Sodium: 110 mg | Fiber: 8 g | Carbohydrates: 27 g

Very Cherry Vanilla

Needing nothing more than three simple ingredients, this smoothie combines sweet cherries, flavorful vanilla bean, and creamy vanilla almond milk for a very vanilla spin on an already delicious treat. Packed with loads of valuable nutrition, like the surprisingly powerful vanillin, which acts to combat colds and flu, this is one smoothie you'd never guess was designed to promote health.

YIELDS: 3 CUPS

Ingredients

2 cups cherries, pitted
1 vanilla bean's pulp
1 cup vanilla almond milk
1 cup ice

1. In a blender, combine the cherries, vanilla bean's pulp, and almond milk with ½ cup ice, and blend until thoroughly combined.

2. While blending, add remaining ice until desired consistency is achieved.

PER 1 CUP SERVING Calories: 102 | Fat: 1 g | Protein: 1 g | Sodium: 30 mg | Fiber: 2 g | Carbohydrates: 26 g

Sparkling Strawberry

The "sparkle" of this smoothie comes from the delectable addition of ginger that makes every sip a striking one! Packed with antioxidants for immunity, protein for strength and endurance, and probiotics for good bacteria protection, the combination of ingredients in this recipe help make living better that much tastier!

YIELDS: 3 CUPS

Ingredients

2 cups strawberries
1 tablespoon grated ginger
1 cup strawberry kefir
1 cup ice

1. In a blender, combine the strawberries, ginger, and kefir with ½ cup ice, and blend until thoroughly combined.

2. While blending, add remaining ice until desired consistency is achieved.

PER 1 CUP SERVING Calories: 78 | Fat: 0 g | Protein: 5 g | Sodium: 64 mg | Fiber: 2 g | Carbohydrates: 14 g

Crazy for Cranberries

Cranberries lend a tart sweetness to any smoothie, and when paired with delicious ginger, there's no end to the amazing depth of flavors. Helping to maintain urinary tract health, the cranberry's powerful benefits make this smoothie a great option for everyone of every age and gender.

YIELDS: 3 CUPS

Ingredients

2 cups cranberries
1 tablespoon grated ginger
1 cup vanilla rice milk
1 cup ice

1. In a blender, combine the cranberries, ginger, and rice milk with ½ cup ice, and blend until thoroughly combined.

2. While blending, add remaining ice until desired consistency is achieved.

PER 1 CUP SERVING Calories: 65 | Fat: 1 g | Protein: 1 g | Sodium: 32 mg | Fiber: 3 g | Carbohydrates: 18 g

Lickity Lime and Berries

The tart sensation of limes gets chilled out with the sweet tastes of strawberries, raspberries, and creamy kefir. When there's a delicious blend like this one that packs a one-two punch of vitamins A and C for immunity-strengthening benefits, it's pretty easy to live healthy!

YIELDS: 2 CUPS

Ingredients

1 cup strawberries
1 cup raspberries
1 lime, peeled and deseeded
1 cup strawberry kefir
1 cup ice
½ cup water

1. In a blender, combine the strawberries, raspberries, lime, and kefir with ½ cup ice, and blend until thoroughly combined.

2. While blending, add water and remaining ice until desired consistency is achieved.

PER 1 CUP SERVING Calories: 110 | Fat: 1 g | Protein: 8 g | Sodium: 96 mg | Fiber: 5 g | Carbohydrates: 20 g

Cherries and Spice

Creamy, spicy, and sweet, this smoothie is a delicious way to pack in some nutritious fruit servings. The vitamin C in the deep red berries helps protect against cardiovascular disease and prenatal problems. This tasty recipe takes healthy living to a whole new level!

YIELDS: 3 CUPS

Ingredients

2 cups cherries, pitted
1 tablespoon grated ginger
1 teaspoon ground cloves
1 teaspoon ground nutmeg
1 cup vanilla almond milk
1 cup ice
½ cup water

1. In a blender, combine the cherries, ginger, cloves, nutmeg, and almond milk with ½ cup ice, and blend until thoroughly combined.

2. While blending, add the water and remaining ice until desired consistency is achieved.

PER 1 CUP SERVING Calories: 106 | Fat: 1 g | Protein: 2 g | Sodium: 32 mg | Fiber: 3 g | Carbohydrates: 27 g

Wonderful Watermelon

This delicious smoothie is packed full of hydrating watermelon, smooth banana, and creamy coconut milk that will brighten your day. With flu-fighting quercetin and cancer-fighting lycopene brimming in every sip of this simple splendor, your vitality can improve without any effort at all!

YIELDS: 3 CUPS

Ingredients

2 cups watermelon
1 banana, peeled
1 cup coconut milk
1 cup ice

1. In a blender, combine the watermelon, banana, and coconut milk with ½ cup ice, and blend until thoroughly combined.

2. While blending, add remaining ice until desired consistency is achieved.

PER 1 CUP SERVING Calories: 214 | Fat: 16 g | Protein: 3 g | Sodium: 11 mg | Fiber: 1 g | Carbohydrates: 19 g

Terrific Tomato Smoothie

When you take the rich antioxidants of tomatoes and blend them into this savory smoothie, the delicious flavor is just an added plus. This smoothie is packed full of cancer-fighting lycopene—and great taste!

YIELDS: 2 CUPS

Ingredients
4 tomatoes
2 garlic cloves
1 tablespoon basil
1 cup water
1 cup ice

1. In a blender, combine the tomatoes, garlic, basil, and ½ cup water with ½ cup ice, and blend until thoroughly combined.

2. While blending, add remaining water and ice until desired consistency is achieved.

PER 1 CUP SERVING Calories: 49 | Fat: 1 g | Protein: 2 g | Sodium: 13 mg | Fiber: 3 g | Carbohydrates: 11 g

Very Cherry "Milk" Shake

If you're in the mood for dessert, you're sure to enjoy this milkshake-like smoothie. The sweet creamy taste is so delicious and actually good for you! This recipe is filled with tons of antioxidants, probiotics, and vitamins A and C for disease-fighting power.

YIELDS: 3 CUPS

Ingredients
2 cups cherries, pitted
1 serving probiotic supplement (see packaging for exact amount)
1 cup strawberry kefir
½ cup coconut milk
1 cup ice

1. In a blender, combine the cherries, probiotic, kefir, and coconut milk with ½ cup ice, and blend until thoroughly combined.

2. While blending, add remaining ice until desired consistency is achieved.

PER 1 CUP SERVING Calories: 185 | Fat: 8 g | Protein: 7 g | Sodium: 68 mg | Fiber: 2 g | Carbohydrates: 24 g

Cooling Cranberry Concoction

While chilled cranberries don't really need anything else to be delicious, this smoothie takes their delicious flavor to a whole new level. Combined with bittersweet mint and sweet, creamy coconut milk, this slushed cranberry concoction is absolutely refreshing.

YIELDS: 3 CUPS

Ingredients

2 cups cranberries
1 tablespoon mint
1 cup coconut milk
1 cup ice

1. In a blender, combine the cranberries, mint, and coconut milk with ½ cup ice, and blend until thoroughly combined.

2. While blending, add remaining ice until desired consistency is achieved.

PER 1 CUP SERVING Calories: 181 | Fat: 16 g | Protein: 2 g | Sodium: 13 mg | Fiber: 3 g | Carbohydrates: 11 g

Cran-Apple Cooler

This simple recipe is light tasting and refreshing enough to tingle your taste buds. The simple sweetness of red apples and pure apple juice mixed with the tart flavor of cranberries makes this smoothie a simple and tasty way to sip the rainbow. However, the rich taste isn't the extent of this smoothie's wonders; factor in the antioxidants like quercetin and anthocyanins that combat cancer-causing free radical damage in cells, and you end up with one tasty, healthy treat!

YIELDS: 3 CUPS

Ingredients

1 cup cranberries
2 red apples, cored
1 cup organic, all-natural apple juice (not from concentrate)
1 cup ice

1. In a blender, combine the cranberries, apples, and juice with ½ cup ice, and blend until thoroughly combined.

2. While blending, add remaining ice until desired consistency is achieved.

PER 1 CUP SERVING Calories: 105 | Fat: 0 g | Protein: 1 g | Sodium: 4 mg | Fiber: 3 g | Carbohydrates: 27 g

Wishful Watermelon

While most people think watermelon's benefits are limited to water, this is definitely not the case. Watermelon deserves much more credit for its unique blend of vitamins, minerals, and phytochemicals: Protein, vitamin C, and lycopene combine for performance-improving and immunity-protecting properties. Delicious in its simplicity, this smoothie is one pretty impressive treat.

YIELDS: 2 CUPS

Ingredients
2 cups watermelon
1 cup water
1 cup ice

1. In a blender, combine the watermelon and ½ cup water with ½ cup ice, and blend until thoroughly combined.

2. While blending, add remaining water and ice until desired consistency is achieved.

PER 1 CUP SERVING Calories: 46 | Fat: 0 g | Protein: 1 g | Sodium: 2 mg | Fiber: 1 g | Carbohydrates: 11 g

Razzle-Dazzle Raspberry

With sharp raspberries as the stars of the show, the supporting ingredients take this smoothie from bright to shining! The special additions of spicy grated ginger, chai-flavored cardamom, and the sweet nectar of apples whirl this smoothie into a flavor combination you've probably never even imagined. In addition, powerful antioxidants like *bromelain* and *anthocyanins* add immunity-boosting power to every delicious sip!

YIELDS: 2 CUPS

Ingredients
2 cups raspberries
1 tablespoon grated ginger
1 teaspoon ground cardamom
1 cup organic, all-natural apple juice (not from concentrate)
1 cup ice

1. In a blender, combine the raspberries, ginger, cardamom, and apple juice with ½ cup ice, and blend until thoroughly combined.

2. While blending, add remaining ice until desired consistency is achieved.

PER 1 CUP SERVING Calories: 130 | Fat: 1 g | Protein: 2 g | Sodium: 7 mg | Fiber: 9 g | Carbohydrates: 31 g

Spiced Up Strawberries

Strawberries don't really need anything else to taste great, but the combination of sweet strawberries, vanilla, and aromatic spices in this deliciously creamy blend takes this berry from great to amazing! Nutritiously packed with immunity-strengthening vitamin C and antioxidants, spiced just right, and deliciously creamy, this strawberry smoothie couldn't get much better!

YIELDS: 3 CUPS

Ingredients

2 cups strawberries
1 vanilla bean's pulp
1 teaspoon ground ginger
1 teaspoon ground cloves
1 teaspoon ground cardamom
1 cup strawberry kefir
1 cup ice
½ cup coconut milk

1. In a blender, combine the strawberries, vanilla bean's pulp, ginger, cloves, cardamom, and kefir with ½ cup ice, and blend until thoroughly combined.

2. While blending, add the coconut milk and remaining ice until desired consistency is achieved.

PER 1 CUP SERVING Calories: 159 | Fat: 9 g | Protein: 6 g | Sodium: 71 mg | Fiber: 2 g | Carbohydrates: 16 g

Simple Strawberry Smoothie

For all of you strawberry lovers who just want to stick with what you know, this smoothie is for you! This smoothie keeps things as natural as they can get, and it delivers tons of nutrition with vitamins A and C and the added benefits of manganese and fiber. The nutrients join forces to boost your metabolism, immune system, and body's defenses against the common cold and cancerous invaders—all on top of the sweet strawberry taste you love!

YIELDS: 2 CUPS

Ingredients

2 cups strawberries
1 cup water
1 cup ice

1. In a blender, combine the strawberries and water with ½ cup ice, and blend until thoroughly combined.

2. While blending, add remaining ice until desired consistency is achieved.

PER 1 CUP SERVING Calories: 46 | Fat: 0 g | Protein: 1 g | Sodium: 1 mg | Fiber: 3 g | Carbohydrates: 11 g

Red-Alert Raspberry

You can't deny it. When citrus meets raspberry, magic happens. The sweet, tart flavors of the powerful citrus fruits combine with the unique flavor of raspberries for a great-tasting smoothie filled with vitamin C and manganese that will get your blood pumping and keep it healthy, too.

YIELDS: 4 CUPS

Ingredients

2 cups raspberries
1 orange, peeled and deseeded
1 lemon, peeled and deseeded
1 lime, peeled and deseeded
1 cup coconut milk
1 cup ice

1. In a blender, combine the raspberries, orange, lemon, lime, and ½ cup coconut milk with ½ cup ice, and blend until thoroughly combined.

2. While blending, add remaining coconut milk and ice until desired consistency is achieved.

PER 1 CUP SERVING Calories: 168 | Fat: 13 g | Protein: 2 g | Sodium: 9 mg | Fiber: 6 g | Carbohydrates: 16 g

Risk-Reducing Red Raspberry

Brimming with strong antioxidants and the powerful phytochemicals that fill these beautiful berries with their unmistakable pink-red coloring, raspberries are great crusaders in the battle for better health. Add a healthy dose of vitamin C–packed oranges to these healthy berries, and you have a sweet smoothie recipe for healthy living!

YIELDS: 4 CUPS

Ingredients

2 cups raspberries
2 oranges, peeled and deseeded
1 cup water
1 cup ice

1. In a blender, combine the raspberries, oranges, and ½ cup water with ½ cup ice, and blend until thoroughly combined.

2. While blending, add remaining water and ice until desired consistency is achieved.

PER 1 CUP SERVING Calories: 63 | Fat: 0 g | Protein: 1 g | Sodium: 0 mg | Fiber: 6 g | Carbohydrates: 15 g

Pomegranate-Watermelon Tart

If you're looking to boost your immune system, then this red smoothie is for you! Pairing watermelon's and pomegranate's powerful doses of beta-carotene, lycopene, vitamin C, and manganese not only multiplies their immunity-helping properties, it also creates a delicious blend of exotic and familiar flavors that you'll want to savor again and again.

YIELDS: 2 CUPS

Ingredients
1 cup watermelon
1 cup pomegranate jewels
¼ cup organic, all-natural granola
1 cup vanilla almond milk
1 cup ice

1. In a blender, combine the watermelon, pomegranate jewels, granola, and almond milk with ½ cup ice, and blend until thoroughly combined.

2. While blending, add remaining ice until desired consistency is achieved.

PER 1 CUP SERVING Calories: 159 | Fat: 2 g | Protein: 2 g | Sodium: 50 mg | Fiber: 4 g | Carbohydrates: 40 g

Grapefruit Grenade

When it comes to fighting illness and promoting overall health, citrus is an amazingly powerful food because of its double dose of vitamins A and C. Both act as immune-system builders and antioxidants that fight off foreign invaders that can cause illness. And when you blend the delicious flavors of grapefruit with sweet orange, you get a smoothie that's packed with healthy nutrients that can get your engines running—and keep them running.

YIELDS: 4 CUPS

Ingredients
2 grapefruits, peeled and deseeded
1 orange, peeled and deseeded
1 lemon, peeled and deseeded
1 cup strawberries
1 cup water
1 cup ice

1. In a blender, combine the grapefruits, orange, lemon, strawberries, and ½ cup water with ½ cup ice, and blend until thoroughly combined.

2. While blending, add remaining water and ice until desired consistency is achieved.

PER 1 CUP SERVING Calories: 72 | Fat: 0 g | Protein: 2 g | Sodium: 1 mg | Fiber: 3 g | Carbohydrates: 18 g

Glorious Grapefruit Smoothie

Toss out your vitamin C supplements and opt instead for this whole food alternative! This recipe unleashes the immunity-promoting powers of grapefruit in a delicious smoothie that's perfect to try any time of the day. Combined with the creaminess of kefir and a hint of extra sweetness with natural maple syrup, this great recipe delivers nutrition *and* taste!

YIELDS: 2 CUPS

Ingredients
2 grapefruits, peeled and deseeded
1 cup plain kefir
1 teaspoon organic, all-natural maple syrup
1 cup ice

1. In a blender, combine the grapefruits, kefir, and maple syrup with ½ cup ice, and blend until thoroughly combined.

2. While blending, add remaining ice until desired consistency is achieved.

PER 1 CUP SERVING Calories: 152 | Fat: 0 g | Protein: 8 g | Sodium: 97 mg | Fiber: 3 g | Carbohydrates: 31 g

Red Grapefruit-Raspberry

Grapefruit and raspberry combine in this recipe to bring essential nutrients to your blender. The lycopene in both fruits, compounded by the quercetin of the apple juice, works wonders in protecting the body's cells from dangerous mutations. Not only for protection, this great-tasting smoothie also works to help your body to perform at its best. Fruit servings never tasted so great!

YIELDS: 4 CUPS

Ingredients
2 grapefruits, peeled and deseeded
2 cups raspberries
1 cup organic, all-natural apple juice (not from concentrate)
1 cup ice

1. In a blender, combine the grapefruits, raspberries, and ½ cup apple juice with ½ cup ice, and blend until thoroughly combined.

2. While blending, add remaining apple juice and ice until desired consistency is achieved.

PER 1 CUP SERVING Calories: 101 | Fat: 1 g | Protein: 2 g | Sodium: 3 mg | Fiber: 6 g | Carbohydrates: 25 g

Pomegranate Jewels

If you're looking for a red smoothie that develops a variety of flavors, colors, and textures, then you've come to the right place. This Pomegranate Jewels smoothie is infused with a unique mix of great beauty, great nutrition, and great taste! This smoothie is high in antioxidant-rich vitamin C and lycopene that work diligently to protect the body from dangerous and deadly illnesses like cancer and heart disease. Once you combine pomegranate jewels, strawberries, and banana in a sweet apple juice blend, you'll have a healthy recipe that you'll never want to put down!

YIELDS: 3 CUPS

Ingredients

1 cup pomegranate jewels
½ cup strawberries
1 banana, peeled
1½ cups organic, all-natural apple juice (not from concentrate)
1 cup ice

1. In a blender, combine the pomegranate jewels, strawberries, banana, and 1 cup apple juice with ½ cup ice, and blend until thoroughly combined.

2. While blending, add remaining apple juice and ice until desired consistency is achieved.

PER 1 CUP SERVING Calories: 148 | Fat: 1 g | Protein: 2 g | Sodium: 7 mg | Fiber: 4 g | Carbohydrates: 36 g

Great Gazpacho

Normally served chilled, this savory delight is commonly seen as a soup. But when you're working with ingredients that are as natural, nutritious, and delicious as those found in this recipe, why not create a savory smoothie for those days when sweet just doesn't fit the bill? Naturally packed with tons of flavor, this great blend of *lutein*-packed red vegetables is sure to make any tomato lover smile.

YIELDS: 4 CUPS

Ingredients

3 tomatoes
½ cucumber, peeled
1 celery stalk
½ cup red onion
2 garlic cloves
2 tablespoons basil
1 cup ice
1 cup water

1. In a blender, combine the tomatoes, cucumber, celery, red onion, garlic, and basil with ½ cup ice, and blend until thoroughly combined.

2. While blending, add the water and remaining ice until desired consistency is achieved.

PER 1 CUP SERVING Calories: 34 | Fat: 0 g | Protein: 1 g | Sodium: 14 mg | Fiber: 2 g | Carbohydrates: 8 g

Creamy, Dreamy Watermelon

When you combine sweet watermelon with creamy kefir, you take this powerful fruit to a new level. Rich in nutrients such as beta-carotene and lycopene, and unlimited health benefits—including improved immunity and endurance—the two key ingredients make this a tasty experience!

YIELDS: 2 CUPS

Ingredients
2 cups watermelon
1 cup plain kefir
1 cup ice

1. In a blender, combine the watermelon and ½ cup kefir with ½ cup ice, and blend until thoroughly combined.

2. While blending, add remaining kefir and ice until desired consistency is achieved.

PER 1 CUP SERVING Calories: 114 | Fat: 0 g | Protein: 8 g | Sodium: 96 mg | Fiber: 1 g | Carbohydrates: 21 g

Sublime Watermelon-Lime

In this recipe, the sweet taste of watermelon gets jazzed up with the tasty, tart flavor of limes and the deliciously creamy texture that only coconut milk can provide. You'll keep your health top-notch with antioxidants that work together to fight off illnesses *and* promote overall well-being.

YIELDS: 3 CUPS

Ingredients
2 cups watermelon
2 limes, peeled and deseeded
1 cup coconut milk
1 cup ice

1. In a blender, combine the watermelon, limes, and coconut milk with ½ cup ice, and blend until thoroughly combined.

2. While blending, add remaining ice until desired consistency is achieved.

PER 1 CUP SERVING Calories: 192 | Fat: 16 g | Protein: 2 g | Sodium: 12 mg | Fiber: 2 g | Carbohydrates: 14 g

Suped-Up Strawberry-Banana

Strawberry-banana is a staple flavor in everything from yogurt to candy to ice cream, so why not take the real things and make them even better? By adding vanilla protein powder and probiotic-rich kefir to the mix, you can enjoy this traditional favorite with all of the added benefits of good bacteria—and reduce the likelihood of invasive bad bacteria growth.

YIELDS: 4 CUPS

Ingredients
2 cups strawberries
1 banana, peeled
1 scoop vanilla protein powder
1 cup strawberry kefir
1 cup ice
½ cup water

1. In a blender, combine the strawberries, banana, protein powder, and kefir with ½ cup ice, and blend until thoroughly combined.

2. While blending, add the water and remaining ice until desired consistency is achieved.

PER 1 CUP SERVING Calories: 112 | Fat: 1 g | Protein: 10 g | Sodium: 48 mg | Fiber: 2 g | Carbohydrates: 17 g

Limey Cherry Smoothie

Sweet cherries need only a small dose of lime to create a completely new identity. Here, both are partnered with creamy coconut milk to create a rich mix of flavors that complement each other perfectly. Frothy smoothies are hard to resist—and this recipe makes sipping the rainbow easy to embrace!

YIELDS: 2 CUPS

Ingredients
2 cups cherries, pitted
1 lime, peeled and deseeded
1 cup coconut milk
1 cup ice

1. In a blender, combine the cherries, lime, and coconut milk with ½ cup ice, and blend until thoroughly combined.

2. While blending, add remaining ice until desired consistency is achieved.

PER 1 CUP SERVING Calories: 329 | Fat: 24 g | Protein: 4 g | Sodium: 15 mg | Fiber: 4 g | Carbohydrates: 31 g

Red Pepper Relief

This savory blend of crisp red peppers, simple tomato, and fragrant basil combine for a smoothie that's packed with antioxidants that act as anti-inflammatory agents, which help to bring your health to optimum levels. Even though it's busy fighting off illness and disease, this smoothie always takes the time to taste great and deliver the benefits!

YIELDS: 2 CUPS

Ingredients

2 red peppers, cored and deseeded
1 tomato, cored
1 tablespoon basil
1 cup water
1 cup ice

1. In a blender, combine the peppers, tomato, basil, and water with ½ cup ice, and blend until thoroughly combined.

2. While blending, add remaining ice until desired consistency is achieved.

PER 1 CUP SERVING Calories: 35 | Fat: 0 g | Protein: 2 g | Sodium: 7 mg | Fiber: 3 g | Carbohydrates: 8 g

Nuts and Berries

Move over, trail mix! The ingredients in this recipe bring the flavors of the traditional woodsy treat to this icy-cold smoothie. Combining the bright flavors of berries with savory nuts and flaxseed, this smoothie is sweetened up with pure maple syrup and creamy almond milk for a taste that's totally on track!

YIELDS: 3 CUPS

Ingredients

1 cup raspberries
1 cup strawberries
¼ cup walnuts
¼ cup almonds
⅛ cup ground flaxseed
1 teaspoon organic, pure maple syrup
1 cup almond milk
1 cup ice

1. In a blender, combine the raspberries, strawberries, walnuts, almonds, flaxseed, maple syrup, and almond milk with ½ cup ice, and blend until thoroughly combined.

2. While blending, add remaining ice until desired consistency is achieved.

PER 1 CUP SERVING Calories: 209 | Fat: 13 g | Protein: 5 g | Sodium: 33 mg | Fiber: 7 g | Carbohydrates: 24 g

Refreshing Raspberries

Packed with bright colors and healthy antioxidants, raspberries take center stage in this quick and easy smoothie. Raspberry's and mint's powerful double dose of anti-inflammatory benefits will help your aches and pains disappear—deliciously!

YIELDS: 2 CUPS

Ingredients

2 cups raspberries
1 tablespoon spearmint leaves
1 cup coconut milk
1 cup ice

1. In a blender, combine the raspberries, spearmint leaves, and coconut milk with ½ cup ice, and blend until thoroughly combined.

2. While blending, add remaining ice until desired consistency is achieved.

PER 1 CUP SERVING Calories: 286 | Fat: 25 g | Protein: 4 g | Sodium: 16 mg | Fiber: 8 g | Carbohydrates: 18 g

Red Apple Sweet Tea

Ditch the sugar-filled, store-bought sweet tea and opt instead for this cool smoothie blend. Red apples and antioxidant-rich white tea will help your body fend off foreign immunity assailants that are responsible for everything from the flu to common cancers. When you finish this smoothie off with just a sweet touch of maple syrup, you'll forget all about manufactured tea blends forever!

YIELDS: 2 CUPS

Ingredients

2 red apples, cored
1 cup white tea
1 teaspoon organic, pure maple syrup
1 cup ice

1. In a blender, combine the apples, tea, and maple syrup with ½ cup ice, and blend until thoroughly combined.

2. While blending, add remaining ice until desired consistency is achieved.

PER 1 CUP SERVING Calories: 89 | Fat: 0 g | Protein: 0 g | Sodium: 4 mg | Fiber: 2 g | Carbohydrates: 24 g

Sinfully Strawberry White Tea

Strawberries are an excellent ingredient for any smoothie—they add great taste and a wealth of powerful antioxidants that promote the health of your cells. Blending these beautiful berries with white tea and maple syrup make this the perfect treat to sweeten your day, and can make living your life better with every delicious sip.

YIELDS: 2 CUPS

Ingredients
1½ cups strawberries
1 cup white tea
1 teaspoon organic, pure maple syrup
1 cup ice

1. In a blender, combine the strawberries, tea, and maple syrup with ½ cup ice, and blend until thoroughly combined.

2. While blending, add remaining ice until desired consistency is achieved.

PER 1 CUP SERVING Calories: 46 | Fat: 0 g | Protein: 1 g | Sodium: 5 mg | Fiber: 2 g | Carbohydrates: 11 g

Raspberry Twist on Tea

Sweet, light, and flavorful, this raspberry twist on tea makes a delicious smoothie. Refreshing and packed full of a variety of nutrients, including powerful antioxidants and immunity-strengthening vitamins like A and C, this cool treat fulfills your daily fruit servings while bringing a little extra brightness to your table!

YIELDS: 2 CUPS

Ingredients
1½ cups raspberries
1 cup white tea
1 teaspoon organic, pure maple syrup
1 cup ice

1. In a blender, combine the raspberries, white tea, and maple syrup with ½ cup ice, and blend until thoroughly combined.

2. While blending, add remaining ice until desired consistency is achieved.

PER 1 CUP SERVING Calories: 60 | Fat: 1 g | Protein: 1 g | Sodium: 4 mg | Fiber: 6 g | Carbohydrates: 14 g

Cherry Tea To-Go

The rich taste of cherry juice fills every sip of this delicious smoothie. And along with this great taste comes a plethora of health-protecting antioxidants (which help with free radical–fighting cancer protection) that pour out of your blender and into your cup! It's true, this visually stimulating smoothie takes the time to tantalize your taste buds, and it doesn't skimp on providing a healthy hook either!

YIELDS: 2 CUPS

Ingredients

1½ cups cherries, pitted
1 cup green tea
1 teaspoon organic, pure maple syrup
1 cup ice

1. In a blender, combine the cherries, green tea, and maple syrup with ½ cup ice, and blend until thoroughly combined.

2. While blending, add remaining ice until desired consistency is achieved.

PER 1 CUP SERVING Calories: 84 | Fat: 0 g | Protein: 1 g | Sodium: 4 mg | Fiber: 2 g | Carbohydrates: 21 g

Very Cherry-Pear

The delightful flavors of cherries and pears meet up in this smoothie to create a sinful celebration of sweet, tart deliciousness. And when you add the creamy texture and hint of strawberry flavor from the kefir, you'll ensure that every sip of this smoothie is full of much-needed probiotics and powerful protein that will keep your body moving and functioning at its best!

YIELDS: 3 CUPS

Ingredients

1½ cups cherries, pitted
1 pear, cored
1 cup strawberry kefir
1 cup water
1 cup ice

1. In a blender, combine the cherries, pear, kefir, and ½ cup water with ½ cup ice, and blend until thoroughly combined.

2. While blending, add remaining water and ice until desired consistency is achieved.

PER 1 CUP SERVING Calories: 106 | Fat: 0 g | Protein: 6 g | Sodium: 63 mg | Fiber: 3 g | Carbohydrates: 22 g

Smooth Cherry Banana

Cherries and bananas seem like they would go great together in anything, and this smoothie is no exception. But the sweet, tart flavor of the cherries and the smoothness of banana isn't all this smoothie has going for it. It's also packed full of slimming potassium, which helps beat the bloat and ensure quality hydration of all the body's cells—and, like this smoothie, that's a beautiful thing!

YIELDS: 3 CUPS

Ingredients

1½ cups cherries, pitted
1 banana, peeled
1 cup strawberry kefir
1 cup water
1 cup ice

1. In a blender, combine the cherries, banana, kefir, and ½ cup water with ½ cup ice, and blend until thoroughly combined.

2. While blending, add remaining water and ice until desired consistency is achieved.

PER 1 CUP SERVING Calories: 130 | Fat: 0 g | Protein: 6 g | Sodium: 63 mg | Fiber: 3 g | Carbohydrates: 28 g

Creamy Cranberry Creation

Cranberries may be delicious and nutritious, but one thing they are not is creamy. However, when you add in strawberry kefir and refreshing coconut milk, you give this simple, tart berry a whole new depth that is out-of-this-world tasty! In addition, this smoothie is full of powerful phytochemicals like lycopene and beta-carotene that work hand in hand for improved immunity and top-notch defenses against cancerous cell transformation.

YIELDS: 3 CUPS

Ingredients

1 cup cranberries
1 cup strawberry kefir
1 cup coconut milk
1 cup ice

1. In a blender, combine the cranberries, kefir, and coconut milk with ½ cup ice, and blend until thoroughly combined.

2. While blending, add remaining ice until desired consistency is achieved.

PER 1 CUP SERVING Calories: 209 | Fat: 16 g | Protein: 6 g | Sodium: 73 mg | Fiber: 2 g | Carbohydrates: 12 g

Cranberry Cucumber-Melon

With the scrumptious combination of tart cranberries, hydrating cucumber, and sweet honeydew melon, this smoothie puts on quite a show! Your body will benefit from every amazing sip of this nutritious, delicious smoothie that's packed with vivacious vitamin C and powerful antioxidants for a combined one-two punch of immunity-boosting power that fights against cancer-causing free radicals!

YIELDS: 3 CUPS

Ingredients
1½ cups cranberries
1 cucumber, peeled
1 cup honeydew melon, peeled and deseeded
1 cup water
1 cup ice

1. In a blender, combine the cranberries, cucumber, honeydew melon and water with ½ cup ice, and blend until thoroughly combined.

2. While blending, add remaining ice until desired consistency is achieved.

PER 1 CUP SERVING Calories: 58 | Fat: 0 g | Protein: 1 g | Sodium: 13 mg | Fiber: 3 g | Carbohydrates: 15 g

Cran-Pear Banana

The combination of the four simple ingredients found in this smoothie creates a taste sensation that's unique *and* healthy. The potassium, vitamin C, and disease-fighting antioxidants all combine for immunity-strengthening benefits found in each and every ounce of this delicious sweet treat! With the deep red cranberries stealing the show, the pear, banana, and coconut milk act as supporting stars that contribute creaminess and striking flavors you're sure to enjoy.

YIELDS: 3 CUPS

Ingredients
1 cup cranberries
1 pear, cored
1 banana, peeled
1 cup coconut milk
1 cup ice

1. In a blender, combine the cranberries, pear, banana, and coconut milk with ½ cup ice, and blend until thoroughly combined.

2. While blending, add remaining ice until desired consistency is achieved.

PER 1 CUP SERVING Calories: 210 | Fat: 16 g | Protein: 2 g | Sodium: 11 mg | Fiber: 4 g | Carbohydrates: 18 g

Minty Watermelon

From every sweet drop of this watermelon smoothie comes a refreshing jolt of much-needed nutrients like muscle-strengthening protein and vision-protecting lycopene. Add the powerful taste of spearmint and the creaminess of coconut milk to the mix, and you have a smoothie that's packed with nutrition and flavor that can help make sipping the rainbow easier than you ever thought possible.

YIELDS: 2 CUPS

Ingredients
2 cups watermelon
1 tablespoon spearmint leaves
1 cup coconut milk
1 cup ice

1. In a blender, combine the watermelon, spearmint, and coconut milk with ½ cup ice, and blend until thoroughly combined.

2. While blending, add remaining ice until desired consistency is achieved.

PER 1 CUP SERVING Calories: 536 | Fat: 48 g | Protein: 6 g | Sodium: 32 mg | Fiber: 1 g | Carbohydrates: 29 g

Herbed and Spicy Tomato

While the delicious taste of tomato brings amazing flavor to any recipe on its own, adding in the spicy flavors of red onion and garlic, and aromatic herbs like basil, oregano, and rosemary, makes this savory smoothie one that will keep you coming back for more!

YIELDS: 2 CUPS

Ingredients
3 tomatoes, cored
¼ cup red onion
2 cloves garlic
1 tablespoon basil leaves
1 tablespoon oregano (fresh or dried)
1 tablespoon rosemary
1 cup water
1 cup ice

1. In a blender, combine the tomatoes, red onion, garlic, basil, oregano, rosemary, and water with ½ cup ice, and blend until thoroughly combined.

2. While blending, add remaining ice until desired consistency is achieved.

PER 1 CUP SERVING Calories: 50 | Fat: 0 g | Protein: 2 g | Sodium: 11 mg | Fiber: 3 g | Carbohydrates: 11 g

Chapter 5

Orange

Apricots • Cantaloupe • Carrots •
Oranges • Papaya • Pumpkin • Yams

If you're eating—and drinking—orange, you know that, above anything else, you're getting your daily dose of vitamin C. This powerful vitamin is well-known for strengthening the immune system, but the most recent attribute credited to the selection of fruits and veggies rich in vitamin C is their powerful ability to act as antiviral, anti-inflammatory, and antibacterial agents. Creating this dual task force designed to fend off illnesses and diseases from the common cold to certain types of cancers, the vitamin C found in these fruits and vegetables is supported and strengthened by the additional vitamin and mineral content also present in these powerful foods.

Consuming the orange spectrum of the rainbow also provides you with the wide variety of vitamins, minerals, and powerful phytochemicals that pack each and every delicious bit of orange produce. With impressive amounts of vitamins A, B1, B2, B3, B5, B6, B9, E, and K,

orange fruits and vegetables offer up health benefits that promote immunity. They also affect the utilization of carbohydrates and the subsequent production of energy, the production and regulation of healthy red blood cells and important hormones, metabolism maintenance, muscle strength, and teeth and bone strength. On top of all those benefits, they even protect cells against free radical damage, and they improve the quality of hair, skin, and nails.

The important minerals calcium, copper, manganese, potassium, selenium, and zinc, which are also found in these foods, lend support to the body's overall functioning by promoting nerve cell communication and functioning, and by sustaining the vitamins' roles in optimizing the production and maintenance of red blood cells, hormones, bone and muscle tissue, the metabolism, the digestive system, and the immune system.

In addition to reaping the benefits of these vitamins and minerals, you'll also find that orange foods are packed full of the powerful phytochemicals *flavanones* and *carotenes* that give this produce its color. While encouraging healthy functioning of the eyes, the brain, cell production, cell growth, and the much-needed optimizing of the immune system, these phytochemicals also play a major role in preventing free radical damage that can lead to various cancers, inflammation that can lead to cardiovascular disease and arthritis, and blood conditions that can raise your cholesterol levels.

But keep this in mind: To benefit from all of the intense nutrition packed into the vibrantly colored orange selection of produce, you have to eat (or drink!) them in as close to their natural state as possible. While drinking orange juice is a great way to get vitamin C, the better alternative is to eat (or sip!) an actual orange. Not only are the whole fruit versions of juices and dried varieties less likely to have additional sugars and preservatives added to them in the manufacturing process, but the whole fruit also contains loads of fiber that is absolutely necessary if you want your digestive system to function well. So, when it comes to sipping the orange part of the rainbow, try to remember that "Nature's Way Is the Best Way"—which shouldn't be a problem once you try the delicious smoothies in this chapter.

Clever Carrots and Spice

Carrot juice is embellished in this recipe, which incorporates aromatic spices, sweet maple syrup, and creamy almond milk for one delicious smoothie that's packed with nutrition! The beta-carotene that gives carrots their delightful shade provides protective defenses for the cells of the skin, eyes, and internal organs against free radical damage from foreign invaders that can mutate healthy cells.

YIELDS: 2 CUPS

Ingredients
2 cups carrots
1 teaspoon ground ginger
1 teaspoon cloves
1 teaspoon cardamom
1 teaspoon organic, natural maple syrup
1 cup vanilla almond milk
1 cup ice

1. In a blender, combine the carrots, ginger, cloves, cardamom, maple syrup, and almond milk with ½ cup ice, and blend until thoroughly combined.

2. While blending, add remaining ice until desired consistency is achieved.

PER 1 CUP SERVING Calories: 112 | Fat: 2 g | Protein: 2 g | Sodium: 126 mg | Fiber: 4 g | Carbohydrates: 29 g

Sweet Potato Surprise

Simple, sweet, and with a little added crunch, this smoothie packs tons of healthy complex carbohydrates that will satisfy your sweet tooth and keep you full. Maintaining your energy for longer periods of time than less nutritious smoothie alternatives, this Sweet Potato Surprise is the way to go!

YIELDS: 2 CUPS

Ingredients
1½ cups sweet potatoes, baked and peeled
½ cup organic, all-natural granola
1 cup almond milk
1 cup ice

1. In a blender, combine the sweet potatoes, granola, and almond milk with ½ cup ice, and blend until thoroughly combined.

2. While blending, add remaining ice until desired consistency is achieved.

PER 1 CUP SERVING Calories: 285 | Fat: 8 g | Protein: 7 g | Sodium: 107 mg | Fiber: 6 g | Carbohydrates: 50 g

Easy on the Eyes

With rich sources of beta-carotene and lutein that promote the quality of your vision, carrots and apricots join forces in this delicious blended fruit concoction. Sweet and loaded with health benefits, this smoothie is a delicious way to get those fruit and vegetable servings easily.

YIELDS: 2 CUPS

Ingredients

2 cups carrots
1 cup water
1 cup apricots, pitted
1 cup ice

1. In a blender, combine the carrots and water, and emulsify completely.

2. Add apricots and ½ cup ice, and blend until thoroughly combined.

3. While blending, add remaining ice until desired consistency is achieved.

PER 1 CUP SERVING Calories: 82 | Fat: 1 g | Protein: 2 g | Sodium: 77 mg | Fiber: 5 g | Carbohydrates: 19 g

Wacky Orange Mango Tango

With only a few simple ingredients, this smoothie is a cinch to make and a delight to enjoy. Packed with unique flavors that pair well together, this smoothie helps you load up on vitamins, minerals, and powerful antioxidants—like B vitamins and vitamin C—that work together to keep your metabolism and energy moving while providing your body with protections against anything that can wreak havoc on your health.

YIELDS: 2 CUPS

Ingredients

3 large oranges, peeled and deseeded
½ cup mango, peeled
1 cup water
1 cup ice

1. In a blender, combine the oranges, mango, and water with ½ cup ice, and blend until thoroughly combined.

2. While blending, add remaining ice until desired consistency is achieved.

PER 1 CUP SERVING Calories: 120 | Fat: 0 g | Protein: 2 g | Sodium: 1 mg | Fiber: 5 g | Carbohydrates: 30 g

Papaya Perfection

Papaya needs only the addition of water and ice to be a perfect pick-me-up at any point in your day. Sweet and unique in flavor, papaya is a tasty treat that comes with the added benefit of quality nutrition. This rich source of vitamin A works wonders on maintaining eye and skin health by protecting the important organs from premature degeneration.

YIELDS: 2 CUPS

Ingredients
2 cups papaya, peeled and deseeded
1 cup water
1 cup ice

1. In a blender, combine the papaya and water with ½ cup ice, and blend until thoroughly combined.

2. While blending, add remaining ice until desired consistency is achieved.

PER 1 CUP SERVING Calories: 54 | Fat: 0 g | Protein: 1 g | Sodium: 4 mg | Fiber: 3 g | Carbohydrates: 14 g

Pumpkin Pie

Who would've thought that pumpkin pie could actually be beneficial to your health? This recipe combines the health-promoting ingredients of beta-carotene- and fiber-rich pumpkin along with antioxidant-packed spices that combine for powerful disease-fighting potential. You'll enjoy delicious traditional pumpkin pie flavor without all of the unhealthy additions.

YIELDS: 2 CUPS

Ingredients
2 cups pure pumpkin purée
1 teaspoon ground ginger
1 teaspoon ground cloves
1 teaspoon ground nutmeg
1 teaspoon ground cinnamon
1 cup vanilla almond milk
1 cup ice

1. In a blender, combine the pumpkin, ginger, cloves, nutmeg, cinnamon, and almond milk with ½ cup ice, and blend until thoroughly combined.

2. While blending, add remaining ice until desired consistency is achieved.

PER 1 CUP SERVING Calories: 90 | Fat: 1 g | Protein: 2 g | Sodium: 49 mg | Fiber: 2 g | Carbohydrates: 24 g

Papaya-nana

Sometimes, simplicity is best. That definitely rings true with this delicious blend of sweet papaya, smooth banana, and creamy coconut milk. Morning, noon, or night, this smoothie is a splendidly sweet treat that packs in plentiful anti-aging vitamin A and bloat-fighting potassium amidst bounds of deliciousness.

YIELDS: 3 CUPS

Ingredients
2 cups papaya, peeled and deseeded
1 banana, peeled
2 cups coconut milk
1 cup ice

1. In a blender, combine the papaya, banana, and 1 cup coconut milk with ½ cup ice, and blend until thoroughly combined.

2. While blending, add remaining coconut milk and ice until desired consistency is achieved.

PER 1 CUP SERVING Calories: 368 | Fat: 32 g | Protein: 4 g | Sodium: 23 mg | Fiber: 3 g | Carbohydrates: 22 g

Papaya Powerhouse

Powerful nutrients and phytochemicals combine in this smoothie: disease-combating beta-carotene in papaya, omega-rich flaxseed, probiotic-packed kefir, and healthy fats and protein in almond milk keep your muscles in tip-top condition. The irresistible taste and strong heath benefits make this a smoothie that can't be beat!

YIELDS: 3 CUPS

Ingredients
2 cups papaya, peeled and deseeded
1 scoop vanilla protein powder
¼ cup ground flaxseed
½ cup plain kefir
1 cup vanilla almond milk
1 cup ice

1. In a blender, combine the papaya, protein powder, flaxseed, kefir, and almond milk with ½ cup ice, and blend until thoroughly combined.

2. While blending, add remaining ice until desired consistency is achieved.

PER 1 CUP SERVING Calories: 142 | Fat: 4 g | Protein: 13 g | Sodium: 34 mg | Fiber: 5 g | Carbohydrates: 15 g

Cool Off with Cantaloupe

You know Mother Nature has done her job when the most nutritious foods need nothing more than ice to tingle your taste buds and help your body function at its best. Cantaloupe and coconut milk combine to provide B vitamins for blood and metabolism health and vitamin C for improved immunity with absolute deliciousness in every delightful sip.

YIELDS: 2 CUPS

Ingredients
2 cups cantaloupe, peeled and deseeded
1 cup coconut milk
1 cup ice

1. In a blender, combine the cantaloupe and coconut milk with ½ cup ice, and blend until thoroughly combined.

2. While blending, add remaining ice until desired consistency is achieved.

PER 1 CUP SERVING Calories: 275 | Fat: 24 g | Protein: 4 g | Sodium: 40 mg | Fiber: 1 g | Carbohydrates: 16 g

Healthy Glow Smoothie

This smoothie is filled to the brim with vitamins, minerals, and powerful antioxidants, including vitamin A, which does double duty as the powerful antioxidant beta-carotene, to promote healthy eyes and skin while preventing premature aging. Here these nutrients work hand in hand to prevent skin damage and give you a healthy glow.

YIELDS: 2 CUPS

Ingredients
2 cups cantaloupe, peeled and deseeded
1 medium cucumber, peeled
1 cup water
1 cup ice

1. In a blender, combine the cantaloupe, cucumber, and water with ½ cup ice, and blend until thoroughly combined.

2. While blending, add remaining ice until desired consistency is achieved.

PER 1 CUP SERVING Calories: 75 | Fat: 0 g | Protein: 2 g | Sodium: 28 mg | Fiber: 2 g | Carbohydrates: 18 g

Papaya with a Kick

Papaya doesn't need much to taste great, but the surprising blend of ingredients found in this recipe brings its flavor to another level. With the addition of fresh grated ginger and a sprinkling of cayenne pepper, the metabolism-promoting antioxidants and B vitamins found in this smoothie will awaken your senses!

YIELDS: 2 CUPS

Ingredients
2 cups papaya, peeled and deseeded
1 tablespoon grated ginger
1 teaspoon cayenne pepper
1 cup coconut milk
1 cup ice

1. In a blender, combine the papaya, ginger, cayenne pepper, and coconut milk with ½ cup ice, and blend until thoroughly combined.

2. While blending, add remaining ice until desired consistency is achieved.

PER 1 CUP SERVING Calories: 282 | Fat: 24 g | Protein: 3 g | Sodium: 20 mg | Fiber: 3 g | Carbohydrates: 18 g

"A" Is for Apricot

Less famous among the orange foods, apricots are more commonly eaten in their dried variety. But while dried apricots are still fruit, fresh apricots can contribute whole, natural supplies of vitamin A that will help protect cells from dangerous disease and mutations while promoting healthy skin and eyes that will resist premature aging and degeneration. These health benefits, combined with the natural sweetness and goodness of the apricot, make this smoothie both delicious *and* nutritious.

YIELDS: 2 CUPS

Ingredients
2 cups apricots, pitted
1 cup water
1 cup ice

1. In a blender, combine the apricots and water with ½ cup ice, and blend until thoroughly combined.

2. While blending, add remaining ice until desired consistency is achieved.

PER 1 CUP SERVING Calories: 74 | Fat: 1 g | Protein: 2 g | Sodium: 2 mg | Fiber: 3 g | Carbohydrates: 17 g

Pleasantly Pumpkin

Pumpkin has healthy amounts of fiber that help the body to maintain regularity and resist cancer-causing collections of foreign bacteria in the colon. By quickly combining the few simple ingredients in this recipe, you can prepare a sweet, healthy, creamy smoothie that benefits both your body and taste buds.

YIELDS: 3 CUPS

Ingredients
2 cups pure pumpkin purée
¼ cup ground flaxseed
1 teaspoon organic, all-natural maple syrup
1½ cups vanilla almond milk
1 cup ice

1. In a blender, combine the pumpkin, flaxseed, maple syrup, and almond milk with ½ cup ice, and blend until thoroughly combined.

2. While blending, add remaining ice until desired consistency is achieved.

PER 1 CUP SERVING Calories: 123 | Fat: 5 g | Protein: 4 g | Sodium: 47 mg | Fiber: 3 g | Carbohydrates: 24 g

Pumpkin and Spice for Everything Nice

With sweet flavors, a hint of spice, and a creamy texture, this pumpkin smoothie is a delicious option to sip your way to better health. From your skin to your cells, your body will benefit from the load of vitamin A that acts as a double agent in preventing illness and disease while regenerating healthy cells . . . deliciously!

YIELDS: 3 CUPS

Ingredients
2 cups pure pumpkin purée
1 tablespoon grated ginger
½ teaspoon cayenne pepper
1½ cups vanilla coconut milk
1 cup ice

1. In a blender, combine the pumpkin, ginger, cayenne, and 1 cup coconut milk with ½ cup ice, and blend until thoroughly combined.

2. While blending, add remaining coconut milk and ice until desired consistency is achieved.

PER 1 CUP SERVING Calories: 250 | Fat: 24 g | Protein: 3 g | Sodium: 16 mg | Fiber: 1 g | Carbohydrates: 10 g

Yummy Yams

While packing this smoothie with tons of intense flavor, yams also add a sweet complex carbohydrate to the mix. This slow release of sugar can help the blood maintain healthy sugar levels—complex carbohydrates benefit the body and the brain by preventing blood sugar spikes and drops that would otherwise create quick energy shortly followed by an inevitable "crash" felt physically and mentally. This orange ingredient takes center stage in a beautiful blend of spices and smooth almond milk.

YIELDS: 2 CUPS

Ingredients

2 cups yams, softened and skins removed
1 vanilla bean's pulp
1 teaspoon ground nutmeg
1½ cups vanilla almond milk
1 cup ice

1. In a blender, combine the yams, vanilla bean's pulp, nutmeg, and 1 cup almond milk with ½ cup ice, and blend until thoroughly combined.

2. While blending, add remaining almond milk and ice until desired consistency is achieved.

PER 1 CUP SERVING Calories: 264 | Fat: 2 g | Protein: 3 g | Sodium: 81 mg | Fiber: 6 g | Carbohydrates: 64 g

Creative with Carrots

The sweetness of fiber-rich apples and carrots collides with smooth banana in a delightful smoothie that needs nothing more than water and ice to turn a variety of produce into an even more scrumptious smoothie! With an abundance of cancer-fighting fiber that also creates a feeling of fullness, this recipe takes the prize for multitasking health benefits and deliciousness!

YIELDS: 3 CUPS

Ingredients

1 cup carrots
2 cups water
1 banana, peeled
1 yellow apple, cored
1 cup ice

1. In a blender, combine the carrots with 1 cup water and blend until emulsified.

2. Add banana, apple, remaining water, and ½ cup ice, and blend until thoroughly combined.

3. While blending, add remaining ice until desired consistency is achieved.

PER 1 CUP SERVING Calories: 76 | Fat: 0 g | Protein: 1 g | Sodium: 26 mg | Fiber: 3 g | Carbohydrates: 19 g

Sweet and Tart Carrot-Apricot

All of the ingredients in this smoothie contribute a different level of sweet flavors, and the tart kick of acidic pineapple acts as a beautifully designed balancer. Here the deep orange carrots and apricots team up with the rich, golden pineapple to launch a nutritious attack of vitamins A and C to act as illness preventers against whatever ails you!

YIELDS: 2 CUPS

Ingredients
1 cup carrots
1½ cups coconut milk
1 cup apricots, pitted
1 cup pineapple
1 cup ice

1. In a blender, combine the carrots with 1 cup coconut milk and blend until emulsified.

2. Add the apricots, pineapple, remaining coconut milk, and ½ cup ice, and blend until thoroughly combined.

3. While blending, add remaining ice until desired consistency is achieved.

PER 1 CUP SERVING Calories: 435 | Fat: 37 g | Protein: 5 g | Sodium: 62 mg | Fiber: 4 g | Carbohydrates: 29 g

Sweet Potato Pie

Everyone loves sweet potato pie, but let's be honest, it's not all that healthy. This smart smoothie allows you to ditch the marshmallows and brown sugar found in traditional sweet potato pie and try this version on for size. With delicious flavors that add unique depth to every sip of this smoothie, you'll be pleasantly surprised that natural and healthy ingredients could taste this great.

YIELDS: 3 CUPS

Ingredients
1½ cups sweet potato, softened and skins removed
2 cups vanilla almond milk
½ cup walnuts
1 teaspoon ground ginger
1 teaspoon ground cloves
1 teaspoon cinnamon
1 cup ice

1. In a blender, combine the sweet potato and ½ cup almond milk with the walnuts and blend until emulsified.

2. Add the ginger, cloves, cinnamon, and remaining almond milk with ½ cup ice, and blend until thoroughly combined.

3. While blending, add remaining ice until desired consistency is achieved.

PER 1 CUP SERVING Calories: 253 | Fat: 14 g | Protein: 5 g | Sodium: 97 mg | Fiber: 3 g | Carbohydrates: 35 g

Pumped Up Pumpkin Chai

On a cold winter day, sitting down with a hot cup of chai just feels right, but the chai you buy at the local coffeehouse doesn't really do a body good. There's good news, though; the pumpkin, protein, and spices used in this recipe make for an antioxidant-packed smoothie that will taste great while also fending off deadly diseases that can wreak havoc on your cells. So by enjoying this Pumped Up Pumpkin Chai smoothie, you can grab that delightful chai taste in a delicious treat that not only feels right, but helps the body feel good, too!

YIELDS: 3 CUPS

Ingredients
2 cups pure pumpkin purée
1 scoop vanilla protein powder
¼ cup ground flaxseed
1 teaspoon ground cardamom
1 teaspoon ground nutmeg
2 cups plain kefir
1 cup ice

1. In a blender, combine the pumpkin purée, protein powder, flaxseed, cardamom, nutmeg, and kefir with ½ cup ice, and blend until thoroughly combined.

2. While blending, add remaining ice until desired consistency is achieved.

PER 1 CUP SERVING Calories: 198 | Fat: 5 g | Protein: 20 g | Sodium: 126 mg | Fiber: 4 g | Carbohydrates: 21 g

Citrus Cantaloupe

In this smoothie, the sweet cantaloupe gets a tart twist from various delicious citrus fruits. With cantaloupe, oranges, and lemons—which are full of vitamins A, C, and E—teaming up for loads of nutritious benefits, including cell protection and healthy cell regeneration, this is a great smoothie that can't be beat!

YIELDS: 2 CUPS

Ingredients
1 cup cantaloupe, peeled and deseeded
2 oranges, peeled and deseeded
1 lemon, peeled and deseeded
1 cup water
1 cup ice

1. In a blender, combine the cantaloupe, oranges, lemon, and water with ½ cup ice, and blend until thoroughly combined.

2. While blending, add remaining ice until desired consistency is achieved.

PER 1 CUP SERVING Calories: 96 | Fat: 0 g | Protein: 2 g | Sodium: 13 mg | Fiber: 5 g | Carbohydrates: 24 g

Sweet and Simple Carrot-Apple

In this smoothie, the use of the natural apple juice enhances the delectable flavors of apple and carrot. By blending these two scrumptious flavors together, you get one sweet treat that's not only tasty, but also delivers valuable nutrition. Rich provisions of vitamin C prevent illness, and quercetin provides antioxidant power against free radical damage.

YIELDS: 2 CUPS

Ingredients
1 cup carrots
1½ cups all-natural apple juice, organic (not from concentrate)
1 yellow apple, cored
1 cup ice

1. In a blender, combine the carrots and 1 cup of apple juice, and blend until completely emulsified.

2. Add the apple, remaining apple juice, and ½ cup ice, and blend until thoroughly combined.

3. While blending, add remaining ice until desired consistency is achieved.

PER 1 CUP SERVING Calories: 147 | Fat: 0 g | Protein: 1 g | Sodium: 45 mg | Fiber: 3 g | Carbohydrates: 37 g

Orange Creamsicle

There's no need to search for store-bought varieties of creamy, fruity ice pops anymore. You'll find the same fruity taste in this delicious, chilly blend of oranges, creamy kefir, and coconut milk—and you'll find more bacteria-fighting probiotics, muscle-strengthening protein, and health-protecting vitamin C than you'd ever find on a stick.

YIELDS: 2 CUPS

Ingredients
4 oranges, peeled and deseeded
1 cup plain kefir
½ cup coconut milk
1 cup ice

1. In a blender, combine the oranges, kefir, and coconut milk with ½ cup ice, and blend until thoroughly combined.

2. While blending, add remaining ice until desired consistency is achieved.

PER 1 CUP SERVING Calories: 303 | Fat: 13 g | Protein: 11 g | Sodium: 102 mg | Fiber: 6 g | Carbohydrates: 42 g

Spicy Cantaloupe

The "spicy" in this smoothie recipe comes from the fragrant gingerroot that we all know and love. Soothing any stomachache while acting as a strong antioxidant, ginger is an amazingly unexpected, sweet and spicy element of any smoothie—especially this one.

YIELDS: 2 CUPS

Ingredients
1 cup cantaloupe, peeled and deseeded
2 oranges, peeled and deseeded
½ lemon, peeled and deseeded
1 tablespoon grated ginger
1 cup water
1 cup ice

1. In a blender, combine the cantaloupe, oranges, lemon, ginger, and ½ cup water with ½ cup ice, and blend until thoroughly combined.

2. While blending, add remaining water and ice until desired consistency is achieved.

PER 1 CUP SERVING Calories: 94 | Fat: 0 g | Protein: 2 g | Sodium: 13 mg | Fiber: 4 g | Carbohydrates: 24 g

Orange You Glad You Woke Up for This!

While waking yourself with orange juice may be delicious and nutritious, this spin on the traditional morning juice drink takes the cake! Packed with real, whole oranges that provide quality nutrition from their abundant beta-carotene, vitamin C, and fiber, this delicious creamy spin on your favorite glass of OJ may make tomorrow morning's wake-up call a little easier to bear.

YIELDS: 2 CUPS

Ingredients
4 oranges, peeled and deseeded
1 scoop vanilla protein powder
1½ cups vanilla almond milk
1 cup ice

1. In a blender, combine the oranges, protein powder, and 1 cup vanilla almond milk with ½ cup ice, and blend until thoroughly combined.

2. While blending, add remaining milk and ice until desired consistency is achieved.

PER 1 CUP SERVING Calories: 253 | Fat: 3 g | Protein: 15 g | Sodium: 68 mg | Fiber: 6 g | Carbohydrates: 52 g

Melon Mender

The sweet nectar of hydrating melons combines with a healthy dose of kefir for an out-of-this-world smoothie that makes it easier than ever to sip the rainbow. Fast, easy, and enjoyable, this smoothie won't take you any time to prepare, but you'll sure want to savor every sip.

YIELDS: 2 CUPS

Ingredients

2 cups cantaloupe, peeled and deseeded
1 cup plain kefir
½ cup water
1 cup ice

1. In a blender, combine the cantaloupe, kefir, and water with ½ cup ice, and blend until thoroughly combined.

2. While blending, add remaining ice until desired consistency is achieved.

PER 1 CUP SERVING Calories: 122 | Fat: 1 g | Protein: 8 g | Sodium: 119 mg | Fiber: 1 g | Carbohydrates: 22 g

Sweet and Smooth Citrus Smoothie

In this smoothie, the sweet, crisp flavors of vitamin C–rich oranges combine with the tart tastes of limonin-packed lemon and lime. The tartness is smoothed and cooled with the potassium-filled flavors of banana and coconut milk. But even better than this smoothie's taste is the nutritional punch it packs! Vitamin C, limonin, and potassium combine for an all-out attack against sickness and disease.

YIELDS: 3 CUPS

Ingredients

3 oranges, peeled and deseeded
½ lemon, peeled and deseeded
½ lime, peeled and deseeded
2 bananas, peeled
1½ cups coconut milk
1 cup ice

1. In a blender, combine the oranges, lemon, lime, bananas, and 1 cup coconut milk with ½ cup ice, and blend until thoroughly combined.

2. While blending, add remaining coconut milk and ice until desired consistency is achieved.

PER 1 CUP SERVING Calories: 360 | Fat: 25 g | Protein: 5 g | Sodium: 16 mg | Fiber: 6 g | Carbohydrates: 39 g

Creamy Vitamin C

Flu season is a great time—and a great excuse—to enjoy this smoothie over and over again! With rich produce that packs a double dose of vitamin C for improved immunity against colds and flu, this smoothie has it all!

YIELDS: 3 CUPS

Ingredients

2 oranges, peeled and deseeded
1 cup cantaloupe, peeled and deseeded
1 banana, peeled
1 cup rice milk
1 cup ice

1. In a blender, combine the oranges, cantaloupe, banana, and rice milk with ½ cup ice, and blend until thoroughly combined.

2. While blending, add remaining ice until desired consistency is achieved.

PER 1 CUP SERVING Calories: 127 | Fat: 1 g | Protein: 2 g | Sodium: 39 mg | Fiber: 4 g | Carbohydrates: 33 g

Thankful Sweet Potato Pie

Forget about not-so-nutritious pastry pies, and opt for a similar smoothie that provides loads of nutrition on top of great taste. This recipe combines delicious winter veggies with complex carbohydrates and aromatic spices that will leave you feeling full but light and refreshed . . . no guilt necessary!

YIELDS: 4 CUPS

Ingredients

1 cup sweet potatoes, softened and skins removed
1 cup pure pumpkin purée
½ cup rolled oats
¼ cup honey wheat germ
1 teaspoon ground cloves
1 teaspoon ground ginger
1 teaspoon cinnamon
2 cups vanilla almond milk
1 cup ice

1. In a blender, combine the sweet potato, pumpkin purée, oats, wheat germ, cloves, ginger, cinnamon, and 1½ cups almond milk with ½ cup ice, and blend until thoroughly combined.

2. While blending, add remaining almond milk and ice until desired consistency is achieved.

PER 1 CUP SERVING Calories: 154 | Fat: 3 g | Protein: 4 g | Sodium: 67 mg | Fiber: 3 g | Carbohydrates: 34 g

Nutty Pumpkin Blend

The combination of flavorful nuts and sweet puréed pumpkin is delicious and nutritious on its own, but when you add it to a delightful mix of omega-rich flaxseed, protein-packed almond milk, and super-sweet maple syrup, you have a dessert smoothie that's healthy enough to enjoy any time of the day!

YIELDS: 4 CUPS

Ingredients
2 cups almond milk
¼ cup walnuts
¼ cup natural almonds
1 cup pure pumpkin purée
¼ cup ground flaxseed
1 teaspoon all-natural, organic maple syrup
1 cup ice

1. In a blender, combine 1 cup almond milk with the walnuts and almonds, and blend until completely emulsified.

2. Add the pumpkin purée, flaxseed, ½ cup almond milk, and maple syrup with ½ cup ice, and blend until thoroughly combined.

3. While blending, add remaining almond milk and ice until desired consistency is achieved.

PER 1 CUP SERVING Calories: 179 | Fat: 11 g | Protein: 5 g | Sodium: 47 mg | Fiber: 4 g | Carbohydrates: 22 g

Crazy for Carrots

If you love carrot juice, this smoothie will knock your socks off! If you haven't yet become an avid lover of the deep orange juice, you certainly will after tasting this unbelievably sweet treat packed with heart-protecting vitamin A and absolutely amazing taste!

YIELDS: 2 CUPS

Ingredients
2 cups carrots
1 cup coconut milk
1 cup ice

1. In a blender, combine the carrots and coconut milk with ½ cup ice, and blend until thoroughly combined.

2. While blending, add remaining ice until desired consistency is achieved.

PER 1 CUP SERVING Calories: 267 | Fat: 24 g | Protein: 3 g | Sodium: 91 mg | Fiber: 3 g | Carbohydrates: 14 g

Tropical Twist on Carrots

Adding tropical-flavored fruits like pineapple, banana, and coconut to something as simple and sweet as carrots may seem like overkill, but one taste of this smoothie will make you a true convert! Brimming with vitamins A and C, beta-carotene and bromelain, and ultra-important fiber that all act to promote your overall health and well-being by fending off illness and promoting healthy intestinal environments, this recipe is a truly tasty tropical twist on something already super-delicious.

YIELDS: 3 CUPS

Ingredients
1 cup carrots
2 cups coconut milk
1 cup pineapple
1 banana, peeled
1 cup ice

1. In a blender, combine the carrots with 1 cup coconut milk and blend until completely emulsified.

2. Add the pineapple, banana, and remaining coconut milk with ½ cup ice, and blend until thoroughly combined.

3. While blending, add remaining ice until desired consistency is achieved.

PER 1 CUP SERVING Calories: 374 | Fat: 32 g | Protein: 4 g | Sodium: 46 mg | Fiber: 3 g | Carbohydrates: 24 g

Creamy Carrot Smoothie

While carrots can work wonders on your body on their own, adding smooth, creamy ingredients like Greek-style yogurt and kefir only serve to add essential doses of much-needed protein that improve the health of the muscles, blood, and brain.

YIELDS: 3 CUPS

Ingredients
2 cups carrots
½ cup plain kefir
½ cup Greek-style yogurt
1 serving probiotic supplement (see packaging for exact amount)
½ cup water
1 cup ice

1. In a blender, combine the carrots, kefir, yogurt, probiotic, and water with ½ cup ice, and blend until thoroughly combined.

2. While blending, add remaining ice until desired consistency is achieved.

PER 1 CUP SERVING Calories: 75 | Fat: 0 g | Protein: 7 g | Sodium: 98 mg | Fiber: 2 g | Carbohydrates: 12 g

Smooth and Sweet Banana-Carrot

Sweet bananas and carrots join up to pack every delicious sip with tons of vitamin A for cell protection, potassium for hydration regulation, and protein for improved strength and endurance. With the added benefits of powerful antioxidants, probiotics, and protein, this is one jam-packed smoothie that's overflowing with nutrition!

YIELDS: 2 CUPS

Ingredients
1 cup carrots, peeled and tops removed
1 banana, peeled
½ cup plain kefir
½ cup Greek-style yogurt
½ cup water
1 cup ice

1. In a blender, combine the carrots, banana, kefir, yogurt, and water with ½ cup ice, and blend until thoroughly combined.

2. While blending, add remaining ice until desired consistency is achieved.

PER 1 CUP SERVING Calories: 142 | Fat: 0 g | Protein: 11 g | Sodium: 109 mg | Fiber: 3 g | Carbohydrates: 26 g

Coconut Milk and Meat Smoothie

By including actual coconut meat as well as coconut milk in this recipe, you ensure that the sweet, unique taste of coconut fills every tasty sip of this smoothie. Coconut provides necessary fats that keep you satiated, and support healthy skin and nails. Lending a slightly sweet and creamy taste, this coconut duo adds depth to the amazing tastes of carrot and orange for a bright orange blend you're sure to enjoy!

YIELDS: 3 CUPS

Ingredients
1 cup carrots, peeled and tops removed
1 cup coconut meat
2 oranges, peeled and deseeded
1 cup coconut milk
1 cup ice

1. In a blender, combine the carrots, coconut meat, oranges, and coconut milk with ½ cup ice, and blend until thoroughly combined.

2. While blending, add remaining ice until desired consistency is achieved.

PER 1 CUP SERVING Calories: 299 | Fat: 25 g | Protein: 4 g | Sodium: 40 mg | Fiber: 6 g | Carbohydrates: 20 g

Color Your Smoothie Cantaloupe

If you love cantaloupe, this smoothie is for you! The sweet, tart flavors of orange—which is packed full of immunity-strengthening vitamin C—and the sweet, smooth taste and texture of cantaloupe, which is brimming with beta-carotene blend into a smoothie that tastes so good, you won't believe it's actually good for you—but it is!

YIELDS: 2 CUPS

Ingredients
1 cup cantaloupe
1 orange, peeled and deseeded
1 cup water
1 cup ice

1. In a blender, combine the cantaloupe, orange, and water with ½ cup ice, and blend until thoroughly combined.

2. While blending, add remaining ice until desired consistency is achieved.

PER 1 CUP SERVING Calories: 57 | Fat: 0 g | Protein: 1 g | Sodium: 13 mg | Fiber: 2 g | Carbohydrates: 14 g

Smooth Cantaloupe Creation

While cantaloupe has a unique splendor in terms of taste and antioxidants, this smoothie contains the powers of protein for improved muscle function and potassium that promotes optimum cell activity. It's a new and improved way to drink the rainbow!

YIELDS: 4 CUPS

Ingredients
2 cups cantaloupe, peeled and deseeded
1 banana, peeled
1 cup Greek-style yogurt
1 cup water
1 cup ice

1. In a blender, combine the cantaloupe, banana, yogurt, and water with ½ cup ice, and blend until thoroughly combined.

2. While blending, add remaining ice until desired consistency is achieved.

PER 1 CUP SERVING Calories: 73 | Fat: 0 g | Protein: 7 g | Sodium: 30 mg | Fiber: 1 g | Carbohydrates: 12 g

Papaya-Pineapple

This tropical smoothie combines the delicious flavors of papaya, pineapple, and creamy coconut milk for a healthy blast of nutrition all in one place. The powerful antioxidants packed into this simple smoothie—like beta-carotene and bromelain—can provide a better life of reversed aging, disease prevention, and healthier cell functioning.

YIELDS: 3 CUPS

Ingredients
1½ cups papaya, peeled and deseeded
1 cup pineapple
1 cup coconut milk
1 cup ice

1. In a blender, combine the papaya, pineapple, and coconut milk with ½ cup ice, and blend until thoroughly combined.

2. While blending, add remaining ice until desired consistency is achieved.

PER 1 CUP SERVING Calories: 203 | Fat: 16 g | Protein: 2 g | Sodium: 12 mg | Fiber: 2 g | Carbohydrates: 16 g

Wake Up and Smell the Smoothie

If you love to jumpstart your mornings with the sweet, tangy flavor of orange juice, this smoothie is for you! But this smoothie is about more than just juice! It combines the delicious flavors of eye-opening oranges, smooth bananas, and special coconut milk for a sweet, creamy breakfast packed with vitamin C and potassium that'll keep your body running at peak performance with reduced incidence of illness and improved energy.

YIELDS: 2 CUPS

Ingredients
2 oranges, peeled and deseeded
2 bananas, peeled
1½ cups coconut milk
1 cup ice

1. In a blender, combine the oranges, bananas, and 1 cup coconut milk with ½ cup ice, and blend until thoroughly combined.

2. While blending, add remaining coconut milk and ice until desired consistency is achieved.

PER 1 CUP SERVING Calories: 500 | Fat: 5 g | Protein: 6 g | Sodium: 23 mg | Fiber: 6 g | Carbohydrates: 47 g

Ginger-Melon

Sweet and simple, this recipe is jazzed up with the splendid addition of gingerroot, which adds its unique taste for an unexpected smoothie that's out of this world! Filled with essential nutrients like vitamins A and C for improved immunity and tons of antioxidants for the best disease prevention possible, this is a delicious and nutritious smoothie perfect any time of year . . . but especially cold and flu season!

YIELDS: 2 CUPS

Ingredients

2 cups cantaloupe, peeled and deseeded
1 tablespoon grated ginger
1 cup coconut milk
1 cup ice

1. In a blender, combine the cantaloupe, ginger, and coconut milk with ½ cup ice, and blend until thoroughly combined.

2. While blending, add remaining ice until desired consistency is achieved.

PER 1 CUP SERVING Calories: 278 | Fat: 24 g | Protein: 4 g | Sodium: 40 mg | Fiber: 1 g | Carbohydrates: 16 g

Coconuts for Cantaloupe

The addition of omega-rich ground flaxseed to the sweet ingredients of this smoothie gives every sip a slightly nutty background taste with unbelievable amounts of quality nutrition essentials, such as omega fatty acids and vitamin C that work together for better brain health and functioning. The combination of the cantaloupe, coconut, and flaxseed creates a powerful smoothie that may change your life—and it tastes great too!

YIELDS: 3 CUPS

Ingredients

2 cups cantaloupe, peeled and deseeded
½ cup coconut meat
⅛ cup ground flaxseed
1 cup coconut milk
1 cup ice

1. In a blender, combine the cantaloupe, coconut meat, flaxseed, and coconut milk with ½ cup ice, and blend until thoroughly combined.

2. While blending, add remaining ice until desired consistency is achieved.

PER 1 CUP SERVING Calories: 254 | Fat: 22 g | Protein: 4 g | Sodium: 29 mg | Fiber: 4 g | Carbohydrates: 14 g

Crisp Carrot-Cauliflower

The cauliflower in this recipe acts as a blank canvas for the sweet flavors of beta-carotene–rich carrot and vitamin B–packed coconut. But even though the cauliflower isn't the star of the show, you can still benefit from the rich stores of vitamin C that fill every white floret.

YIELDS: 3 CUPS

Ingredients

1½ cups carrots, peeled and tops removed
1 cup cauliflower
1 cup coconut milk
1 cup ice

1. In a blender, combine the carrots, cauliflower, and coconut milk with ½ cup ice, and blend until thoroughly combined.

2. While blending, add remaining ice until desired consistency is achieved.

PER 1 CUP SERVING Calories: 179 | Fat: 16 g | Protein: 3 g | Sodium: 58 mg | Fiber: 2 g | Carbohydrates: 9 g

Carrot-Pear

The sweet blend of carrots and pear join up with creamy coconut milk for a unique taste sensation that's actually good for you! Packed with powerful antioxidants and tons of fiber that act together to benefit your health by promoting regularity and cleaning out dangerous "left behind" food particles, you can sip this smoothie happily knowing you've made a sweet, smart choice for better health!

YIELDS: 2 CUPS

Ingredients

1½ cups carrots, peeled and tops removed
1 pear, cored
1 cup coconut milk
1 cup ice

1. In a blender, combine the carrots, pear, and coconut milk with ½ cup ice, and blend until thoroughly combined.

2. While blending, add remaining ice until desired consistency is achieved.

PER 1 CUP SERVING Calories: 182 | Fat: 16 g | Protein: 2 g | Sodium: 48 mg | Fiber: 3 g | Carbohydrates: 10 g

Cucumber-Carrot

Refreshing and sweet, this smoothie combines the vibrant color and flavor of carrots with the more subdued intensity of cucumber. Lending little color or taste, but tons of important minerals—including silica and magnesium, which work together to maintain an optimum environment of fluids and healthy chemicals in your body—the cucumber in this amazing smoothie keeps your body healthy from the inside, out.

YIELDS: 2 CUPS

Ingredients
1½ cups carrots, peeled and tops removed
1 cucumber, peeled
1 cup water
1 cup ice

1. In a blender, combine the carrots, cucumber, and water with ½ cup ice, and blend until thoroughly combined.

2. While blending, add remaining ice until desired consistency is achieved.

PER 1 CUP SERVING Calories: 56 | Fat: 0 g | Protein: 2 g | Sodium: 60 mg | Fiber: 3 g | Carbohydrates: 13 g

Orange Sunrise

The refreshing dew of cantaloupe joins the intense flavors of oranges and bananas in this amazing breakfast smoothie that packs tons of nutrition with tons of taste. Vitamins A and C, potassium, and amazing phytochemicals like beta-carotene and bromelain act together to combat illness and promote healthy organ functioning. It's an easy and delicious way to sip your nutrition . . . all with the added plus of satisfying those important fruit servings!

YIELDS: 4 CUPS

Ingredients
2 cups cantaloupe, peeled and deseeded
2 oranges, peeled and deseeded
1 banana, peeled
1 cup water
1 cup ice

1. In a blender, combine the cantaloupe, oranges, banana, and water with ½ cup ice, and blend until thoroughly combined.

2. While blending, add remaining ice until desired consistency is achieved.

PER 1 CUP SERVING Calories: 83 | Fat: 0 g | Protein: 2 g | Sodium: 13 mg | Fiber: 3 g | Carbohydrates: 21 g

Chapter 6

Yellow

Acorn Squash • Corn • Lemons and Limes • Mangoes •
Peaches and Nectarines • Pineapple • Yellow Squash

When you're drinking the yellow spectrum of the rainbow, you're in for a variety of light and sweet fruits and flavorful, hearty veggies that can pack any smoothie full of valuable nutrients. Vitamins found in yellow produce include A, C, E, and a variety of B vitamins. Because of their high amounts of each B vitamin, these foods are packed with mood-improving, hormone-regulating, weight-managing, metabolism-optimizing benefits that combine to keep your body's energy production at a stable level throughout the entire day. B vitamins also help out with the quality of the blood by supporting blood cell production and promoting healthy cell growth. The plentiful vitamin A that is found in yellow fruits and vegetables also helps in the production of red blood cells, the maintenance of vision health, and the optimization of protein synthesis. Vitamins C and E work hand in hand as powerful antioxidants that get even more support from the numerous phytochemicals found in the same foods.

Yellow fruits and vegetables also contain plenty of minerals, including iron, manganese, potassium, and phosphorous, which support healthy blood composition and improve the absorption of certain nutrients. (For instance, iron enhances the absorption of vitamin C, and manganese supports the utilization of carbohydrates, proteins, and fats.) In addition, the minerals ensure adequate hydration of the body and its cells, and they promote proper nerve cell functioning.

While the vitamins and minerals found in this color group are impressive on their own, the phytochemicals that give these foods their bright yellow hue take their health-promoting powers from impressive to amazing. The beta-carotene found in all of the yellow fruits and vegetables promotes healthy vision, clearer skin, improved immunity against common colds and illnesses, and reduced cancer risk among healthy cells. In addition, limonins, the unique phytochemicals found in lemons and limes, are powerful antioxidants that fight free radical damage and act as anti-inflammatory elements. And bromelain, the phytochemical found in pineapples, acts as a powerful anti-inflammatory antioxidant that joins forces with pineapple's high vitamin C content to combat illnesses, promote immunity, prevent free radical damage, and support healthy cell growth and functioning.

As you can see, the majority of the benefits provided by yellow fruits and vegetables includes improved immunity and protection against serious life-threatening illnesses, which makes it absolutely imperative to include them in your diet. And with their wide spectrum of tastes and textures, any and all of these foods can easily be paired with fruits and vegetables of other color schemes to create an even more nutritious, balanced taste sensation that promotes health in a number of delicious ways. Enjoy!

Pineapple Pleasure

The two ingredients in this simple smoothie are packed with powerful B vitamins that protect and promote the healthy production of blood cells, and vibrant antioxidants like bromelain, which empowers your cells to fend off harmful chemicals.

YIELDS: 2 CUPS

Ingredients

2 cups pineapple
1 cup coconut milk
1 cup ice

1. In a blender, combine the pineapple and coconut milk with ½ cup ice, and blend until thoroughly combined.

2. While blending, add remaining ice until desired consistency is achieved.

PER 1 CUP SERVING Calories: 305 | Fat: 24 g | Protein: 3 g | Sodium: 16 mg | Fiber: 16 g | Carbohydrates: 25 g

Yearning for Yellow Smoothie

If you're looking for a smoothie with flavors so amazing that it will knock your socks off, you've found it! This surprisingly bright blend of colorful, tasty pineapple, lemon, and grapefruit is balanced with the addition of vanilla coconut milk.

YIELDS: 2 CUPS

Ingredients

1 cup pineapple
½ lemon, peeled and deseeded
½ white grapefruit, peeled and deseeded
1 cup vanilla coconut milk
1 cup ice

1. In a blender, combine the pineapple, lemon, grapefruit, and coconut milk with ½ cup ice, and blend until thoroughly combined.

2. While blending, add remaining ice until desired consistency is achieved.

PER 1 CUP SERVING Calories: 288 | Fat: 24 g | Protein: 3 g | Sodium: 16 mg | Fiber: 2 g | Carbohydrates: 21 g

Tangy Tropical Treat

If you're in the mood for a tropical treat this smoothie is just perfect! Real pineapple, citrus, and coconut blend together with creamy coconut milk and crushed ice for a frothy glow. You'll feel like you've landed in paradise. The drink umbrella is optional, but go for if you want to take things up a notch!

YIELDS: 2 CUPS

Ingredients

1 cup pineapple
½ lemon, peeled and deseeded
½ cup coconut meat
1 cup coconut milk
1 cup ice

1. In a blender, combine the pineapple, lemon, coconut meat, and coconut milk with ½ cup ice, and blend until thoroughly combined.

2. While blending, add remaining ice until desired consistency is achieved.

PER 1 CUP SERVING Calories: 338 | Fat: 31 g | Protein: 4 g | Sodium: 20 mg | Fiber: 3 g | Carbohydrates: 18 g

Passionate Pineapple Perfection

Who would've thought that the sweet (but tart!) flavors of pineapple could go so well with the light taste of an apple? Powerful antioxidants from both the apple and pineapple join forces to protect the health of your cells, making this smoothie delicious *and* disease-fighting. Simple, sweet, and whipped up in just minutes, this smoothie provides a delicious treat any time of day.

YIELDS: 2 CUPS

Ingredients

2 cups pineapple
1 yellow apple, cored
1 cup organic, pure apple juice (not from concentrate)
1 cup ice

1. In a blender, combine the pineapple, apple, and apple juice with ½ cup ice, and blend until thoroughly combined.

2. While blending, add remaining ice until desired consistency is achieved.

PER 1 CUP SERVING Calories: 178 | Fat: 0 g | Protein: 1 g | Sodium: 7 mg | Fiber: 4 g | Carbohydrates: 46 g

Pleasure Island

Who needs a vacation when you can just take a trip with your taste buds! This smoothie combines the tropical flavors of pineapple and real coconut in a creamy blend for one delicious, nutritious recipe that will really take you places! In addition to the amazing taste, the valuable B vitamins in this recipe help promote metabolic functioning while the powerful antioxidants help cells better absorb and utilize important nutrients. This smoothie can lead an increased well-being of all your body's systems.

YIELDS: 2 CUPS

Ingredients
2 cups pineapple
1 cup coconut meat
1 cup coconut milk
1 cup ice

1. In a blender, combine the pineapple, coconut meat, and coconut milk with ½ cup ice, and blend until thoroughly combined.

2. While blending, add remaining ice until desired consistency is achieved.

PER 1 CUP SERVING Calories: 446 | Fat: 38 g | Protein: 5 g | Sodium: 24 mg | Fiber: 6 g | Carbohydrates: 31 g

Mango Banana Madness

If you can't remember the last time you enjoyed a mango, now is the time! Not only does this vibrant yellow fruit make for a beautiful ingredient, but also, mango is a rich source of vitamin A, which promotes the health of the skin and eyes with each and every delicious, nutritious sip!

YIELDS: 2 CUPS

Ingredients
1 cup mango, peeled
1 banana, peeled
1 cup coconut milk
1 cup ice

1. In a blender, combine the mango, banana, and coconut milk with ½ cup ice, and blend until thoroughly combined.

2. While blending, add remaining ice until desired consistency is achieved.

PER 1 CUP SERVING Calories: 328 | Fat: 25 g | Protein: 3 g | Sodium: 17 mg | Fiber: 3 g | Carbohydrates: 31 g

Lightly Lemon

If you're not a big fan of lemons, this recipe is the perfect way to ease you into this yellow fruit. This smoothie blends lemons with subtly sweet apples to balance the tart taste perfectly. With their potent content of vitamin C and unique antioxidants called *limonins*, lemons make an important immunity-protecting addition to any diet. Before you know it, you'll be enjoying a delicious smoothie packed with nutrients that will refresh your body and your mind!

YIELDS: 2 CUPS

Ingredients
2 lemons, peeled and deseeded
2 yellow apples, cored
1 cup organic apple juice (not from concentrate)
1 cup ice

1. In a blender, combine the lemons, apples, and apple juice with ½ cup ice, and blend until thoroughly combined.

2. While blending, add remaining ice until desired consistency is achieved.

PER 1 CUP SERVING Calories: 151 | Fat: 1 g | Protein: 1.4 g | Sodium: 63 mg | Fiber: 3 g | Carbohydrates: 13 g

Perfect Peach Potion

The key to perfection is simplicity, and this smoothie is definitely simple! When you combine sweet peaches with the smooth taste of banana, you create a flavorful smoothie packed with vitamin A and B vitamins that will both improve cell health and your mood.

YIELDS: 2 CUPS

Ingredients
2 cups peaches
1 banana, peeled
1 cup water
1 cup ice

1. In a blender, combine the peaches, banana, and water with ½ cup ice, and blend until thoroughly combined.

2. While blending, add remaining ice until desired consistency is achieved.

PER 1 CUP SERVING Calories: 112 | Fat: 1 g | Protein: 2 g | Sodium: 1 mg | Fiber: 4 g | Carbohydrates: 28 g

Peaches 'n' Cream

It's hard to resist the temptation of not-so-nutritious dishes, like the calorie-packed traditional peaches 'n' cream. The good news is that now you don't have to give up the dishes you love in order to live a healthy life. This smoothie blends the rich, flavorful, natural ingredients that give Peaches 'n' Cream its amazing taste, but since it's a smoothie, it helps you get healthy without weighing you down.

YIELDS: 2 CUPS

Ingredients

2 cups peaches, pits removed
1 cup plain kefir
½ cup water
1 cup ice

1. In a blender, combine the peaches, kefir, and water with ½ cup ice, and blend until thoroughly combined.

2. While blending, add remaining ice until desired consistency is achieved.

PER 1 CUP SERVING Calories: 128 | Fat: 1 g | Protein: 8 g | Sodium: 94 mg | Fiber: 2 g | Carbohydrates: 24 g

Mellow Yellow Chiller

Packed with peaches and nectarines, this smoothie loads up on powerful antioxidants like beta-carotene while tasting absolutely amazing! It pulls its weight in terms of protecting your total body health, too!

YIELDS: 2 CUPS

Ingredients

1 cup peaches, pits removed
1 cup nectarines, pits removed
1 banana, peeled
1 cup white tea, chilled
1 cup ice

1. In a blender, combine the peaches, nectarines, banana, and white tea with ½ cup ice, and blend until thoroughly combined.

2. While blending, add remaining ice until desired consistency is achieved.

PER 1 CUP SERVING Calories: 96 | Fat: 0 g | Protein: 2 g | Sodium: 2 mg | Fiber: 3 g | Carbohydrates: 24 g

Minty Mango Smoothie

If you're having trouble concentrating, this smoothie will get you back on track. Just these few simple ingredients provide the benefits of better blood quality and improved blood flow that combine to supply the brain with more efficient oxygen—resulting in better brain functioning. Delicious, beautiful, and nutritious, these ingredients pack a punch of antioxidant-rich, fragrant, and flavorful benefits that do a body (and a brain!) good!

YIELDS: 2 CUPS

Ingredients

2 cups mango, peeled
1 tablespoon chopped mint
1 cup white tea, chilled
1 cup ice

1. In a blender, combine the mango, mint, and white tea with ½ cup ice, and blend until thoroughly combined.

2. While blending, add remaining ice until desired consistency is achieved.

PER 1 CUP SERVING Calories: 110 | Fat: 0 g | Protein: 1 g | Sodium: 7 mg | Fiber: 3 g | Carbohydrates: 29 g

Creamy Dreamy Nectarine Smoothie

Juicy nectarines take center stage in this smoothie with their vibrant, yellow color and simple, sweet flavor. In this delicious blend, the probiotic- and vitamin-rich kefir and coconut milk combine to create a smooth texture and give a boost to your brain functioning.

YIELDS: 2 CUPS

Ingredients

2 cups nectarines, pits removed
1 cup plain kefir
½ cup vanilla coconut milk
1 cup ice

1. In a blender, combine the nectarines, kefir, and coconut milk with ½ cup ice, and blend until thoroughly combined.

2. While blending, add remaining ice until desired consistency is achieved.

PER 1 CUP SERVING Calories: 204 | Fat: 12 g | Protein: 9 g | Sodium: 58 g | Fiber: 3 g | Carbohydrates: 17 g

Pumped Up Pineapple

Though it is already full of protein and probiotics for improved muscle function and good bacteria promotion, this smoothie makes pineapple even more nutritious! The vitamin C, manganese, *bromelain*, probiotics, and protein that pour into your cup will protect, prepare, and help your body with whatever life has to throw at it with benefits like improved immunity to better blood quality.

YIELDS: 2 CUPS

Ingredients
2 cups pineapple
1 cup plain kefir
1 serving probiotic supplement (see packaging for exact amount)
1 scoop vanilla protein powder
1 cup water
1 cup ice

1. In a blender, combine the pineapple, kefir, probiotic, protein powder, and ½ cup water with ½ cup ice, and blend until thoroughly combined.

2. While blending, add remaining water and ice until desired consistency is achieved.

PER 1 CUP SERVING Calories: 206 | Fat: 1 g | Protein: 20 g | Sodium: 96 mg | Fiber: 2 g | Carbohydrates: 32 g

Tempting Tropical Citrus Twist

Plain old orange juice or coffee *is* nutritious, but slightly boring. Wouldn't you rather wake up and jolt your senses with a power-packed smoothie brimming with a variety of sweet and sour citrus flavors, smooth and sweet banana, and creamy coconut milk, instead? Providing protection against illness with the added benefit of cell repair, this is a delicious way to blend ingredients that will better your health and taste great!

YIELDS: 3 CUPS

Ingredients
1 cup pineapple
1 banana, peeled
½ lemon, peeled and deseeded
½ lime, peeled and deseeded
½ white grapefruit, peeled and deseeded
1 cup coconut milk
1 cup ice

1. In a blender, combine the pineapple, banana, lemon, lime, grapefruit, and ½ cup coconut milk with ½ cup ice, and blend until thoroughly combined.

2. While blending, add remaining coconut milk and ice until desired consistency is achieved.

PER 1 CUP SERVING Calories: 230 | Fat: 16 g | Protein: 3 g | Sodium: 11 mg | Fiber: 3 g | Carbohydrates: 24 g

Yummy Yellow Smoothie

The plentiful B vitamins and protein in this smoothie work hand in hand for mood enhancement and balance and load this delicious concoction with the important health benefits hidden behind sweet, succulent flavors. This creamy, sweet, fruit-packed, probiotic-pounding smoothie will please even the harshest judge!

YIELDS: 2 CUPS

Ingredients
1 cup pineapple
1 cup peaches, pitted
1 cup organic apple juice (not from concentrate)
½ cup plain kefir
1 cup ice

1. In a blender, combine the pineapple, peaches, apple juice, and kefir with ½ cup ice, and blend until thoroughly combined.

2. While blending, add remaining ice until desired consistency is achieved.

PER 1 CUP SERVING Calories: 163 | Fat: 1 g | Protein: 5 g | Sodium: 53 mg | Fiber: 3 g | Carbohydrates: 37 g

Super-Powered Squash Sweetness

While most people consider acorn squash as a beautiful side dish and not much else, this delicious winter squash can add brightness, nutrition, and flavor to any smoothie. Providing the body with important vitamin A for eye health, and omega-3s and omega-6s for better brain health, this is a smoothie of delicious nutrition! Add some amazing spices and creamy coconut milk to it, and you have a smoothie that fills you up and tastes great!

YIELDS: 3 CUPS

Ingredients
2 cups acorn squash
¼ cup ground flaxseed
1 scoop vanilla protein powder
2 cups coconut milk
1 teaspoon organic, natural maple syrup
1 cup ice

1. In a blender, combine the acorn squash, flaxseed, protein powder, coconut milk, and maple syrup with ½ cup ice, and blend until thoroughly combined.

2. While blending, add remaining ice until desired consistency is achieved.

PER 1 CUP SERVING Calories: 422 | Fat: 36 g | Protein: 14 g | Sodium: 23 mg | Fiber: 4 g | Carbohydrates: 19 g

Hold the Cob Corn Smoothie

The creaminess of corn becomes even more decadent when it's blended with a delicious banana. But this smoothie is full of more than just sweet, creamy froth. Packed with tons of vitamin A and fiber for better digestion, regularity, and protection from serious illnesses that strike the colon, this nutritious and delicious smoothie is a sweet way to enjoy the little-known health benefits of corn.

YIELDS: 2 CUPS

Ingredients
2 cups yellow corn kernels
1 banana, peeled
1 cup vanilla coconut milk
1 cup Ice

1. In a blender, combine the corn, banana, and coconut milk with ½ cup ice, and blend until thoroughly combined.

2. While blending, add remaining ice until desired consistency is achieved.

PER 1 CUP SERVING Calories: 419 | Fat: 26 g | Protein: 8 g | Sodium: 20 mg | Fiber: 5 g | Carbohydrates: 51 g

Peak of the Season Peach Delight

Whether you're sweltering in the dead of summer or chilling out during the frostiest time of winter, peak season for this smoothie is any time at all. Simply blend deliciously dewy peaches—either fresh or frozen—with scrumptious apple and creamy coconut milk, for a pleasurable peach delight that suits you no matter the time of year.

YIELDS: 2 CUPS

Ingredients
2 cups peaches, pitted
1 apple, cored
1½ cups coconut milk
1 cup ice

1. In a blender, combine the peaches, apple, and 1 cup coconut milk with ½ cup ice, and blend until thoroughly combined.

2. While blending, add remaining coconut milk and ice until desired consistency is achieved.

PER 1 CUP SERVING Calories: 432 | Fat: 36 g | Protein: 5 g | Sodium: 22 mg | Fiber: 3 g | Carbohydrates: 30 g

Coolest Peach Cobbler

Ditch the baked-good variety of this tasty treat, and opt instead for this nutrition-packed go-to that will keep you moving. With rich, complex carbohydrates, bountiful spices, and thick, protein-rich almond milk, this delicious alternative to a fat- and calorie-laden treat will stimulate your senses with sweetness while providing your body with lasting energy, better muscle functioning, and improved stamina.

YIELDS: 3 CUPS

Ingredients

2 cups peaches
¼ cup organic granola
1 teaspoon ground cloves
1 teaspoon ground ginger
1 teaspoon ground cinnamon
1½ cups vanilla almond milk
1 cup ice

1. In a blender, combine the peaches, granola, cloves, ginger, cinnamon, and 1 cup almond milk with ½ cup ice, and blend until thoroughly combined.

2. While blending, add remaining almond milk and ice until desired consistency is achieved.

PER 1 CUP SERVING Calories: 146 | Fat: 4 g | Protein: 3 g | Sodium: 50 mg | Fiber: 3 g | Carbohydrates: 31 g

Pineapple Banana Cream

You can't go wrong making a creamy delight out of sweet pineapple and bananas, creamy kefir and coconut milk, and a little bit of ice. Why? Well, this smoothie is full of powerful antioxidants like bromelain and minerals like calcium and potassium that combine for a strong defense against illness and a unified front for promoting stronger bones and respiratory health. These benefits all contribute to powerful protection against common colds and serious illnesses in a refreshing, creamy, fruity concoction that is sure to please!

YIELDS: 2 CUPS

Ingredients

1 cup pineapple
1 banana, peeled
1 cup plain kefir
½ cup coconut milk
1 cup ice

1. In a blender, combine the pineapple, banana, kefir, and coconut milk with ½ cup ice, and blend until thoroughly combined.

2. While blending, add remaining ice until desired consistency is achieved.

PER 1 CUP SERVING Calories: 273 | Fat: 13 g | Protein: 9 g | Sodium: 103 mg | Fiber: 3 g | Carbohydrates: 35 g

Limitless Lemon

With ingredients that all pack a punch in nutrition, this smoothie is a surprising way to enjoy the sweet and sour citrus taste of lemon. Beautifully balanced with sweet, subtle banana, and blended into a creamy cocktail with coconut milk, this refreshing smoothie's plentiful potassium, B vitamins, and bromelain combine for better blood and brain health that will take your mind and your body to peak performance levels, inside and out!

YIELDS: 2 CUPS

Ingredients
3 lemons, peeled and deseeded
1 banana, peeled
1 cup coconut milk
1 cup ice

1. In a blender, combine the lemons, banana, and coconut milk with ½ cup ice, and blend until thoroughly combined.

2. While blending, add remaining ice until desired consistency is achieved.

PER 1 CUP SERVING Calories: 300 | Fat: 24 g | Protein: 4 g | Sodium: 17 mg | Fiber: 4 g | Carbohydrates: 25 g

Luscious Lemon Mango Melon

What do you get when you combine yellow fruits that all have completely different tastes and nutritional backgrounds? A tasty cocktail with loads of health benefits that improve all aspects of the body and mind by supplying essential antioxidants like beta-carotenes and limonins to fend off illnesses. Enjoy!

YIELDS: 2 CUPS

Ingredients
2 lemons, peeled and deseeded
1 cup mango, peeled
1 cup honeydew, rind and seeds removed
1 cup coconut milk
1 cup ice

1. In a blender, combine the lemons, mango, honeydew, and coconut milk with ½ cup ice, and blend until thoroughly combined.

2. While blending, add remaining ice until desired consistency is achieved.

PER 1 CUP SERVING Calories: 323 | Fat: 25 g | Protein: 4 g | Sodium: 33 mg | Fiber: 4 g | Carbohydrates: 30 g

Scrumptious Spiced Squash

Move over calorie- and sugar-laden squash sides at the holiday table! This healthy—and delicious—combination of sweet squash, aromatic spices, and creamy almond milk is enough to take the place of any family favorite. This smoothie has a sweet, smooth texture and taste *and* the added benefits of vitamins A and C that combine for amazing immunity protection . . . perfect for the holiday (and flu) season!

YIELDS: 3 CUPS

Ingredients
2 cups acorn squash, softened and peeled
1 teaspoon ground cloves
1 teaspoon ground cardamom
1½ cups vanilla almond milk
1 cup ice

1. In a blender, combine the squash, cloves, cardamom, and almond milk with ½ cup ice, and blend until thoroughly combined.

2. While blending, add remaining ice until desired consistency is achieved.

PER 1 CUP SERVING Calories: 46 | Fat: 0 g | Protein: 1 g | Sodium: 11 mg | Fiber: 2 g | Carbohydrates: 12 g

Delightfully Dewy Peach

The grated ginger in this recipe takes the delightful sweet flavors of peaches to a whole new level. The slightly spicy ginger gently heats this smoothie up and the dewy peaches cool it down with a sweet and spicy flavor that's as full of illness-fighting beta-carotene, vitamin C, and manganese as it is taste.

YIELDS: 2 CUPS

Ingredients
2 cups peaches
1 tablespoon grated ginger
1 cup organic apple juice (not from concentrate)
1 cup ice

1. In a blender, combine the peaches, ginger, and apple juice with ½ cup ice, and blend until thoroughly combined.

2. While blending, add remaining ice until desired consistency is achieved.

PER 1 CUP SERVING Calories: 120 | Fat: 1 g | Protein: 2 g | Sodium: 5 mg | Fiber: 3 g | Carbohydrates: 29 g

Nutritious Nectar of Nectarines

Nectarines are delicious enough on their own, but when you add cloves and maple syrup to the mix, you make this super-healthy fruit even more amazing! Nectarines are already full of powerful cell-protecting beta-carotene, but when you add in these extra ingredients, you also add in amazing antioxidants that boost the body's defenses against damaging free radicals. Needing nothing more than water for blending purposes, this recipe is a simple, spiced-up version you're sure to enjoy!

YIELDS: 2 CUPS

Ingredients
2 cups nectarines, pits removed
1 teaspoon ground cloves
1 teaspoon organic, natural maple syrup
1 cup water
1 cup ice

1. In a blender, combine the nectarines, cloves, maple syrup, and water with ½ cup ice, and blend until thoroughly combined.

2. While blending, add remaining ice until desired consistency is achieved.

PER 1 CUP SERVING Calories: 37 | Fat: 0 g | Protein: 1 g | Sodium: 3 mg | Fiber: 1 g | Carbohydrates: 9 g

Move-It Mango

This delicious mango smoothie goes to work quickly and unleashes some powerful antioxidants, including beta-carotene and vitamins C and E, which work to protect the body and its cells from disastrous free radical damage! Spiced up just right with a light addition of cardamom, this is one smoothie that will be a sure go-to anytime you need to get in gear!

YIELDS: 2 CUPS

Ingredients
2 cups mangoes, peeled
1 scoop vanilla protein powder
1 teaspoon ground cardamom
1 cup apple juice (not from concentrate)
1 cup ice

1. In a blender, combine the mangoes, protein powder, cardamom, and apple juice with ½ cup ice, and blend until thoroughly combined.

2. While blending, add remaining ice until desired consistency is achieved.

PER 1 CUP SERVING Calories: 219 | Fat: 1 g | Protein: 13 g | Sodium: 8 mg | Fiber: 3 g | Carbohydrates: 43 g

Perfect Sweet Peach

The peaches in this recipe get a slightly sweeter twist with a creamy combination of maple syrup, vanilla bean, and cool coconut milk. But just because you're satisfying your sweet tooth doesn't mean you have to sacrifice your health! Adding to the appeal of this delightful smoothie is the astounding amount of powerful antioxidants, vitamin C, and calcium for improved immunity and a better mood!

YIELDS: 2 CUPS

Ingredients
1 cup peaches, pits removed
1 teaspoon organic, natural maple syrup
1 vanilla bean's pulp
1 cup coconut milk
1 cup ice

1. In a blender, combine the peaches, maple syrup, vanilla bean's pulp, and coconut milk with ½ cup ice, and blend until thoroughly combined.

2. While blending, add remaining ice until desired consistency is achieved.

PER 1 CUP SERVING Calories: 268 | Fat: 24 g | Protein: 3 g | Sodium: 15 mg | Fiber: 1 g | Carbohydrates: 13 g

Sweet and Sour Citrus Power

Whether you're a fan of citrus already, or just jumping on the bandwagon, this sweet and sour smoothie may be just what you're looking for! The antioxidants, bromelain and limonins, which are specific to pineapple and lemons and limes respectively, combine for powerful protection against respiratory infections. Combining the tart flavors of lemon and lime with sweet pineapple, all blended in a creamy whirl of icy goodness, this is one great breathe-easy smoothie for all!

YIELDS: 2 CUPS

Ingredients
2 lemons, peeled and deseeded
2 limes, peeled and deseeded
1 cup pineapple
1 cup coconut milk
1 cup ice

1. In a blender, combine the lemons, limes, pineapple, and coconut milk with ½ cup ice, and blend until thoroughly combined.

2. While blending, add remaining ice until desired consistency is achieved.

PER 1 CUP SERVING Calories: 300 | Fat: 25 g | Protein: 4 g | Sodium: 18 mg | Fiber: 5 g | Carbohydrates: 26 g

Golden Goodness

Pineapples pack tons of important vitamins, nutrients, and powerful bromelain, an antioxidant that promotes health from head to toe. Pack a punch in taste and nutrition with ginger and pour in some creamy almond milk, and you have golden goodness in a cup!

YIELDS: 2 CUPS

Ingredients

2 cups pineapple
1 tablespoon grated ginger
1 teaspoon organic, natural maple syrup
1 cup vanilla almond milk
1 cup ice

1. In a blender, combine the pineapple, ginger, maple syrup, and almond milk with ½ cup ice, and blend until thoroughly combined.

2. While blending, add remaining ice until desired consistency is achieved.

PER 1 CUP SERVING Calories: 143 | Fat: 1 g | Protein: 1 g | Sodium: 47 mg | Fiber: 2 g | Carbohydrates: 38 g

Pineapple Pickers' Persuasion

In this smoothie, bananas and coconut milk create a creamy texture, while powerful cardamom pumps up the flavor and bring out the brightness in every sip! But cardamom does more than just spice up this smoothie; it also packs a punch of plentiful minerals like magnesium and selenium for better metabolic functioning and improved energy supplies.

YIELDS: 2 CUPS

Ingredients

2 cups pineapple
1 banana, peeled
1 teaspoon ground cardamom
1½ cups coconut milk
1 cup ice

1. In a blender, combine the pineapple, banana, cardamom, and 1 cup coconut milk with ½ cup ice, and blend until thoroughly combined.

2. While blending, add remaining coconut milk and ice until desired consistency is achieved.

PER 1 CUP SERVING Calories: 469 | Fat: 37 g | Protein: 5 g | Sodium: 24 mg | Fiber: 4 g | Carbohydrates: 40 g

Mango-Pear

The unique flavors of mangoes and pears team up in this sensually sweet, simple smoothie. And all you have to do is look at its bright yellow coloring to know that it's full of polyphenols and antioxidants that will give you energy and act as a great pick-me-up for any point in the day!

YIELDS: 3 CUPS

Ingredients
2 cups mango
1 pear, cored
1 cup rice milk
1 cup ice

1. In a blender, combine the mango, pear, and rice milk with ½ cup ice, and blend until thoroughly combined.

2. While blending, add remaining ice until desired consistency is achieved.

PER 1 CUP SERVING Calories: 150 | Fat: 1 g | Protein: 2 g | Sodium: 47 mg | Fiber: 4 g | Carbohydrates: 40 g

Mango-Kiwi Confection

When you take the deliciousness of mango and combine it with the sweet flavor of kiwifruit, you get one amazing taste. But, add coconut milk to that combination, and you have a great-tasting, vitamin B– and C–packed smoothie that'll awaken your senses and help you bounce back from any slump.

YIELDS: 2 CUPS

Ingredients
1 cup mango
1 kiwifruit, peeled
1 cup coconut milk
1 cup ice

1. In a blender, combine the mango, kiwifruit, and coconut milk with ½ cup ice, and blend until thoroughly combined.

2. While blending, add remaining ice until desired consistency is achieved.

PER 1 CUP SERVING Calories: 299 | Fat: 24 g | Protein: 3 g | Sodium: 18 mg | Fiber: 3 g | Carbohydrates: 23 g

Mango-Apple

This smoothie contains only three ingredients, but they're all delicious! And while this smoothie is full of great taste, it's also packed full of powerful antioxidants like *beta-carotene* and *quercetin* that double up for top-notch immune-system protection. Tasting great and packed with essential nutrition, this is a great simple smoothie that makes living healthy that much easier.

YIELDS: 2 CUPS

Ingredients
1 cup mango
1 yellow apple, cored
1 cup rice milk
1 cup ice

1. In a blender, combine the mango, apple, and rice milk with ½ cup ice, and blend until thoroughly combined.

2. While blending, add remaining ice until desired consistency is achieved.

PER 1 CUP SERVING Calories: 142 | Fat: 1 g | Protein: 1 g | Sodium: 47 mg | Fiber: 3 g | Carbohydrates: 38 g

Minty Corn Concoction

When you combine the sweet, creamy, uniquely textured kernels of vibrant yellow corn with crisp spearmint, sweet maple syrup, and light rice milk, you get one heck of a smoothie that'll make you think again about the delicious capability of corn. The natural sugar content of fiber-rich corn provides a touch of sweetness along with the benefits of improved regularity and reduced chances of colon illnesses to any smoothie recipe—just like this one!

YIELDS: 2 CUPS

Ingredients
1½ cups corn kernels
1 tablespoon mint leaves
½ teaspoon organic, pure maple syrup
1 cup vanilla rice milk
1 cup ice

1. In a blender, combine the corn, mint, maple syrup, and rice milk with ½ cup ice, and blend until thoroughly combined.

2. While blending, add remaining ice until desired consistency is achieved.

PER 1 CUP SERVING Calories: 165 | Fat: 2 g | Protein: 4 g | Sodium: 52 mg | Fiber: 3 g | Carbohydrates: 41 g

Mighty Mango Citrus

The color of mango alone shows off its mighty health-promoting powers. The plentiful vitamin A (aka beta-carotene) that gives mango its beautiful shade also acts as a major protector of the body's important cell processes, including production, functioning, and regeneration. Absolutely delicious, this smoothie's appeal doesn't stop at the amazing flavor!

YIELDS: 4 CUPS

Ingredients
2 cups mango
1 orange, peeled and deseeded
½ red grapefruit, peeled and deseeded
1 cup coconut milk
1 cup ice

1. In a blender, combine the mango, orange, grapefruit, and coconut milk with ½ cup ice, and blend until thoroughly combined.

2. While blending, add remaining ice until desired consistency is achieved.

PER 1 CUP SERVING Calories: 190 | Fat: 12 g | Protein: 2 g | Sodium: 9 mg | Fiber: 3 g | Carbohydrates: 22 g

Peachy Mango

The beautiful, bright yellow color of this smoothie advertises the health benefits that you'll find here! Bursting with bright antioxidants that act as powerful crusaders in the war for better health, these vibrant yellow ingredients join forces for a sweet treat packed with intense health benefits that range from protecting the respiratory system to improving the health of your eyes!

YIELDS: 3 CUPS

Ingredients
1 cup mango
2 peaches, pitted
1 cup coconut milk
1 cup ice

1. In a blender, combine the mango, peaches, and coconut milk with ½ cup ice, and blend until thoroughly combined.

2. While blending, add remaining ice until desired consistency is achieved.

PER 1 CUP SERVING Calories: 222 | Fat: 16 g | Protein: 3 g | Sodium: 11 mg | Fiber: 2 g | Carbohydrates: 21 g

Clean Nectarine

As the sprinkling of nutmeg brings out the flavor of the beautiful fruit, this smoothie recipe serves up sweet nectarine intensity in a cool, refreshing way! Nutmeg is known for being a perfect addition to almost every culinary creation, but its plentiful minerals and powerful health benefits to the metabolism and mood make it a smart, nutritious, and delicious addition to any smoothie.

YIELDS: 2 CUPS

Ingredients
4 nectarines, pitted
1 teaspoon ground nutmeg
1 cup water
1 cup ice

1. In a blender, combine the nectarines, nutmeg, and water with ½ cup ice, and blend until thoroughly combined.

2. While blending, add remaining ice until desired consistency is achieved.

PER 1 CUP SERVING Calories: 129 | Fat: 1 g | Protein: 3 g | Sodium: 0 mg | Fiber: 5 g | Carbohydrates: 30 g

Bright Citrus Nectarine

While nectarines bring their unique taste and sweetness to this smoothie, the tart citrus taste of orange and grapefruit adds a depth of flavor and tons of vitamins, including vitamins C and E, which multitask as powerful bacteria-fighting antioxidants for improved health benefits along with the amazingly great taste. With a delightful variety of delicious ingredients packing every sip, your mouth (and your body) will thank you.

YIELDS: 3 CUPS

Ingredients
2 nectarines, pitted
1 orange, peeled and deseeded
½ white grapefruit, peeled and deseeded
1 cup water
1 cup ice

1. In a blender, combine the nectarines, orange, grapefruit, and water with ½ cup ice, and blend until thoroughly combined.

2. While blending, add remaining ice until desired consistency is achieved.

PER 1 CUP SERVING Calories: 75 | Fat: 0 g | Protein: 2 g | Sodium: 0 mg | Fiber: 3 g | Carbohydrates: 18 g

Nutty Nectarine

This smoothie combines the unexpected taste of sweet nectarines, flavorful nuts, and creamy kefir in a smoothie that will shock your senses. Beautiful and packed with tons of essential protein for improved muscle function and stamina, this smoothie is a surprisingly delicious spin on the everyday favorites you love.

YIELDS: 2 CUPS

Ingredients
2 nectarines, pitted
¼ cup walnuts
⅛ cup ground flaxseed
1 cup plain kefir
½ cup water
1 cup ice

1. In a blender, combine the nectarines, walnuts, flaxseed, kefir, and water with ½ cup ice, and blend until thoroughly combined.

2. While blending, add remaining ice until desired consistency is achieved.

PER 1 CUP SERVING Calories: 260 | Fat: 13 g | Protein: 12 g | Sodium: 95 mg | Fiber: 6 g | Carbohydrates: 28 g

Herbal Peach-Tea Twist

Why just enjoy a peach or simply sip your favorite tea when you can combine the two in a delicious smoothie? Building upon their own unique health benefits, including the white tea's plentiful antioxidants and the vitamin A and C content of the peaches, these two amazing ingredients come together beautifully with spearmint for a delicious combination of flavor and health benefits you're sure to enjoy that much more!

YIELDS: 2 CUPS

Ingredients
3 peaches, pitted
1 cup white tea
1 teaspoon spearmint leaves
1 cup ice

1. In a blender, combine the peaches, tea, and mint leaves with ½ cup ice, and blend until thoroughly combined.

2. While blending, add remaining ice until desired consistency is achieved.

PER 1 CUP SERVING Calories: 87 | Fat: 1 g | Protein: 2 g | Sodium: 1 mg | Fiber: 3 g | Carbohydrates: 21 g

Just Peachy!

Heightened with the vibrant flavor of cinnamon, the essence of this delicious drink is as smooth as a peach. Brightly colored and brimming with powerful vitamin C and beta-carotene, which help protect your cells from illness and your eyes from degeneration, this is a great recipe any peach lover is sure to enjoy!

YIELDS: 2 CUPS

Ingredients
3 peaches, pitted
1 teaspoon ground cinnamon
1 cup water
1 cup ice

1. In a blender, combine the peaches, cinnamon, and water with ½ cup ice, and blend until thoroughly combined.

2. While blending, add remaining ice until desired consistency is achieved.

PER 1 CUP SERVING Calories: 89 | Fat: 1 g | Protein: 2 g | Sodium: 0 mg | Fiber: 4 g | Carbohydrates: 22 g

Peachy Banana Citrus

In this recipe, peaches blend beautifully with the creamy sweetness of a banana and coconut milk—and they get an unexpected kick from the delightful addition of orange. Packed with tons of quality nutrients like vitamin C and potassium—which can help protect your body against illness by improving immunity, preventing free radical damage, and reversing damage already done—this smoothie packs a punch in bettering your life . . . one delicious sip at a time!

YIELDS: 4 CUPS

Ingredients
2 peaches, pitted
1 banana, peeled
1 orange, peeled and deseeded
1 cup coconut milk
1 cup ice

1. In a blender, combine the peaches, banana, orange, and coconut milk with ½ cup ice, and blend until thoroughly combined.

2. While blending, add remaining ice until desired consistency is achieved.

PER 1 CUP SERVING Calories: 181 | Fat: 12 g | Protein: 2 g | Sodium: 8 mg | Fiber: 3 g | Carbohydrates: 19 g

Pineapple-Melon

The sweet, unique flavors of pineapple and canta-loupe come together in one smoothie that has the perfect combination of B vitamins and vitamin C for an immune system and metabolic boost that is both refreshing and sure to give you the energy you need. These delicious ingredients pack antioxidants into every single slurp of this deliciously nutritious smoothie.

YIELDS: 2 CUPS

Ingredients
1½ cups pineapple
½ cup cantaloupe
1 cup water
1 cup ice

1. In a blender, combine the pineapple, can-taloupe, and ½ cup water with ½ cup ice, and blend until thoroughly combined.

2. While blending, add remaining water and ice until desired consistency is achieved.

PER 1 CUP SERVING Calories: 75 | Fat: 0 g | Protein: 1 g | Sodium: 7 mg | Fiber: 2 g | Carbohydrates: 19 g

Very Vital Pineapple-Apple

Replacing lost vitamins is no chore with this deli-cious sweet treat! Here, each fresh, fruity ingredient is packed with its own variety of vitamins that help to replenish your stores. The pineapple's brome-lain, apple's quercetin, and coconut milk's potas-sium combine for essential restoration of adequate hydration for all of the body's cells.

YIELDS: 3 CUPS

Ingredients
2 cups pineapple
1 yellow apple, cored
1 cup coconut milk
1 cup ice

1. In a blender, combine the pineapple, apple, and coconut milk with ½ cup ice, and blend until thoroughly combined.

2. While blending, add remaining ice until desired consistency is achieved.

PER 1 CUP SERVING Calories: 175 | Fat: 9 g | Protein: 2 g | Sodium: 6 mg | Fiber: 5 g | Carbohydrates: 25 g

Chapter 7

Green

Asparagus · Avocados · Broccoli · Celery · Cucumbers · Honeydew Melon · Kiwifruit · Leeks · Peas · Romaine Lettuce · Scallions · Spinach · Spirulina · Wheatgrass · Zucchini

Maybe you want to try green smoothies, but hesitate because they're, well ... green! But don't let their coloring deter you from giving this part of the rainbow a try. Even though you may not think of greens as sweet and delicious, they certainly can be! The green smoothies in this chapter are made up of a delicious blend of green super-foods and compatible ingredients that either complement or soften the taste of the greens. For example, the apples and spices combined with the greens in the Apple Pie smoothie make for a sweet, splendid treat that just so happens to include an entire cup of spinach, which qualifies as a day's serving! Even the green smoothies that are designed to heighten the taste sensation of the greens are simply delicious. But great taste isn't all a green smoothie has to give; the recipes in this chapter are also filled with a variety of vitamins, minerals, and other nutrients designed to make you healthier than ever.

Especially rich in vitamin B9 (otherwise known as *folate* or *folic acid*), leafy deep greens help aid in the production of red blood cells, promote optimal brain function and neuron activity, and actually contribute to the composition of the fluid in and around your spinal cord. And, if you're a woman of childbearing age, B9 is especially important; there's a strong correlation between B9 and the proper formation and functioning of all of these systems and their parts in a developing fetus. In addition to B9, green produce contains a list of minerals, including calcium (with celery and broccoli containing more than other vegetables); copper (especially high in spirulina); iron (spinach, spinach, and more spinach!); magnesium; manganese; phosphorous; selenium; sodium; and zinc. Each of these minerals contributes to vision health, helps control the body's cholesterol by reducing the "bad" (LDL) and improving the "good" (HDL), aids the digestive system by regulating bacteria growth, fends off free radicals, and promotes a healthy immune system.

And while the vitamin and mineral content of greens is quite extraordinary, the components that attract even more attention for their astounding health benefits are the phytochemicals responsible for the vibrant coloring of green fruits and vegetables. *Chlorophyll*, which contains the actual genetic material and chemical makeup of a plant, is arguably the most potent element in greens. Rich in carbon, hydrogen, nitrogen, and oxygen, chlorophyll has the same elements that make up human blood. Because of this similarity in genetic makeup and the specific combination of these four elements in particular, chlorophyll powerfully affects almost all of the major components of your body, including your body's systems and functioning, from the circulatory and immune systems to the digestive and endocrine systems. It also improves your body's ability to use oxygen, and it raises the quality of your blood through its own oxygen concentration, which promotes your body's production of healthy red blood cells. Protecting the body from free radical damage at the molecular level, chlorophyll is also a well-known cancer-fighting agent.

What are you waiting for? Get ready to blend up a green smoothie that's out of this world!

Go Green with Bananas

As a very light-flavored green smoothie, the full 2 cups of spinach and 3 servings of fruit in this recipe offer an excellent amount of nutrition from vitamin K to vitamin C for better blood health and improved mood and balance. And if you want to change the taste up a little and boost the nutritional value, the water in this recipe can be swapped out for any of the alternative milks.

YIELDS: 4 CUPS

Ingredients
2 cups spinach leaves
2 ripe bananas, peeled
1 apple, peeled and cored
1 cup water

1. Combine spinach, bananas, apple, and ½ cup water in a blender, and blend thoroughly.

2. While blending, add remaining water until desired consistency is achieved.

PER 1 CUP SERVING Calories: 75 | Fat: 0 g | Protein: 1 g | Sodium: 14 mg | Fiber: 2 g | Carbohydrates: 19 g

Go Nutty for Greens!

In addition to the potassium brought in by the banana in this smoothie, the almond milk and Greek-style yogurt provide protein for muscle functioning, which makes this smoothie a powerful start to any day.

YIELDS: 4 CUPS

Ingredients
½ cup Greek-style yogurt
1 cup iceberg lettuce
1 banana, peeled
1 cup vanilla almond milk

1. Combine yogurt, lettuce, and banana in a blender with ½ cup almond milk, and blend thoroughly.

2. Continue adding remaining almond milk while blending until desired consistency is reached.

PER 1 CUP SERVING Calories: 68 | Fat: 1 g | Protein: 4 g | Sodium: 51 mg | Fiber: 1 g | Carbohydrates: 12 g

The Green Go-Getter

Some people who are new to creating green smoothies can have a hard time enjoying the powerful taste of the greens. In this recipe, the combination of banana, apples, and spinach with more fruit than greens provides an appetizing taste that is more sweet and lessens the intensity of the spinach. This smoothie, which is packed with total body-benefitting essential amino acids, vitamin K, and iron, is a great green starter.

YIELDS: 3–4 CUPS

Ingredients
1 cup spinach
2 green apples, peeled and cored
1 banana, peeled
1 cup water

1. Combine spinach, apples, and banana with ½ cup water in a blender, and blend until thoroughly combined.

2. Continue adding remaining water while blending until desired texture is achieved.

PER 1 CUP SERVING Calories: 89 | Fat: 0 g | Protein: 1 g | Sodium: 10 mg | Fiber: 3 g | Carbohydrates: 23 g

An Apple Pie Day

The cloves in this smoothie add a flavor reminiscent of apple pie and add to the immunity-strengthening health benefits already present in the spinach, apples, and coconut milk. Although most consider cloves an essential when it comes time to make pies for the holidays, Ayurvedic healers utilize this spice for its healing powers—it's believed to alleviate symptoms of irregular digestion and malfunctioning metabolism. Although it is used in only small amounts, its antibacterial and antiviral properties in any amount can only help you stay healthy!

YIELD: 4 CUPS

Ingredients
2 cups spinach
1 teaspoon cloves
1 teaspoon cinnamon
3 apples, peeled and cored
1½ cups coconut milk

1. Place the spinach in the blender.

2. Add the spices, followed by the apples.

3. Add coconut milk slowly while blending until desired texture is achieved.

PER 1 CUP SERVING Calories: 232 | Fat: 18 g | Protein: 3 g | Sodium: 24 mg | Fiber: 2 g | Carbohydrates: 19 g

Calming Cucumber

Even though a cucumber is mostly water (and fiber), it is far more than a tasty, hydrating, and filling snack option. These green veggies are a great addition to a diet in need of moisture and clarity . . . for the skin! By consuming one serving of cucumbers per day, you'll not only fulfill a full serving of veggies and stave off hunger, you'll also ensure that your complexion remains—or becomes—clear and hydrated!

YIELDS: 3–4 CUPS

Ingredients
1 cup romaine lettuce
2 cucumbers, peeled
¼ cup mint, chopped
1 cup water

1. Combine romaine lettuce, cucumbers, mint, and ½ cup water in a blender, and blend thoroughly.

2. Add remaining water while blending until desired texture is achieved.

PER 1 CUP SERVING Calories: 24 | Fat: 0 g | Protein: 1 g | Sodium: 9 mg | Fiber: 2 g | Carbohydrates: 4 g

Super Celery

This combination of greens and rich vegetables offers a healthy dose of fiber; vitamins A, C, and K; B vitamins; and a wealth of minerals, including iron and potassium, which combine to effectively fight water retention. But, even though this smoothie is healthy, the best part is that it's absolutely delicious!

YIELDS: 3–4 CUPS

Ingredients
1 cup spinach
3 celery stalks
1 cucumber, peeled
1 carrot, peeled
1 cup water

1. Combine spinach, celery, cucumber, carrot, and ½ cup water in a blender, and blend until thoroughly combined.

2. Continue adding remaining water as you blend until desired texture is achieved.

PER 1 CUP SERVING Calories: 34 | Fat: 0 g | Protein: 1 g | Sodium: 72 mg | Fiber: 3 g | Carbohydrates: 7 g

Very Veggie

The parsley in this recipe is rich in vitamins and minerals. In just one serving of this cleansing green, there are impressive amounts of vitamins C and A as well as iron and folate. But the main benefit here comes from the huge amounts of vitamin K. In fact, by including just 2 tablespoons of parsley in your daily diet, you'll consume more than 153 percent of your needed vitamin K daily, which adds to the quality of your blood and the strength of your bones!

YIELDS: 3–4 CUPS

Ingredients

1 cup spinach
2 celery stalks
2 carrots, peeled
1 tomato
1 green onion
1 small sprig parsley
1 cup water

1. Combine the spinach, celery, carrots, tomato, green onion, parsley, and ½ cup water in a blender, and blend until combined thoroughly.

2. Continue adding remaining water while blending until desired texture is achieved.

PER 1 CUP SERVING Calories: 32 | Fat: 0 g | Protein: 1 g | Sodium: 62 mg | Fiber: 2 g | Carbohydrates: 7 g

Go, Go, Garlic!

The amazing cancer-fighting benefits and strong antiviral and antibacterial properties in the antioxidants found in garlic are maximized when the garlic clove has been crushed and allowed to set at room temperature. Heating garlic cloves inhibits the full ability of important enzymes to do their work. Maximize garlic's full potential by preparing it at room temperature in your green smoothies.

YIELDS: 3–4 CUPS

Ingredients

1 cup romaine lettuce
2 tomatoes
½ cup basil leaves
3 garlic cloves, crushed and allowed to sit for 1 hour
½ cup water (if necessary)

1. Combine romaine lettuce, tomatoes, basil, and garlic in a blender and combine thoroughly until all garlic is emulsified.

2. Add water while blending, if needed, until desired consistency is reached.

PER 1 CUP SERVING Calories: 23 | Fat: 0 g | Protein: 1 g | Sodium: 6 mg | Fiber: 1 g | Carbohydrates: 5 g

Awesome Asparagus

Rich in vitamins K, A, C, Bs, folate, and a variety of minerals, including iron and zinc, this veggie's benefits surpass many others. Considering all of these nutrients, it should come as no surprise that introducing 1 cup of asparagus to your daily diet promotes heart health, digestive health and regularity—and satisfies a daily serving requirement of vegetables.

YIELDS: 3–4 CUPS

Ingredients
1 cup romaine lettuce
1 cup asparagus
1 green onion
1 celery stalk
1 garlic clove
2 cups water
Juice of ½ lemon

1. Combine romaine lettuce, asparagus, onion, celery, garlic, and 1 cup water in a blender, and blend until thoroughly combined.

2. Add remaining water and lemon juice while blending until desired texture and taste are achieved.

PER 1 CUP SERVING Calories: 12 | Fat: 0 g | Protein: 1 g | Sodium: 3 mg | Fiber: 1 g | Carbohydrates: 3 g

Blazing Broccoli

If you're like most people, you probably grew up hearing, "You need to finish your broccoli." The truth is that broccoli is one of the most powerfully packed super-foods you can find! Combining vitamin K, iron, and fiber, this veggie can improve regularity while reducing the chances for colon cancers and ulcers. And it's delicious, too!

YIELDS: 3–4 CUPS

Ingredients
1 cup spinach
1 cup broccoli
1 carrot, peeled
1 green pepper, cored
½ lime, peeled
2 cups water

1. Combine spinach, broccoli, carrot, pepper, lime, and 1 cup water in a blender, and blend until thoroughly combined.

2. Add remaining water while blending until desired texture is achieved.

PER 1 CUP SERVING Calories: 24 | Fat: 0 g | Protein: 1 g | Sodium: 27 mg | Fiber: 2 g | Carbohydrates: 6 g

Spicy Garlic Spinach

The garlic in this smoothie may be one of the healthiest vegetables you can add. Studies credit it with fighting bladder, skin, colon, and stomach cancers. Consuming one to three cloves per day is recommended for optimum results and, while eating—or drinking!—that much garlic may seem difficult, placing garlic in your smoothies is an easy way to meet that requirement.

YIELDS: 3–4 CUPS

Ingredients
1 cup spinach
1 tomato
1 celery stalk
1–2 tablespoons cilantro
1 garlic clove
2 cups water

1. Combine spinach, tomato, celery, cilantro, garlic, and 1 cup water in a blender, and blend until thoroughly combined.

2. Add remaining water while blending until desired texture is achieved.

PER 1 CUP SERVING Calories: 13 | Fat: 0 g | Protein: 1 g | Sodium: 24 mg | Fiber: 1 g | Carbohydrates: 3 g

Zippy Zucchini

Zucchini is well-known for being a blank canvas in terms of flavor, but it doesn't stand in the background when it comes to health benefits. This vegetable is full of essential nutrients like vitamins C and K, iron, and potassium, which work together to improve your blood health and protect your heart from cardiovascular disease. Adding this healthy and savory ingredient in with the spicy arugula used in this recipe delivers a smoothie with a bite.

YIELDS: 3–4 CUPS

Ingredients
1 cup arugula
2 zucchini
1 celery stalk
1 tomato
1 garlic clove
2 cups water

1. Combine arugula, zucchini, celery, tomato, garlic, and 1 cup water in a blender, and blend until thoroughly combined.

2. Add remaining water while blending until desired texture is achieved.

PER 1 CUP SERVING Calories: 25 | Fat: 0 g | Protein: 2 g | Sodium: 23 mg | Fiber: 2 g | Carbohydrates: 5 g

Great Garlic

Not only may it keep vampires away, but the strong addition of garlic to this smoothie can also do so much for your health. Just one small clove of garlic helps promote a strong heart and makes almost anything taste absolutely delightful.

YIELDS: 3–4 CUPS

Ingredients
1 cup spinach
1 celery stalk
1 tomato
3 garlic cloves
2 cups water

1. Combine spinach, celery, tomato, garlic, and 1 cup water in a blender, and blend until thoroughly combined.

2. Add remaining water, if needed, while blending until desired texture is achieved.

PER 1 CUP SERVING Calories: 12 | Fat: 0 g | Protein: 1 g | Sodium: 18 mg | Fiber: 1 g | Carbohydrates: 3 g

Ahhh, Sweet Greens!

Apples and spinach in the same smoothie may seem like an unlikely pair, but one sip of this blend will have even the harshest skeptic agreeing that the duo makes a delicious treat. These veggies are full of fiber, and because fiber is almost completely unable to be digested by the human body, it makes your stomach feel full, and clears your intestinal tract by remaining nearly intact throughout digestion. Although fiber is available in pill and powder forms, those options are a far cry from a healthy bowl of spinach, broccoli, or fresh fruit.

YIELDS: 3–4 CUPS

Ingredients
1 cup spinach
2 bananas, peeled
2 apples, cored and peeled
2 cups almond milk

1. Combine spinach, bananas, apples, and 1 cup almond milk in a blender, and blend until thoroughly combined.

2. Add remaining almond milk while blending until desired texture is achieved.

PER 1 CUP SERVING Calories: 147 | Fat: 2 g | Protein: 2 g | Sodium: 82 mg | Fiber: 4 g | Carbohydrates: 34 g

Broccoli Carrot

Broccoli is not only a vitamin- and mineral-packed green veggie, it also contains more protein than most other veggie options. Due to its high amounts of this essential macronutrient, this smoothie will help you maintain muscle functioning and mental clarity, which could suffer if you're eating inadequate amounts of protein.

YIELDS: 3–4 CUPS

Ingredients
1 cup romaine lettuce
1 cup broccoli
2 carrots
2 cups water

1. Combine romaine lettuce, broccoli, carrots, and 1 cup water in a blender, and blend until thoroughly combined.

2. Add remaining water while blending until desired texture is achieved.

PER 1 CUP SERVING Calories: 22 | Fat: 0 g | Protein: 1 g | Sodium: 32 mg | Fiber: 2 g | Carbohydrates: 5 g

Veggie Delight

If you're in the mood for a refreshingly savory smoothie, this one might be just what you're looking for! These ingredients create a splendid smoothie that may be delicious and filling enough to take the place of dinner. With a wide variety of veggies that combine for great taste while contributing a range of phytochemicals from lycopene to allicin, this smoothie's impressive amount of powerful antioxidants helps your body fend off illness and disease.

YIELDS: 4–6 CUPS

Ingredients
1 cup romaine lettuce
2 tomatoes
1 zucchini
2 celery stalks
1 cucumber
½ cup green onions
2 garlic cloves
2 cups water

1. Combine romaine lettuce, tomatoes, zucchini, celery, cucumber, green onions, garlic, and 1 cup water in a blender, and blend until thoroughly combined.

2. Add remaining water, if needed, while blending until desired texture is achieved.

PER 1 CUP SERVING Calories: 28 | Fat: 0 g | Protein: 1 g | Sodium: 6 mg | Fiber: 1 g | Carbohydrates: 6g

Cucumber Zing!

Cucumbers offer up a wide variety of important vitamins and minerals, including vitamin C and silica, while lending a refreshing and hydrating background to the spicy ginger in this smoothie. This blend will whet your appetite while cleansing your body and building your immunity!

YIELDS: 3–4 CUPS

Ingredients

1 cup watercress
2 cucumbers, peeled
2 oranges, peeled and deseeded
1 tablespoon grated ginger
1 cup water

1. Combine watercress, cucumbers, oranges, ginger, and ⅛ cup water in a blender, and blend until thoroughly combined.

2. Add remaining water while blending, as needed, until desired texture is achieved.

PER 1 CUP SERVING Calories: 57 | Fat: 0 g | Protein: 2 g | Sodium: 7 mg | Fiber: 3 g | Carbohydrates: 13 g

The Spicy Savior

The ginger in this recipe is what gives this smoothie the spicy zing! But ginger also provides a rich amount of helpful anti-aging, antibacterial, and antiviral properties that multitask as powerful antioxidants that will bring you better health in one easy-to-drink smoothie full of delicious flavor!

YIELDS: 3–4 CUPS

Ingredients

1 cup watercress
1 cup broccoli
3 carrots, peeled
1 tablespoon grated ginger
2 cups water

1. Combine watercress, broccoli, carrots, ginger, and 1 cup water in a blender, and blend until thoroughly combined.

2. Add remaining water while blending, as needed, until desired texture is achieved.

PER 1 CUP SERVING Calories: 28 | Fat: 0 g | Protein: 1 g | Sodium: 45 mg | Fiber: 2 g | Carbohydrates: 6 g

Green Garlic

This savory delight is sure to excite every one of your senses with the potent smell, flavor, and antioxidants in each and every bit of the amazing garlic in this smoothie. Not only does the flavor blend nicely with the other ingredients, but the unique addition of the antioxidant allicin also provides liver-cleansing health benefits.

YIELDS: 3–4 CUPS

Ingredients
1 cup spinach
1 zucchini, unpeeled
¼ cup parsley
2–3 cloves of garlic, depending upon size
2 cups water

1. Combine the spinach, zucchini, parsley, garlic, and 1 cup water in a blender, and blend until thoroughly combined.

2. Add remaining water while blending, as needed, until desired texture is achieved.

PER 1 CUP SERVING Calories: 13 | Fat: 0 g | Protein: 1 g | Sodium: 16 mg | Fiber: 1 g | Carbohydrates: 3 g

Fabulous Fiber Flush

Kale provides an abundance of vitamins A and K, which help with your blood, liver, and brain functioning. Combined with the iron- and folate-rich broccoli, pectin-providing apples, and beta-carotene–filled carrot, the kale makes this smoothie a fiber-filled masterpiece that will improve regularity and keep you feeling more satisfied longer.

YIELDS: 3–4 CUPS

Ingredients
2 large kale leaves
1 cup broccoli
2 apples, peeled and cored
1 carrot, peeled
½ lemon, peeled
2 cups water

1. Combine kale, broccoli, apples, carrot, lemon, and 1 cup water in a blender, and blend until thoroughly combined.

2. Add remaining water while blending, as needed, until desired texture is achieved.

PER 1 CUP SERVING Calories: 71 | Fat: 0 g | Protein: 2 g | Sodium: 35 mg | Fiber: 3 g | Carbohydrates: 17 g

Apple-Celery Smoothie

The fruits and greens in this smoothie provide natural sugars, sodium, and complex carbohydrates that help your body maintain a regular blood sugar level. But this smoothie doesn't stop there—the added benefits of the antioxidants in the apples help your body to fend off illness, and the celery helps to regulate the water levels in your body. And it's delicious, too! What better way to drink the rainbow!

YIELDS: 3–4 CUPS

Ingredients

1 cup romaine lettuce
3 Granny Smith apples, peeled and cored
2 celery stalks
¼" gingerroot, peeled
2 cups water

1. Combine romaine lettuce, apples, celery, ginger, and 1 cup water in a blender, and blend until thoroughly combined.

2. Add remaining water as needed while blending until desired consistency is achieved.

PER 1 CUP SERVING Calories: 64 | Fat: 0 g | Protein: 1 g | Sodium: 19 mg | Fiber: 2 g | Carbohydrates: 17 g

"Pea" Is for Prevention

Sweetening this smoothie with green peas makes a delightful treat. And adding just 1 cup of this sweet veggie to your daily diet provides more than 50 percent of your daily recommended intake of vitamin K, along with vitamins B and C, manganese, folate, fiber, and protein. This results in stronger bones; heightened disease prevention; efficient metabolism of carbohydrates, fats, and proteins; improved cardiac health; and more energy.

YIELDS: 3–4 CUPS

Ingredients

1 cup watercress
2 cucumbers, peeled
1 cup petite sweet green peas
2 cups water

1. Combine watercress, cucumbers, peas, and 1 cup water in a blender, and blend until thoroughly combined.

2. Add remaining water as needed while blending until desired consistency is achieved.

PER 1 CUP SERVING Calories: 39 | Fat: 0 g | Protein: 3 g | Sodium: 44 mg | Fiber: 2 g | Carbohydrates: 7 g

Romaine to the Rescue!

Crisp romaine lettuce, broccoli, carrots, garlic, and ginger combine into one satisfying, savory smoothie that will promote health for your eyes, digestion, muscle repair, and mental clarity. The fiber, vitamins C and K, and abundance of iron all join to bring these amazing health benefits to this terrific smoothie!

YIELDS: 3–4 CUPS

Ingredients

2 cups romaine lettuce
½ cup broccoli
2 carrots
1 garlic clove
½" gingerroot, peeled
2 cups water

1. Combine romaine lettuce, broccoli, carrots, garlic, ginger, and 1 cup water in a blender, and blend until thoroughly combined.

2. Add remaining water as needed while blending until desired consistency is achieved.

PER 1 CUP SERVING Calories: 22 | Fat: 0 g | Protein: 1 g | Sodium: 29 mg | Fiber: 2 g | Carbohydrates: 5 g

Rapid Recovery

Tasty and powerful, this recipe's intense vitamin- and mineral-rich veggies act as a powerful protein source that helps with everything from muscle function and repair to mental clarity and focus. The addition of the lemon and garlic benefit your body by promoting a healthy metabolic level for even more efficient fat burning.

YIELDS: 3–4 CUPS

Ingredients

1 cup watercress
1 cup broccoli
1 celery stalk
½ lemon, peeled
1 garlic clove
2 cups Greek-style yogurt

1. Combine watercress, broccoli, celery, lemon, garlic, and 1 cup yogurt in a blender, and blend until thoroughly combined.

2. Add remaining yogurt as needed while blending until desired consistency is achieved.

PER 1 CUP SERVING Calories: 78 | Fat: 0 g | Protein: 13 g | Sodium: 67 mg | Fiber: 1 g | Carbohydrates: 7 g

Broccoli Blast-Off

Broccoli and kale add a great dose of protein in this smoothie, but if you're looking for even more, there is the delightful option of protein powders available in a variety of flavors, including plain, vanilla, almond, and chocolate, which would blend nicely with savory smoothies such as this.

YIELDS: 3–4 CUPS

Ingredients

2 kale leaves
1 cup broccoli
½ red bell pepper, seeded
2 celery stalks
1 green onion
1–2 garlic cloves, depending on size
2 cups water

1. Combine kale, broccoli, pepper, celery, onion, garlic, and 1 cup water in a blender, and blend until thoroughly combined.

2. Add remaining water as needed while blending until desired consistency is achieved.

PER 1 CUP SERVING Calories: 23 | Fat: 0 g | Protein: 1 g | Sodium: 18 mg | Fiber: 1 g | Carbohydrates: 1 g

Zoom with Zucchini

If you're looking for a smoothie that will help boost your metabolism, you've come to the right place. The vibrant veggies and cayenne pepper in this recipe make for a fat-burning, calorie-zapping smoothie that will fill you up and fire up your metabolic engines! Burn, baby, burn!

YIELDS: 3–4 CUPS

Ingredients

1 cup spinach
1 zucchini
1 tomato
2 celery stalks
1 green onion
2 garlic cloves
⅛ teaspoon cayenne pepper
2 cups water

1. Combine spinach, zucchini, tomato, celery, onion, garlic, cayenne, and 1 cup water in a blender, and blend until thoroughly combined.

2. Add remaining water as needed while blending until desired consistency is achieved.

PER 1 CUP SERVING Calories: 22 | Fat: 0 g | Protein: 1 g | Sodium: 32 mg | Fiber: 2 g | Carbohydrates: 5 g

Popeye's Favorite

When you were a kid, Popeye was one amazing example of what could happen if you ate your spinach! How many times did your parents reference Popeye when trying to get you to finish your greens? Spinach is packed with vitamins A, C, E, K, and B vitamins, as well as iron, phosphorous, and fiber. With all of that nutrition delivered in each serving, spinach should be in every athlete's daily diet . . . for strength like Popeye's!

YIELDS: 3–4 CUPS

Ingredients
1 cup spinach
1 kale leaf
1 cup broccoli
3 apples, peeled and cored
2 cups water

1. Combine spinach, kale, broccoli, apples, and 1 cup water in a blender, and blend until thoroughly combined.

2. Add remaining water as needed while blending until desired consistency is achieved.

PER 1 CUP SERVING Calories: 76 | Fat: 0 g | Protein: 2 g | Sodium: 23 mg | Fiber: 3 g | Carbohydrates: 19 g

Baby, Be Happy

This simple recipe makes for a deliciously sweet veggie smoothie that you're sure to come back to again and again. In this recipe, the iron-rich spinach and peas combine with carrots that are full of vitamins C and A for a splendid creation that will satisfy your iron needs for better blood quality.

YIELDS: 3–4 CUPS

Ingredients
1 cup spinach
1 cup sweet peas
3 carrots, peeled
2 cups red raspberry tea

1. Combine spinach, peas, carrots, and 1 cup tea in a blender, and blend until thoroughly combined.

2. Add remaining tea as needed while blending until desired consistency is achieved.

PER 1 CUP SERVING Calories: 46 | Fat: 0 g | Protein: 2 g | Sodium: 76 mg | Fiber: 3 g | Carbohydrates: 9 g

Veggies for Vitamins

This delicious savory blend of spicy arugula, tomato, cucumber, celery, onion, and garlic combine with natural tea to give your body an amazing amount of vitamins and minerals for improved immunity, brain functioning, and blood health.

YIELDS: 3–4 CUPS

Ingredients

1 cup arugula
1 tomato
1 cucumber, peeled
1 celery stalk
1 green onion
1 garlic clove
2 cups red raspberry tea

1. Combine arugula, tomato, cucumber, celery, onion, garlic, and 1 cup tea in a blender, and blend until thoroughly combined.

2. Add remaining tea as needed while blending until desired consistency is achieved.

PER 1 CUP SERVING Calories: 17 | Fat: 0 g | Protein: 1 g | Sodium: 15 mg | Fiber: 1 g | Carbohydrates: 3 g

Perfect Pea Smoothie

Although probably not the veggie that comes to mind when you think "super-food," peas are an excellent source of iron and folate—both important vitamins and minerals for promoting the best health in women and infants! Men can improve the quality of their blood and reduce the incidence of heart-related illnesses by increasing their healthy intake of iron, too, so drink up!

YIELDS: 3–4 CUPS

Ingredients

1 cup arugula
1 cup sweet peas
2 celery stalks
1 cucumber, peeled
1 cup red raspberry tea

1. Combine arugula, sweet peas, celery, cucumber, and ½ cup tea in a blender, and blend until thoroughly combined.

2. Add remaining tea as needed while blending until desired consistency is achieved.

PER 1 CUP SERVING Calories: 36 | Fat: 0 g | Protein: 2 g | Sodium: 56 mg | Fiber: 2 g | Carbohydrates: 8 g

Delicious Bananas and Berries

While satisfying your sweet tooth with this delicious blend of bananas, blueberries, and strawberries, consider boosting your daily protein intake by adding a scoop of whey protein or soy protein powder to the mix. Soy protein has absolutely no milk derivatives in its makeup and is acceptable for a strict dairy-free diet. Whey is made from milk byproducts, making it suitable for those who include dairy in their diet.

YIELDS: 3–4 CUPS

Ingredients
1 cup romaine lettuce
2 bananas, peeled
2 cups strawberries
1 pint blueberries
2 cups almond milk

1. Combine romaine lettuce, bananas, berries, and 1 cup almond milk in a blender, and blend until thoroughly combined.

2. Add remaining almond milk while blending until desired texture is achieved.

PER 1 CUP SERVING Calories: 316 | Fat: 19 g | Protein: 4 g | Sodium: 18 mg | Fiber: 12 g | Carbohydrates: 39 g

Green Ginger Apple

Ginger is hailed as one of nature's most potent medicinal plants, particularly in terms of curing stomach ailments. Combining ginger with the fiber found in fruits and leafy greens is an effective way to clean out the digestive tract, promote the release of good digestive enzymes, and soothe the stomach.

YIELDS: 3–4 CUPS

Ingredients
1 cup romaine lettuce
3 apples, cored and peeled
1 tablespoon ginger, grated
2 cups almond milk

1. Combine romaine lettuce, apples, ginger, and 1 cup almond milk in a blender, and blend until thoroughly combined.

2. Add remaining almond milk while blending until desired texture is achieved.

PER 1 CUP SERVING Calories: 119 | Fat: 2 g | Protein: 1 g | Sodium: 78 mg | Fiber: 4 g | Carbohydrates: 28 g

Green Pears with a Tart Twist

Providing an amazing amount of essential vitamins and minerals, including vitamin C and the plentiful B vitamins needed for the optimal functioning of your mind and body, this smoothie is a sweet, tart, and smart way to pep up your day—and drink green!

YIELDS: 4–6 CUPS

Ingredients
4 cups romaine lettuce
4 pears, cored
1 banana, peeled
6 tablespoons lemon juice
2 cups water

1. Combine romaine lettuce, pears, banana, lemon juice, and 1 cup water in a blender, and blend until thoroughly combined.

2. Add remaining water while blending until desired texture is achieved.

PER 1 CUP SERVING Calories: 94 | Fat: 0 g | Protein: 1 g | Sodium: 6 mg | Fiber: 5 g | Carbohydrates: 25 g

Amazing Avocados

Although avocados have been found to fight the free radicals that can cause colon, breast, and prostate cancers, the most notable protective benefit avocados create in the human body is the protection against oral cancer. With a 50 percent mortality rate most commonly due to late detection, oral cancer is a cancer that can be helped with the addition of just 2 ounces of avocado to your diet.

YIELDS: 3–4 CUPS

Ingredients
1 cup spinach
2 avocados, peeled and seeds removed
1 lime, peeled
1 cup water
1 cup Greek-style yogurt

1. Combine spinach, avocados, lime, ½ cup water, and ½ cup yogurt in a blender, and blend until thoroughly combined.

2. Add remaining water and yogurt while blending until desired texture is achieved.

PER 1 CUP SERVING Calories: 200 | Fat: 15 g | Protein: 8 g | Sodium: 38 mg | Fiber: 7 g | Carbohydrates: 13 g

Zucchini-Apple

Raw food enthusiasts embrace the idea of consuming minimally cooked foods because heat (above 115°F) drastically reduces the vitamins, minerals, phytochemicals, and antioxidants found in fruits and vegetables. Zucchini is usually sautéed, baked, or roasted with salt and seasonings to add flavor. By blending this healthy veggie in your smoothie, you'll benefit from it in its pure form, without destructive heat and counterproductive seasonings.

YIELDS: 3–4 CUPS

Ingredients
1 cup spinach
1 zucchini
3 carrots, peeled
2 red apples, cored and peeled
2 cups water

1. Combine spinach, zucchini, carrots, apples, and 1 cup water in a blender, and blend until thoroughly combined.

2. Add remaining water while blending until desired texture is achieved.

PER 1 CUP SERVING Calories: 76 | Fat: 0 g | Protein: 1 g | Sodium: 46 mg | Fiber: 4 g | Carbohydrates: 19 g

Red Apple, Green Smoothie

The ingredients in this recipe offer a wide variety of health benefits, including cold and flu protection, better blood quality, and improved mood. Iron, powerful vitamin C, fiber, antioxidants, and natural diuretics combine to make this a flavorful treat that packs plenty of bonus health benefits like reduced water retention and stronger, shinier hair, too! What a way to make sipping the rainbow easy!

YIELDS: 3–4 CUPS

Ingredients
1 cup spinach
1 cucumber, peeled
2 celery stalks
2 red apples, cored and peeled
1 lemon, peeled
1 lime, peeled
1 cup water

1. Combine spinach, cucumber, celery, apples, lemon, lime, and ½ cup water in a blender, and blend until thoroughly combined.

2. Add remaining water, if needed, while blending until desired texture is achieved.

PER 1 CUP SERVING Calories: 68 | Fat: 0 g | Protein: 1 g | Sodium: 25 mg | Fiber: 4 g | Carbohydrates: 18 g

Ginger and Apple Cleansing Blend

Apples are sometimes referred to as "nature's scrub brushes" because of the powerful amount of fiber they contain. Found in deep greens, vegetables, and fruits, fiber plays an important role in helping your body rid itself of waste products that may be causing irregularity. The indigestible fibers that pass through your digestive system literally sweep lingering waste with them as they leave your body.

YIELDS: 3–4 CUPS

Ingredients
1 cup spinach
3 apples, peeled and cored
½" gingerroot, peeled
2 cups water

1. Combine spinach, apples, ginger, and 1 cup water in a blender, and blend until thoroughly combined.

2. Add remaining water while blending, as needed, until desired texture is achieved.

PER 1 CUP SERVING Calories: 60 | Fat: 0 g | Protein: 1 g | Sodium: 8 mg | Fiber: 2 g | Carbohydrates: 16 g

Sweet Spinach Smoothie

Combining spinach with deliciously sweet apples and bananas can make even the most devout spinach skeptic enjoy this nutritious rich-green veggie as a part of a healthier diet. Essential iron and calcium—along with bounds of B vitamins like folate—boost your blood health . . . and it tastes good, too!

YIELDS: 3–4 CUPS

Ingredients
1 cup spinach
3 apples, cored and peeled
2 bananas, peeled
½ lemon, peeled
2 cups water

1. Combine spinach, apples, bananas, lemon, and 1 cup water in a blender, and blend until thoroughly combined.

2. Add remaining water while blending, as needed, until desired texture is achieved.

PER 1 CUP SERVING Calories: 114 | Fat: 0 g | Protein: 1 g | Sodium: 9 mg | Fiber: 3 g | Carbohydrates: 30 g

Greens and Berries Smoothie

Well-known for promoting urinary tract health, the antioxidant-rich berries in this recipe also promote a healthy bladder. Combining a variety of these rich berries only compounds their benefits. The berries help alleviate symptoms associated with bladder and urinary tract issues, including minimizing discomfort associated with frequent urination, bladder infections, and urinary tract infections.

YIELDS: 3–4 CUPS

Ingredients

1 cup romaine lettuce
2 cups blueberries
1 cup cranberries
1 apple, cored and peeled
1 banana, peeled
½" gingerroot, peeled
2 cups water

1. Combine romaine lettuce, blueberries, cranberries, apple, banana, ginger, and 1 cup water in a blender, and blend until thoroughly combined.

2. Add remaining water while blending, as needed, until desired texture is achieved.

PER 1 CUP SERVING Calories: 102 | Fat: 0 g | Protein: 1 g | Sodium: 5 mg | Fiber: 4 g | Carbohydrates: 26 g

Apple-Broccoli Blend

If you want to drink the rainbow, you have to try this amazing recipe! Packed with fiber that will clear out your digestive system, B vitamins that work to optimize brain functioning and mental clarity, and vitamin C to revitalize your body's many systems of operation, this smoothie is a must-have!

YIELDS: 3–4 CUPS

Ingredients

1 cup romaine lettuce
2 apples, peeled and cored
1 cup broccoli
1 orange, peeled
⅛ cup parsley
2 cups water

1. Combine romaine lettuce, apples, broccoli, orange, parsley, and 1 cup water in a blender, and blend until thoroughly combined.

2. Add remaining water while blending, as needed, until desired texture is achieved.

PER 1 CUP SERVING Calories: 71 | Fat: 0 g | Protein: 1 g | Sodium: 12 mg | Fiber: 3 g | Carbohydrates: 18 g

Spinach-Asparagus Smoothie

Bile acids made in the liver and used by the small intestine for breaking down foods in digestion are stored in the gallbladder. A cleansed gallbladder is one that is free of toxins and waste, which ensures that it's able to function properly and at an optimal level. Fortunately, the vitamins C and K, lycopene, iron, and B vitamins found in the green produce in this recipe work to promote a healthy gallbladder and keep you feeling your best.

YIELDS: 3–4 CUPS

Ingredients

1 cup spinach
1 cup asparagus
½ lemon, peeled
1 tomato
1–2 cloves garlic, depending upon size
2 cups water

1. Combine spinach, asparagus, lemon, tomato, garlic, and 1 cup water in a blender, and blend until thoroughly combined.

2. Add remaining water while blending, as needed, until desired texture is achieved.

PER 1 CUP SERVING Calories: 17 | Fat: 0 g | Protein: 1 g | Sodium: 11 mg | Fiber: 1 g | Carbohydrates: 4 g

The Deep Colors of Dreamy Health

The vibrant colors of the kale, carrot, tomato, celery, and cucumber combine with potent garlic to develop an intensely flavored, savory smoothie that provides a variety of vitamins and minerals. The vitamin K, vitamin C, iron, manganese, and antioxidants in this smoothie all work together to improve everything from the quality of the blood to a better balanced mood, and cardiovascular and colon health.

YIELDS: 3–4 CUPS

Ingredients

2 kale leaves
1 cucumber, peeled
2 celery stalks
1 carrot, peeled
1 tomato
1 garlic clove
2 cups water

1. Combine kale, cucumber, celery, carrot, tomato, garlic, and 1 cup water in a blender, and blend until thoroughly combined.

2. Add remaining water while blending, as needed, until desired texture is achieved.

PER 1 CUP SERVING Calories: 31 | Fat: 0 g | Protein: 1 g | Sodium: 39 mg | Fiber: 2 g | Carbohydrates: 6 g

Refreshing Reprieve

Refreshing flavors can keep a healthy diet on track. Calming cravings for sweets or salty foods can help you keep your focus on your health. In addition, this smoothie is full of rich vitamins, minerals, and phytochemicals like vitamins C and K, beta-carotene, and lutein that promote health and fight illness, which makes this smoothie the perfect green answer to "what's for dinner?" . . . or breakfast, or lunch.

YIELDS: 3–4 CUPS

Ingredients

1 cup romaine lettuce
1 apple, peeled and cored
1 cucumber, peeled
1 celery stalk
1 carrot, peeled
1 garlic clove
2 cups water

1. Combine romaine lettuce, apple, cucumber, celery, carrot, garlic, and 1 cup water in a blender, and blend until thoroughly combined.

2. Add remaining water while blending, as needed, until desired texture is achieved.

PER 1 CUP SERVING Calories: 35 | Fat: 0 g | Protein: 1 g | Sodium: 15 mg | Fiber: 2 g | Carbohydrates: 8 g

Chapter 8

Blue

Blueberries

As you can see, there isn't a lot of produce to choose from when it comes to the blue spectrum of the rainbow; the vibrant, luscious blueberry stands alone here. But the good news is that you don't need a wide selection of fruits and veggies to get the most from this color.

The blueberry is a powerful fruit packed with rich nutrients that provide a myriad of health benefits. The vitamins and minerals that dominate this bluest of berries are vitamins A, E, K, and B vitamins, as well as the minerals calcium and manganese. In terms of benefits, this powerful combination can improve many areas of your health. The vitamin A has the ability to maintain eye health, the quality of your vision, and the strength of your bones, teeth, hair, skin, and nails (all benefits improved significantly by the presence of vitamin E). Further, the vitamin K offers impressive health properties for blood circulation that promote the healthy "glow" of skin.

In this way, the vitamins in blueberries act as a triple treat for your body's aesthetic qualities.

Internally, these same vitamins promote clean and clear blood quality, optimal immune-system functioning, metabolic stability, proper blood sugar maintenance, and hormone regulation. The minerals calcium and manganese take those benefits even further, while also promoting smooth nerve communication to and from the brain.

And the benefits aren't done yet. The impressive list of critical phytochemicals and phytonutrients that give the blueberry its striking blue coloring pack a punch when it comes to their antibacterial, antioxidant, and anti-inflammatory properties. It's true! From the ability to stop cell damage by free radicals, improve the quality of the immune system, promote ideal blood pressure, and reduce "bad" (LDL) cholesterol while improving the "good" (HDL), each and every health benefit from the nutrients contained in these luscious berries is enough to make them an important staple in your refrigerator—and your blender.

Adding to their beautiful coloring and complex nutrition, versatile and powerful blueberries tastefully combine with a number of other fruits, liquids, and additions to create an extraordinary variety of smoothies. And when these power fruits combine with the array of vitamins, minerals, and phytochemicals found in other fruits and veggies, they become even more powerful in fighting off health assailants—and in promoting your quality of life! So let's take a look at some blue smoothies!

A Berry Beautiful Morning

Combining a double dose of luscious berries with the creamy flavors of kefir and rice milk, this is a delicious breakfast smoothie packed with vitamin C, protein, and probiotics. Protecting your health with immunity-boosting nutrition, fighting free radicals with powerful antioxidants, and improving your mental well-being with B vitamins, this delicious smoothie will make your morning great and get your day off to the right start!

YIELDS: 2½ CUPS

Ingredients
1 cup blueberries
½ cup blackberries
1 cup blueberry kefir
½ cup vanilla rice milk
1 cup ice

1. In a blender, combine the blueberries, blackberries, kefir, and rice milk with ½ cup ice, and blend until thoroughly combined.

2. While blending, add remaining ice until desired consistency is achieved.

PER 1 CUP SERVING Calories: 118 | Fat: 1 g | Protein: 6 g | Sodium: 83 mg | Fiber: 3 g | Carbohydrates: 22 g

Blue Blast of Banana

Sometimes simple is best, and simplicity takes over with this four-ingredient smoothie. Blending blueberries and banana with nothing but water and ice allows this smoothie to highlight these fruits' unique flavors! The vitamin C– and antioxidant-packed blueberries lend a sweet, tart flavor to the potassium-rich sweet, smooth banana to make for a total health–boosting, sensational smoothie combination.

YIELDS: 2 CUPS

Ingredients
1 cup blueberries
1 banana, peeled
1½ cups water
1 cup ice

1. In a blender, combine the blueberries, banana, and 1 cup water with ½ cup ice, and blend until thoroughly combined.

2. While blending, add remaining water and ice until desired consistency is achieved.

PER 1 CUP SERVING Calories: 120 | Fat: 1 g | Protein: 2 g | Sodium: 7 mg | Fiber: 4 g | Carbohydrates: 27 g

No Blues Except the Berries

Feeling down can stink, but by packing your body and brain with the bright anthocyanadins, vitamin C, and magnesium found in the vibrant, juicy blueberries and rich almond milk in this recipe, you're well on your way to improving your mood—and your day!

YIELDS: 2½ CUPS

Ingredients
2 cups blueberries
1 cup almond milk
1 cup ice

1. In a blender, combine the blueberries and almond milk with ½ cup ice, and blend until thoroughly combined.

2. While blending, add remaining ice until desired consistency is achieved.

PER 1 CUP SERVING Calories: 124 | Fat: 2 g | Protein: 2 g | Sodium: 39 mg | Fiber: 4 g | Carbohydrates: 28 g

True Blue Tropical Treat

The tropical tastes of pineapple and coconut combine with sweet blueberries for a new and improved blue smoothie that will do more than just shock your taste buds. The fruits found in this recipe are full of vitamin C and bright phytochemicals like bromelain and anthocyanadins, which combine to protect your immune system and make your mouth sing!

YIELDS: 2 CUPS

Ingredients
1½ cups blueberries
½ cup pineapple
1 cup coconut milk
1 cup ice

1. In a blender, combine the blueberries, pineapple, and coconut milk with ½ cup ice, and blend until thoroughly combined.

2. While blending, add remaining ice until desired consistency is achieved.

PER 1 CUP SERVING Calories: 346 | Fat: 25 g | Protein: 5 g | Sodium: 25 mg | Fiber: 5 g | Carbohydrates: 29 g

Beautiful Blue Berry Smoothie

While the berries in this smoothie are colored with different pigments, when mixed together they combine to create a beautifully bright blue smoothie that's packed with vitamins A and C, calcium and manganese, and powerful antioxidants that promote blood health, mental clarity, and increased metabolic functioning. Healthy and delicious! What's not to love?

YIELDS: 3 CUPS

Ingredients
1 cup blueberries
½ cup strawberries
½ cup blackberries
1 cup blueberry kefir
1 cup water
1 cup ice

1. In a blender, combine the blueberries, strawberries, blackberries, kefir, and ½ cup water with ½ cup ice, and blend until thoroughly combined.

2. While blending, add remaining water and ice until desired consistency is achieved.

PER 1 CUP SERVING Calories: 109 | Fat: 1 g | Protein: 6 g | Sodium: 68 mg | Fiber: 4 g | Carbohydrates: 20 g

Banana Berry with a Cherry

Smooth, sweet, and packed with a variety of flavors, this smoothie is a delicious way to enjoy your favorite fruits in a chilly, nutritious smoothie sure to please! Packed with potassium, B vitamins, and fiber, this smoothie helps your body flush out unwanted toxins and restores healthy vitality to both your body and mind.

YIELDS: 3 CUPS

Ingredients
1 cup blueberries
1 banana, peeled
¼ cup cherries, pitted
1 cup blueberry kefir
1 cup water
1 cup ice

1. In a blender, combine the blueberries, banana, cherries, kefir, and ½ cup water with ½ cup ice, and blend until thoroughly combined.

2. While blending, add remaining water and ice until desired consistency is achieved.

PER 1 CUP SERVING Calories: 134 | Fat: 1 g | Protein: 6 g | Sodium: 67 mg | Fiber: 3 g | Carbohydrates: 27 g

Blue Yogurt Smoothie

Far better than a plain cup of yogurt—and much prettier—this smoothie will appeal to anyone who's having some tummy trouble and needs a little extra nutritional TLC from the inside out. With healthy probiotics that fight off bad intestinal bacteria and fiber that keeps food moving through your system, this smoothie packs a delicious one-two punch for better belly health.

YIELDS: 2 CUPS

Ingredients

1 cup blueberries
1 cup blueberry kefir
1 serving probiotic supplement (see packaging for exact amount)
1 teaspoon grated ginger
1 cup water
1 cup ice

1. In a blender, combine the blueberries, kefir, probiotic, ginger, and ½ cup water with ½ cup ice, and blend until thoroughly combined.

2. While blending, add remaining water and ice until desired consistency is achieved.

PER 1 CUP SERVING Calories: 137 | Fat: 1 g | Protein: 8 g | Sodium: 101 mg | Fiber: 3 g | Carbohydrates: 23 g

Very Vanilla Berry

Mixed with bright blueberries, smooth banana, and creamy almond milk, the delicious vanilla bean's pulp gives this scrumptious smoothie a little extra "oomph!" Providing powerful antioxidants like vanillin, minerals like potassium, and loads of vitamin C, this smoothie's ingredients benefit your immune system, cardiovascular system, and the digestive system.

YIELDS: 3 CUPS

Ingredients

1½ cups blueberries
1 banana, peeled
1 vanilla bean's pulp
1½ cups vanilla almond milk
1 cup ice

1. In a blender, combine the blueberries, banana, vanilla bean's pulp, and 1 cup almond milk with ½ cup ice, and blend until thoroughly combined.

2. While blending, add remaining almond milk and ice until desired consistency is achieved.

PER 1 CUP SERVING Calories: 157 | Fat: 2 g | Protein: 2 g | Sodium: 52 mg | Fiber: 4 g | Carbohydrates: 37 g

A "Berry" Beneficial Blend

Blueberries and blackberries combine their powerful anthocyanadins and vitamin A to create a potent smoothie that works to boost your immunity. In addition, the fragrant spices and creamy kefir load this smoothie up with antioxidants that fight free radical damage and protect the entire body from illnesses.

YIELDS: 3 CUPS

Ingredients

1 cup blueberries
1 cup blackberries
½ cup wheat germ
1 teaspoon cinnamon
1 cup blueberry kefir
1 cup water
1½ cups ice

1. In a blender, combine the blueberries, blackberries, wheat germ, cinnamon, kefir, and ½ cup water with 1 cup ice, and blend until thoroughly combined.

2. While blending, add remaining water and ice until desired consistency is achieved.

PER 1 CUP SERVING Calories: 183 | Fat: 3 g | Protein: 11 g | Sodium: 70 mg | Fiber: 7 g | Carbohydrates: 31 g

Blueberries 'n' Cream

If dessert for breakfast sounds like a great idea, this simple, smooth concoction of blueberries, thick yogurt, and creamy coconut milk is for you! Packed with B vitamins, vitamin C, and powerful antioxidants that work together to boost your energy and promote mental clarity by improving blood quality and circulation, this is a great smoothie for any time of day.

YIELDS: 2½ CUPS

Ingredients

1½ cups blueberries
½ cup Greek-style yogurt
1 cup coconut milk
1 cup ice

1. In a blender, combine the blueberries, yogurt, and coconut milk with ½ cup ice, and blend until thoroughly combined.

2. While blending, add remaining ice until desired consistency is achieved.

PER 1 CUP SERVING Calories: 239 | Fat: 17 g | Protein: 7 g | Sodium: 32 mg | Fiber: 3 g | Carbohydrates: 17 g

Blueberry Crumble

If your stomach isn't feeling quite right, this delicious smoothie can be what you need to get things back on track. With rich probiotics, carbohydrate-rich additions, and spices shown to calm indigestion, this smoothie gives you a delicious dose of natural medicine that will contribute to a better-feeling belly.

YIELDS: 2½ CUPS

Ingredients

1 cup blueberries
½ cup rolled oats
¼ cup wheat germ
2 teaspoons grated ginger
1 teaspoon cinnamon
1 cup blueberry kefir
1 cup water
1 cup ice

1. In a blender, combine the blueberries, rolled oats, wheat germ, ginger, cinnamon, kefir, and ½ cup water with ½ cup ice, and blend until thoroughly combined.

2. While blending, add remaining water and ice until desired consistency is achieved.

PER 1 CUP SERVING Calories: 179 | Fat: 5 g | Protein: 4 g | Sodium: 63 mg | Fiber: 3 g | Carbohydrates: 13 g

Healthy Blue Helper

If you're looking to clear out your system and start fresh, this is the smoothie for you! Full of ingredients that have been shown to aid in respiratory health and detoxify the body's organs of foreign invaders, this delicious smoothie packs a double whammy of nutrition that can help your body repair and restore itself so you start your day feeling great!

YIELDS: 3 CUPS

Ingredients

1 cup blueberries
½ cup prunes, pitted
½ cup Concord grapes
1½ cups water
1 cup ice

1. In a blender, combine the blueberries, prunes, grapes, and 1 cup water with ½ cup ice, and blend until thoroughly combined.

2. While blending, add remaining water and ice until desired consistency is achieved.

PER 1 CUP SERVING Calories: 114 | Fat: 1 g | Protein: 2 g | Sodium: 5 mg | Fiber: 4 g | Carbohydrates: 27 g

Bundles of Berries Bursting with Benefits

The three delicious berry varieties in this smoothie combine with sweet maple syrup and creamy coconut milk to contribute a powerful barrage of antioxidants that work together to protect all of your body's cells from damaging free radicals and harmful chemical changes. It's good for your taste buds and good for your health!

YIELDS: 2½ CUPS

Ingredients
1 cup blueberries
½ cup raspberries
½ cup blackberries
1 teaspoon maple syrup
1 cup coconut milk
1 cup ice

1. In a blender, combine the blueberries, raspberries, blackberries, maple syrup, and coconut milk with ½ cup ice, and blend until thoroughly combined.

2. While blending, add remaining ice until desired consistency is achieved.

PER 1 CUP SERVING Calories: 210 | Fat: 17 g | Protein: 3 g | Sodium: 15 mg | Fiber: 3 g | Carbohydrates: 15 g

Blueberry Oatmeal Delight

If you're craving something comforting, forget the store-bought flavored oatmeal, and opt instead for this thick and delicious homemade smoothie that combines tasty fruit, carb-rich oats, and aromatic spices—a healthy mix of ingredients that will jump-start any old breakfast routine! The vibrant blueberries; energy-producing, carbohydrate-rich oats; protein-packed almond milk; and unique blend of spices will awaken your senses and get your body moving!

YIELDS: 2 CUPS

Ingredients
1 cup blueberries
½ cup rolled oats
1 teaspoon cinnamon
1 teaspoon nutmeg
1½ cups vanilla almond milk
1 cup ice

1. In a blender, combine the blueberries, oats, cinnamon, nutmeg, and 1 cup almond milk with ½ cup ice, and blend until thoroughly combined.

2. While blending, add remaining almond milk and ice until desired consistency is achieved.

PER 1 CUP SERVING Calories: 228 | Fat: 4 g | Protein: 5 g | Sodium: 76 mg | Fiber: 6 g | Carbohydrates: 50 g

Blueberry Crunch Kick-Start

If you're looking to amp up your energy level as you walk out the door, and you want that energy to last, then this is the recipe for you! This smoothie is packed with protein and complex carbohydrates and rounded out in a sweet, creamy package. So pick yourself up off the floor and try this smoothie on for size.

YIELDS: 3 CUPS

Ingredients

1½ cups blueberries
¼ cup wheat germ
1 scoop vanilla protein powder
1½ cups almond milk
1 cup ice

1. In a blender, combine the blueberries, wheat germ, protein powder, and 1 cup almond milk with ½ cup ice, and blend until thoroughly combined.

2. While blending, add remaining almond milk and ice until desired consistency is achieved.

PER 1 CUP SERVING Calories: 189 | Fat: 3 g | Protein: 12 g | Sodium: 53 mg | Fiber: 4 g | Carbohydrates: 33 g

Smart Blue Start for Your Heart

This smoothie is full of delicious ingredients that each work to promote an important aspect of your cardiovascular system's health. These fruits are full of antioxidants that will protect your body from free-radical damage; vitamin C, which works to improve your immune system; B vitamins for improved blood content; and magnesium for better circulation. Seems like the perfect recipe for any day when you want to pay your health a little extra attention.

YIELDS: 3 CUPS

Ingredients

1½ cups blueberries
½ cup strawberries
1 banana, peeled
1½ cups green tea
1 teaspoon agave nectar
1 cup ice

1. In a blender, combine the blueberries, strawberries, banana, green tea, and agave nectar with ½ cup ice, and blend until thoroughly combined.

2. While blending, add remaining ice until desired consistency is achieved.

PER 1 CUP SERVING Calories: 119 | Fat: 1 g | Protein: 2 g | Sodium: 11 mg | Fiber: 4 g | Carbohydrates: 27 g

True Blue Smoothie

If you're feeling under the weather, this is the perfect smoothie to kick those blues to the curb. The vitamin C found in this recipe is a delicious and nutritious way to pump up your body's immune system and fend off any flu!

YIELDS: 3 CUPS

Ingredients

2 cups blueberries
1 serving probiotic supplement (see packaging for exact amount)
½ orange, peeled and seeded
1 cup blueberry kefir
½ cup water
1 cup ice

1. In a blender, combine the blueberries, probiotic, orange, kefir, and water with ½ cup ice, and blend until thoroughly combined.

2. While blending, add remaining ice until desired consistency is achieved.

PER 1 CUP SERVING Calories: 147 | Fat: 1 g | Protein: 7 g | Sodium: 72 mg | Fiber: 4 g | Carbohydrates: 27 g

Beat the Blues with the Blues . . . Berries, That Is!

Combining sweet berries with creamy kefir and fragrant spices will put a swing in your step and a smile on your face! Why? Because all of the B vitamins that are found in the ingredients in this delicious smoothie have been shown to improve mood on a regular basis. Packed with excellent nutrition, this smoothie feeds your body, your brain, and your mood!

YIELDS: 2½ CUPS

Ingredients

1 cup blueberries
½ cup blackberries
1 teaspoon cardamom
1 teaspoon cloves
1 cup blueberry kefir
½ cup water
1 cup ice

1. In a blender, combine the blueberries, blackberries, cardamom, cloves, kefir, and water with ½ cup ice, and blend until thoroughly combined.

2. While blending, add remaining ice until desired consistency is achieved.

PER 1 CUP SERVING Calories: 103 | Fat: 6 g | Protein: 6 g | Sodium: 69 mg | Fiber: 3 g | Carbohydrates: 18 g

Blueberry-Banana Blitz

Just when you think blueberries and bananas make for delicious smoothies by themselves, a simple addition of some creative ingredients takes "delicious" to a whole new level! The spicy antioxidant-rich ginger and citrusy *limonin*-packed lemons combine to fight illness, prevent free radical damage, and even improve the respiratory conditions that can result from common illnesses.

YIELDS: 3 CUPS

Ingredients

1½ cups blueberries
1½ bananas, peeled
1 teaspoon grated ginger
Juice of ¼ lemon
1 cup coconut milk
1 cup ice

1. In a blender, combine the blueberries, bananas, ginger, lemon juice, and coconut milk with ½ cup ice, and blend until thoroughly combined.

2. While blending, add remaining ice until desired consistency is achieved.

PER 1 CUP SERVING Calories: 269 | Fat: 17 g | Protein: 4 g | Sodium: 17 mg | Fiber: 4 g | Carbohydrates: 29 g

Blueberry Citrus Smoothie

This smoothie is perfect if you're feeling a little under the weather. The tasty ingredients in this recipe contain nutrients like vitamin C, anthocyanadins, and vitamin E, which all work together as powerful antioxidants to fight off anything that may lower your immune system's resistance. So if you're not feeling great, instead of reaching into your medicine cabinet, reach for a full glass of this delicious smoothie instead!

YIELDS: 3 CUPS

Ingredients

2 cups blueberries
½ orange, peeled and deseeded
½ grapefruit, peeled and deseeded
1½ cups water
1 serving probiotic supplement (see packaging for exact amount)
1 cup ice

1. In a blender, combine the blueberries, orange, grapefruit, 1 cup water and probiotic with ½ cup ice, and blend until thoroughly combined.

2. While blending, add remaining water and ice until desired consistency is achieved.

PER 1 CUP SERVING Calories: 115 | Fat: 1 g | Protein: 2 g | Sodium: 9 mg | Fiber: 5 g | Carbohydrates: 24 g

Blue Spiced Ice

The powerful illness-combating antioxidants found in the potent cloves and cardamom give this creamy blue smoothie a whole new sensation that will tantalize your taste buds, clear out your sinuses, and make for one delicious way to enjoy some healthy fruit!

YIELDS: 3 CUPS

Ingredients
1 cup blueberries
1 banana, peeled
¼ teaspoon cloves
½ teaspoon cardamom
1 vanilla bean's pulp
1½ cups coconut milk
1 cup ice

1. In a blender, combine the blueberries, banana, cloves, cardamom, vanilla bean's pulp, and coconut milk with ½ cup ice, and blend until thoroughly combined.

2. While blending, add remaining ice until desired consistency is achieved.

PER 1 CUP SERVING Calories: 307 | Fat: 25 g | Protein: 4 g | Sodium: 20 mg | Fiber: 3 g | Carbohydrates: 22 g

Blue Tea for a Good Night's Sleep

Everyone suffers from insomnia every once in a while. If you find yourself awake counting sheep, try this sleep-inducing smoothie. With a base of soothing chamomile tea, it includes sweet blueberries and zippy ginger to create a sweet treat that will have you nodding off in no time.

YIELDS: 1½ CUPS

Ingredients
1 cup blueberries
¼ teaspoon ginger, grated
1 cup chamomile tea, chilled
1 cup ice

1. In a blender, combine the blueberries, ginger, and tea with ½ cup ice, and blend until thoroughly combined.

2. While blending, add remaining ice until desired consistency is achieved.

PER 1 CUP SERVING Calories: 70 | Fat: 1 g | Protein: 1 g | Sodium: 8 mg | Fiber: 3 g | Carbohydrates: 14 g

Blueberry Citrus Twist

Who would have guessed that the blueberries in this recipe would combine so deliciously with smooth banana and sweet-tart citrus fruits? It's not just their taste that's complementary, though! The abundant vitamin C and antioxidants that combine for improved immune-system functioning also benefit your health by relieving the stress on that system and allowing your body to exert energy toward other areas in need.

YIELDS: 3 CUPS

Ingredients

1 cup blueberries
1 banana, peeled
½ cup pineapple
½ orange, peeled
½ grapefruit, peeled
Juice of ¼ lime
1 cup water
1 cup ice

1. In a blender, combine the blueberries, banana, pineapple, orange, grapefruit, lime juice, and water with ½ cup ice, and blend until thoroughly combined.

2. While blending, add remaining ice until desired consistency is achieved.

PER 1 CUP SERVING Calories: 118 | Fat: 1 g | Protein: 2 g | Sodium: 5 mg | Fiber: 4 g | Carbohydrates: 28 g

Dreamy Creamy Blueberry

Move over ice cream and frozen yogurts, and make way for this delicious smoothie! This recipe packs potent fruits, creamy deliciousness, and flavorful additions that all combine to make a sweet treat that's not only scrumptious . . . it's healthy, too! In fact, the protein- and probiotic-packed kefir boosts the body's defenses against illness while promoting optimal muscle functioning—which benefits even the smallest of involuntary muscles in the body!

YIELDS: 3 CUPS

Ingredients

1 cup blueberries
1 banana, peeled
1 vanilla bean's pulp
1 cup plain kefir
½ cup coconut milk
½ teaspoon maple syrup
1 cup ice

1. In a blender, combine the blueberries, banana, vanilla bean's pulp, kefir, coconut milk, and maple syrup with ½ cup ice, and blend until thoroughly combined.

2. While blending, add remaining ice until desired consistency is achieved.

PER 1 CUP SERVING Calories: 207 | Fat: 9 g | Protein: 7 g | Sodium: 73 mg | Fiber: 3 g | Carbohydrates: 26 g

Amazing Blueberry Almond

The protein-rich almonds in this recipe add quality sustainable energy to your morning! They tastefully take center stage in this delicious smoothie that is an amazingly delicious way to gain improved energy, mental clarity, and focus that will last the whole day through!

YIELDS: 3 CUPS

Ingredients
¼ cup almonds
1½ cups almond milk
2 cups blueberries
1 cup ice

1. In a blender, combine the almonds and almond milk and emulsify completely.

2. Add blueberries with ½ cup ice, and blend until thoroughly combined.

3. While blending, add remaining ice until desired consistency is achieved.

PER 1 CUP SERVING Calories: 186 | Fat: 6 g | Protein: 4 g | Sodium: 54 mg | Fiber: 5 g | Carbohydrates: 34 g

Blueberries, Baby!

This delicious smoothie is made from healthy ingredients full of disease-fighting antioxidants and creamy probiotics. These ingredients work together to create a sensational-tasting smoothie that will keep you healthy from head to toe. Give it a try!

YIELDS: 2 CUPS

Ingredients
2 cups blueberries
1 serving probiotic supplement (see packaging for exact amount)
1 cup blueberry kefir
½ cup water
1 cup ice

1. In a blender, combine the blueberries, probiotic, kefir, and water with ½ cup ice, and blend until thoroughly combined.

2. While blending, add remaining ice until desired consistency is achieved.

PER 1 CUP SERVING Calories: 136 | Fat: 1 g | Protein: 7 g | Sodium: 71 mg | Fiber: 4 g | Carbohydrates: 25 g

Blue Banana Berry

Mixing up a delicious concoction of sweet berries and smooth banana has never been easier (or tastier!) than in this recipe. With tons of flavor-filled nutritious ingredients like potassium-packed bananas and *anthocyanadin*-rich blueberries, this is a beautiful smoothie that tastes great while promoting health in oh-so-many ways! From breathing easier to speeding up your metabolism, these amazing ingredients work wonders *and* taste great!

YIELDS: 4 CUPS

Ingredients
1 cup blueberries
½ cup strawberries
½ cup blackberries
1 banana, peeled
1 cup blueberry kefir
½ cup water
1 cup ice

1. In a blender, combine the blueberries, strawberries, blackberries, banana, kefir, and water with ½ cup ice, and blend until thoroughly combined.

2. While blending, add remaining ice until desired consistency is achieved.

PER 1 CUP SERVING Calories: 108 | Fat: 1 g | Protein: 5 g | Sodium: 51 mg | Fiber: 4 g | Carbohydrates: 21 g

Blueberry Blast-Off

Get your morning off to a great start with this delicious blueberry smoothie! This recipe combines all of the amazing ingredients of a blueberry-packed bowl of oatmeal, in a creamy, protein-packed smoothie. You'll be sipping your way to great health in no time!

YIELDS: 4 CUPS

Ingredients
2 cups blueberries
½ cup rolled oats
¼ cup honey wheat germ
½ teaspoon organic, all-natural maple syrup
1 scoop protein powder
1 cup blueberry kefir
½ cup water
1 cup ice

1. In a blender, combine the blueberries, rolled oats, wheat germ, maple syrup, protein powder, kefir, and water with ½ cup ice, and blend until thoroughly combined.

2. While blending, add remaining ice until desired consistency is achieved.

PER 1 CUP SERVING Calories: 185 | Fat: 3 g | Protein: 11 g | Sodium: 56 mg | Fiber: 5 g | Carbohydrates: 30 g

Blueberry Supreme

The sweet, juicy blueberries that pack this smoothie don't lose their flavor with the whirl of the blender. And the flavor intensity of these rich, blended berries and creamy blueberry kefir gets even better when you add whole blueberries that'll burst in your mouth with vivacious vitamin-C splendor for an extra blueberry kick!

YIELDS: 3 CUPS

Ingredients
2 cups blueberries
1 cup blueberry kefir
½ cup water
1 cup ice
¼ cup whole blueberries (for mixing in)

1. In a blender, combine 2 cups blueberries, kefir, and water with ½ cup ice, and blend until thoroughly combined.

2. While blending, add remaining ice until desired consistency is achieved.

3. Pour the smoothie into desired containers, and mix in remaining whole blueberries.

PER 1 CUP SERVING Calories: 148 | Fat: 1 g | Protein: 7 g | Sodium: 73 mg | Fiber: 4 g | Carbohydrates: 27 g

Basic Blueberry Smoothie

Sometimes, you just have to get back to basics! In this smoothie, there's nothing else needed but the sweet deliciousness of blueberries to make for an insanely healthy blueberry treat that will give your health and vitality an unexpected, yet much-needed, boost from these delicious, nutritious immunity-building and cell-protecting powerful ingredients!

YIELDS: 2 CUPS

Ingredients
2 cups blueberries
½ cup water
½ cup ice

1. In a blender, combine the blueberries and water with the ice, and blend until thoroughly combined.

PER 1 CUP SERVING Calories: 136 | Fat: 2 g | Protein: 3 g | Sodium: 13 mg | Fiber: 6 g | Carbohydrates: 28 g

Blueberry Bliss

If you're active, your body needs plenty of protein. To make sure you're giving your body what it craves, this smoothie is the way to go. Here, you'll find tons of stamina-building protein from the creamy Greek-style yogurt, which blends perfectly into a delicious, nutritious combination of bright blue ingredients that will keep your mind sharp and your body working at its peak!

YIELDS: 2 CUPS

Ingredients

1 cup blueberries
½ cup blueberry kefir
½ cup Greek-style yogurt
½ cup rice milk
1 cup ice

1. In a blender, combine the blueberries, kefir, Greek yogurt, and rice milk with ½ cup ice, and blend until thoroughly combined.

2. While blending, add remaining ice until desired consistency is achieved.

PER 1 CUP SERVING Calories: 127 | Fat: 1 g | Protein: 5 g | Sodium: 76 mg | Fiber: 3 g | Carbohydrates: 25 g

Blue Apple-Berry

Brimming with health-protecting antioxidants that fight illness and protect cells, and tons of flavor from the fresh blueberries, the depth of this smoothie's flavor far surpasses the quality and intensity of a store-bought or restaurant smoothie. And, when you make your smoothies at home, you know that you'll get out what you put in: healthy, delicious food!

YIELDS: 2 CUPS

Ingredients

1 cup blueberries
1 yellow apple, cored
1 cup blueberry kefir
1 cup coconut milk
1 cup ice

1. In a blender, combine the blueberries, apple, kefir, and coconut milk with ½ cup ice, and blend until thoroughly combined.

2. While blending, add remaining ice until desired consistency is achieved.

PER 1 CUP SERVING Calories: 398 | Fat: 25 g | Protein: 11 g | Sodium: 116 mg | Fiber: 4 g | Carbohydrates: 37 g

Spiced Blue Pears

Pears get a blue, spicy twist in this smooth blend of powerful ingredients, which each provide a unique blend of powerful antioxidants that fight off free radical damage to healthy cells. This smoothie gives your body a multitude of defenses against illness and disease—and it does so deliciously.

YIELDS: 3 CUPS

Ingredients
1 cup blueberries
1 pear, cored
1 teaspoon grated ginger
1 teaspoon ground nutmeg
1 cup vanilla almond milk
1 cup ice

1. In a blender, combine the blueberries, pear, ginger, nutmeg, and almond milk with ½ cup ice, and blend until thoroughly combined.

2. While blending, add remaining ice until desired consistency is achieved.

PER 1 CUP SERVING Calories: 91 | Fat: 1 g | Protein: 1 g | Sodium: 35 mg | Fiber: 3 g | Carbohydrates: 22 g

Blueberry Parfait with Crunch

While a simple berry parfait may sound appetizing, this smoothie takes the nutrition and flavor to a whole new level. Once you add the probiotics, tons of protein, crunchy goodness, and sweet creamy nuttiness that are found in this delightful smoothie recipe, a regular parfait looks downright boring!

YIELDS: 3 CUPS

Ingredients
1 cup blueberries
½ cup blueberry kefir
½ cup Greek-style yogurt
½ cup all-natural, organic granola
1 cup vanilla almond milk
1 cup ice

1. In a blender, combine the blueberries, kefir, Greek-style yogurt, granola, and almond milk with ½ cup ice, and blend until thoroughly combined.

2. While blending, add remaining ice until desired consistency is achieved.

PER 1 CUP SERVING Calories: 223 | Fat: 1 g | Protein: 11 g | Sodium: 87 mg | Fiber: 4 g | Carbohydrates: 34 g

Blueberry Staple Sweetened with Maple

The additions of pure maple syrup and creamy rice milk make this simple smoothie a little sweeter. But these added ingredients bring more than simply added taste; the rich antioxidants that add tons of health-protecting benefits to your immune system, blood, and brain only improve the appeal of this delicious taste combination!

YIELDS: 2 CUPS

Ingredients
2 cups blueberries
1 teaspoon organic, pure maple syrup
1 cup rice milk
1 cup ice

1. In a blender, combine the blueberries, maple syrup, and rice milk with ½ cup ice, and blend until thoroughly combined.

2. While blending, add remaining ice until desired consistency is achieved.

PER 1 CUP SERVING Calories: 195 | Fat: 3 g | Protein: 3 g | Sodium: 59 mg | Fiber: 6 g | Carbohydrates: 44 g

Blue Rainbow Smoothie

With tons of color, flavor, and intense nutrition, this recipe gives you a lot of nutrients that you need to keep your body healthy. More so than any other nutrient, however, the probiotics that promote the growth of good bacteria while inhibiting the growth of undesirable bacteria take this smoothie to a whole new level. If you want to ensure that your body's immunity is at its peak, this is the smoothie for you! Simply and easily, you can enjoy this recipe on your path to better health.

YIELDS: 3 CUPS

Ingredients
2 cups blueberries
1 cup blueberry kefir
1 serving probiotic supplement (see packaging for exact amount)
1 cup water
1 cup ice

1. In a blender, combine the blueberries, kefir, probiotics, and ½ cup water with ½ cup ice, and blend until thoroughly combined.

2. While blending, add remaining water and ice until desired consistency is achieved.

PER 1 CUP SERVING Calories: 136 | Fat: 1 g | Protein: 7 g | Sodium: 71 mg | Fiber: 4 g | Carbohydrates: 25 g

Sweet Burst of Berries

Combining three different types of berries with creaminess and added sweetness, this smoothie will tickle your taste buds and help your body be better! With more antioxidants, probiotics, and vitamins and minerals than any one berry could provide on its own, the amazing blend of these ingredients makes for a great-tasting way to do your body good!

YIELDS: 4 CUPS

Ingredients

2 cups blueberries
½ cup raspberries
½ cup blackberries
1 cup blueberry kefir
1 teaspoon organic, pure maple syrup
½ cup water
1 cup ice

1. In a blender, combine the blueberries, raspberries, blackberries, kefir, maple syrup, and water with ½ cup ice, and blend until thoroughly combined.

2. While blending, add remaining ice until desired consistency is achieved.

PER 1 CUP SERVING Calories: 123 | Fat: 1 g | Protein: 5 g | Sodium: 54 mg | Fiber: 5 g | Carbohydrates: 23 g

Vibrant Berry Smoothie

When you're able to create a delicious smoothie like the one in this recipe, it's easy to fit in your daily fruit servings. Packed with vibrantly colored berries that promote health and well-being while also helping you feel full for longer, this is one multitasking blend of beauty, taste, and health—and it tastes great, too!

YIELDS: 3 CUPS

Ingredients

1 cup blueberries
1 cup blackberries
½ cup cherries, pitted
½ cup raspberries
1 cup water
1 cup ice

1. In a blender, combine the blueberries, blackberries, cherries, raspberries, and ½ cup water with ½ cup ice, and blend until thoroughly combined.

2. While blending, add remaining water and ice until desired consistency is achieved.

PER 1 CUP SERVING Calories: 93 | Fat: 1 g | Protein: 2 g | Sodium: 5 mg | Fiber: 6 g | Carbohydrates: 20 g

Cool Blue Coconut Chiller

Color your coconuts blue with this smoothie's tropical twist on berry flavor. The sweet taste of coconut not only jazzes up the intense flavor of the blueberries, it also adds a variety of B vitamins, protein, and complex carbohydrates to the existing health benefits provided by the antioxidant-rich berries. Brimming with valuable nutrition that can improve your mind's focus, your body's fat-burning potential, and your overall energy levels, this is a tasty tropical treat of the true blue variety!

YIELDS: 2 CUPS

Ingredients
1 cup blueberries
½ cup coconut meat
1 cup coconut milk
1 cup ice

1. In a blender, combine the blueberries, coconut meat, and coconut milk with ½ cup ice, and blend until thoroughly combined.

2. While blending, add remaining ice until desired consistency is achieved.

PER 1 CUP SERVING Calories: 362 | Fat: 32 g | Protein: 4 g | Sodium: 25 mg | Fiber: 5 g | Carbohydrates: 20 g

Chapter 9

Violet

Beets • Blackberries • Concord Grapes • Eggplant •
Figs • Plums • Prunes • Red Cabbage

Without a doubt, some of the most vibrantly colored fruits and vegetables in the produce area are those with the deep purple hues. Those hues are caused by powerful disease-fighting antioxidants called *flavonoids*, which offer the almost magical capacity to protect and reverse damage to the body's cells.

When you look at the purple produce that's out there, the types of phytochemicals (naturally occurring chemicals produced by plants) and phytonutrients (naturally occurring nutrients produced by plants) are quite impressive, and their health benefits are even more remarkable. The flavonoids protect cells from free radical damage, which can turn healthy cells into cancerous ones. Protecting the body by fighting off cancer, disease, and various infections, purple foods are commonly recommended to those at risk for such conditions.

Working hand in hand with these powerful antioxidants are the calming anti-inflammatory effects that can help many illnesses, from slight aches and pains to heart disease. Consuming just 1 cup of any of these naturally anti-inflammatory fruits and vegetables four to six times a week has been suggested to reduce or relieve the symptoms and the underlying causes of any number of frightening health situations that can affect your bones, joints, heart, blood, and brain. Just think, drinking a delicious smoothie that contains 1 cup of delicious grapes, blackberries, or sliced figs—or 1 medium-sized plum—four or more days per week can change your quality of life . . . now *that's* impressive!

The benefits of purple produce don't end there, though. By incorporating any of the fruits listed at the beginning of this chapter into a smoothie, you can also enjoy a sweet treat that may actually help control your blood sugar levels. Because of their low glycemic index classification, purple produce has a natural type of sugar that affects the blood's sugar levels in a healthier way than other sugary alternatives. Whenever you choose to drink a purple smoothie for a snack, you choose ingredients that may help balance your blood sugar levels and regulate your body's release of insulin.

With all these benefits to gain, what are you waiting for?

Deep Purple Passion

The blackberries found in this recipe pack this smoothie with tons of flavor and rich antioxidants that help prepare your body's cells for healthy functioning and regeneration, and provide those cells with amazing protection from harmful free radical damage that can cause cancers.

YIELDS: 2 CUPS

Ingredients

1 cup blackberries
1 cup blueberry kefir
1 medium banana, peeled
1 cup ice

1. In a blender, combine blackberries, kefir, and banana with ½ cup ice and blend until thoroughly combined.

2. While blending, add remaining ice until desired consistency is achieved.

PER 1 CUP SERVING Calories: 152 | Fat: 1 g | Protein: 9 g | Sodium: 96 mg | Fiber: 5 g | Carbohydrates: 30 g

Blackberry Blast Smoothie

The taste of the blackberries found in this recipe is taken to whole new level with creamy almond milk and delicious vanilla protein powder. These three nutritional powerhouses pack this smoothie full of complex carbohydrates and protein, which combine to give you increased energy and muscle functioning—and they taste amazing, too!

YIELDS: 2 CUPS

Ingredients

1 cup blackberries
1 cup vanilla almond milk
1 scoop vanilla protein powder
1 cup ice

1. In a blender, combine blackberries, almond milk, and protein powder with ½ cup ice and blend until thoroughly combined.

2. While blending, add remaining ice until desired consistency is achieved.

PER 1 CUP SERVING Calories: 136 | Fat: 2 g | Protein: 14 g | Sodium: 46 mg | Fiber: 4 g | Carbohydrates: 21 g

Super Smart Purple Tart

Ahhh, smart and delicious . . . breakfast can't get any better! Deep purple berries and sweet tangy citrus combine with creamy coconut milk for an antioxidant-rich blend of B vitamins and vitamin C that work to improve your immune system, help with mental clarity and focus, and give you sustained energy. At the same time, the belly-healthy fiber will keeps your digestive system on track!

YIELDS: 2 CUPS

Ingredients
1 cup bilberries
½ cup pineapple, peeled and cored
1½ cups coconut milk
1 cup ice

1. In a blender, combine bilberries, pineapple, and coconut milk with ½ cup ice.

2. While blending, add remaining ice until desired consistency is achieved.

PER 1 CUP SERVING Calories: 423 | Fat: 37 g | Protein: 5 g | Sodium: 29 mg | Fiber: 3 g | Carbohydrates: 24 g

Grape Greatness

Deep purple grapes combine with the subtle, smooth texture of banana for a beautiful tasty blend that gets even better with the simple addition of pure apple juice. With quercetin and anthocyanadins that work to boost your immune system, these beautiful ingredients make following a healthy diet easy—and delicious!

YIELDS: 2 CUPS

Ingredients
1½ cups Concord grapes
1 medium banana, peeled
1½ cups apple juice (organic and not from concentrate)
1 cup ice

1. In a blender, combine grapes, banana, and 1 cup juice with ½ cup ice, and blend until thoroughly combined.

2. While blending, add remaining juice and ice until desired consistency is achieved.

PER 1 CUP SERVING Calories: 216 | Fat: 1 g | Protein: 2 g | Sodium: 10 mg | Fiber: 3 g | Carbohydrates: 55 g

The Purple Care Bear

If you're not feeling 100 percent and need a little extra TLC, this is the perfect smoothie to try. With vibrant fruits packed with vitamin C and antioxidants, creamy protein-rich kefir, and probiotics that work to protect the immune system, this is a sure favorite for any patient feeling under the weather.

YIELDS: 2 CUPS

Ingredients

½ cup bilberries
½ cup blueberries
1 medium banana, peeled
1 cup blueberry kefir
1 teaspoon probiotic supplement
1 cup ice

1. In a blender, combine the bilberries, blueberries, banana, kefir, and probiotic powder with ½ cup ice, and blend until thoroughly combined.

2. While blending, add remaining ice until desired consistency is achieved.

PER 1 CUP SERVING Calories: 141 | Fat: 1 g | Protein: 8 g | Sodium: 95 mg | Fiber: 3 g | Carbohydrates: 28 g

Sweet Beets

You may not have thought to add beets to a smoothie, but you'll be surprised at how sweet and nutritious these veggies actually are. The truth is that beets are full of phytochemicals like *betalain*, which work to aid breathing and even help your heart's vessels and blood-pumping functioning!

YIELDS: 2 CUPS

Ingredients

1 cup boiled, peeled beets
1 cup coconut milk
1 cup ice

1. In a blender, combine the beets and coconut milk with ½ cup ice, and blend until thoroughly combined.

2. While blending, add remaining ice until desired consistency is achieved.

PER 1 CUP SERVING Calories: 251 | Fat: 24 g | Protein: 3 g | Sodium: 68 mg | Fiber: 2 g | Carbohydrates: 10 g

Blackberry-Banana Bliss

Designed to give you optimum nutrition in just a few ingredients, this blackberry-banana combo makes for a smooth sweet treat that's packed with all of the essential vitamins, minerals, and antioxidants that will keep you moving! With complex carbs for energy, antioxidants for cell health, and vitamin C for immunity, this is a delicious and nutritious smoothie that will optimize every aspect of your health.

YIELDS: 2½ CUPS

Ingredients
1 cup blackberries
1 banana, peeled
1 cup water
1 cup ice

1. In a blender, combine the blackberries, banana, and water with ½ cup ice, and blend until thoroughly combined.

2. While blending, add remaining ice until desired consistency is achieved.

PER 1 CUP SERVING Calories: 83 | Fat: 1 g | Protein: 2 g | Sodium: 1 mg | Fiber: 5 g | Carbohydrates: 20 g

Fruity Fig Blend

In this violet smoothie, figs blend with deliciously smooth banana and sweet blackberries for a flavor combination that puts a new twist on some favorite fruits! Packed with B vitamins, vitamin C, potassium, and anthocyanadins, this smoothie works hard to keep your immune system in tip-top shape. Enjoy this delicious blend as you sip your way to better health!

YIELDS: 2½ CUPS

Ingredients
1 cup figs, peeled and cored
1 banana, peeled
1 cup blackberries
1½ cups water
1 cup ice

1. In a blender, combine the figs, banana, blackberries, and water with ½ cup ice, and blend until thoroughly combined.

2. While blending, add remaining ice until desired consistency is achieved.

PER 1 CUP SERVING Calories: 111 | Fat: 1 g | Protein: 2 g | Sodium: 2 mg | Fiber: 6 g | Carbohydrates: 28 g

Fabulous Fig Fusion

Sweet figs sparkle with this spice-infused blend that packs tons of fiber and antioxidants, which combine to protect against illness while promoting regularity. All these health benefits are whirled up in a smoothie with a creamy taste that will take you by surprise!

YIELDS: 2 CUPS

Ingredients
1 cup figs, peeled and cored
1 teaspoon cardamom
1 teaspoon ginger
1 cup almond milk
1 cup ice

1. In a blender, combine the figs, cardamom, ginger, and almond milk with ½ cup ice, and blend until thoroughly combined.

2. While blending, add remaining ice until desired consistency is achieved.

PER 1 CUP SERVING Calories: 136 | Fat: 1 g | Protein: 1 g | Sodium: 46 mg | Fiber: 3 g | Carbohydrates: 36 g

Sweet Cabbage Collaboration

Cabbage: it's not just for coleslaw anymore! This recipe uses deep purple cabbage for its vibrant violet hues, loads of nutrition, and a delightful taste that's even better when sweet berries, smooth banana, and creamy coconut milk are added. In this smoothie, vitamins C and K and calcium and potassium work hard to benefit everything from quality cell production to stronger immunity against illness and disease. This combination of healthy ingredients truly is a delicious way to consume essential foods for better health—and to keep you drinking the rainbow, too!

YIELDS: 2 CUPS

Ingredients
1 cup cabbage
½ cup blackberries
1 banana, peeled
1 cup coconut milk
1 cup ice

1. In a blender, combine the cabbage, blackberries, banana, and coconut milk with ½ cup ice, and blend until thoroughly combined.

2. While blending, add remaining ice until desired consistency is achieved.

PER 1 CUP SERVING Calories: 299 | Fat: 25 g | Protein: 4 g | Sodium: 22 mg | Fiber: 4 g | Carbohydrates: 22 g

Pleasantly Prune

The pleasant taste of prunes gets a creamy texture in this smoothie from its pairing with the banana and coconut milk. Sweet, smooth, and packed with vitamins and minerals, this is one impressive smoothie that gets most of its attention for its rich fiber content. Helping the stomach by aiding in digestion, promoting regularity, and protecting the entire digestive system from invasive diseases like certain cancers, fiber is an essential part of any diet . . . and this smoothie provides a healthy helping!

YIELDS: 2 CUPS

Ingredients
1 cup prunes, pitted
1 banana, peeled
½ cup coconut milk
1 cup water
1 cup ice

1. In a blender, combine the prunes, banana, coconut milk, and ½ cup water with ½ cup ice, and blend until thoroughly combined.

2. While blending, add remaining water and ice until desired consistency is achieved.

PER 1 CUP SERVING Calories: 367 | Fat: 13 g | Protein: 4 g | Sodium: 10 mg | Fiber: 8 g | Carbohydrates: 69 g

Sweet Spiced Blackberries

Packed with protein, omegas, and tons of vitamins and minerals, this smoothie is sweet and spicy in a great way that will get your day off to a uniquely tasty, healthy start! And why shouldn't it? All of these nutrients combine to provide immunity-protecting vitamin C and antioxidants like anthocy-anadins that act as damage-correcting agents for otherwise healthy cells.

YIELDS: 2 CUPS

Ingredients
1 cup blackberries
1 teaspoon cardamom
⅛ cup ground flaxseed
1 cup almond milk
1 cup ice

1. In a blender, combine the blackberries, cardamom, flaxseed, and almond milk with ½ cup ice, and blend until thoroughly combined.

2. While blending, add remaining ice until desired consistency is achieved.

PER 1 CUP SERVING Calories: 367 | Fat: 13 g | Protein: 4 g | Sodium: 10 mg | Fiber: 8 g | Carbohydrates: 69 g

Blackberry Cream Dream

A different take on nutrition, this creamy concoction of antioxidant-rich berries, probiotic- and vitamin-rich kefir, and aromatic vanilla makes for a simple and delicious way to get major health benefits from a truly sweet treat. By combining ingredients that provide protein, probiotics, and antioxidants, this smoothie offers up a triple threat against illness while also working to boost your overall health.

YIELDS: 2 CUPS

Ingredients

1 cup blackberries
1 vanilla bean's pulp
1 cup blueberry kefir
½ cup water
1 cup ice

1. In a blender, combine the blackberries, vanilla bean's pulp, kefir, and ¼ cup water with ½ cup ice, and blend until thoroughly combined.

2. While blending, add remaining water and ice until desired consistency is achieved.

PER 1 CUP SERVING Calories: 106 | Fat: 1 g | Protein: 8 g | Sodium: 95 mg | Fiber: 4 g | Carbohydrates: 17 g

Blueberry Prunes Perfection

With fiber-rich fruits that offer up loads of B vitamins and vitamin C, magnesium, and fiber, this hard-working smoothie promotes the health of the immune system, the blood, and the heart—all while improving the functioning of your metabolism and promoting regularity. Each and every benefit offered up by this delicious smoothie is an essential aspect of good health that's easy to improve by sipping this sweet treat.

YIELDS: 2 CUPS

Ingredients

1 cup prunes, pitted
1 cup blueberry kefir
½ cup water
1 cup ice

1. In a blender, combine the prunes, kefir, and water with ½ cup ice, and blend until thoroughly combined.

2. While blending, add remaining ice until desired consistency is achieved.

PER 1 CUP SERVING Calories: 273 | Fat: 1 g | Protein: 9 g | Sodium: 96 mg | Fiber: 6 g | Carbohydrates: 64 g

Protein-Powered Prune Smoothie

This recipe improves upon the healing powers of prunes by adding imperative protein and probiotics to create a creamy blend full of health benefits and long-lasting energy that will keep your days—and you—moving smoothly!

YIELDS: 2½ CUPS

Ingredients

1 cup prunes, pitted
½ cup Greek-style yogurt
½ cup blueberry kefir
1 cup water
1 scoop of vanilla protein powder
1 cup ice

1. In a blender, combine the prunes, yogurt, kefir, ½ cup water, and protein powder with ½ cup ice, and blend until thoroughly combined.

2. While blending, add remaining water and ice until desired consistency is achieved.

PER 1 CUP SERVING Calories: 193 | Fat: 0 g | Protein: 10 g | Sodium: 48 mg | Fiber: 4 g | Carbohydrates: 41 g

Vibrant Violet Smoothie

In this vibrantly violet smoothie, absolutely beautiful berries, grapes, and figs are blended in deep blue kefir to create a creamy concoction that's both aesthetically pleasing and beneficial for your health. With probiotics that will help maintain a healthy balance of good and bad bacteria, this smoothie is a great addition to any diet in need of a little bit of a cleanse or healthy jumpstart.

YIELDS: 2½ CUPS

Ingredients

½ cup blackberries
½ cup Concord grapes
½ cup figs, peeled and pitted
½ cup blueberry kefir
1 cup water
1 cup ice

1. In a blender, combine the blackberries, grapes, figs, kefir, and ½ cup water with ½ cup ice, and blend until thoroughly combined.

2. While blending, add remaining water and ice until desired consistency is achieved.

PER 1 CUP SERVING Calories: 78 | Fat: 0 g | Protein: 3 g | Sodium: 33 mg | Fiber: 3 g | Carbohydrates: 17 g

Va-Va-Va-Voom Violet!

Creamy purple smoothies can be as beautiful as they are delicious and nutritious, and this recipe is no exception! Spiced with potassium- and calcium-rich cardamom, this smoothie blends the essential phytochemicals and antioxidants of deep purple fruits with the creamy flavors of banana and almond milk for a great taste that also works to help the blood, brain, and heart function properly.

YIELDS: 3 CUPS

Ingredients

1 cup Concord grapes
1 cup blackberries
1 banana, peeled
1 teaspoon cardamom
1½ cups almond milk
1 cup ice

1. In a blender, combine the grapes, blackberries, banana, cardamom, and 1 cup almond milk with ½ cup ice, and blend until thoroughly combined.

2. While blending, add remaining almond milk and ice until desired consistency is achieved.

PER 1 CUP SERVING Calories: 210 | Fat: 2 g | Protein: 3 g | Sodium: 70 mg | Fiber: 6 g | Carbohydrates: 55 g

Purple Plum Thunder

Plums and blackberries take on the sweet heat of ginger in this healthy concoction. Cooled with creamy coconut milk, this cocktail of insane ingredients is a delicious way to get your B vitamins, vitamin C, potassium, and antioxidants that work together to promote and protect your total health.

YIELDS: 2 CUPS

Ingredients

1 cup plums
½ cup blackberries
1 tablespoon grated ginger
1 cup coconut milk
1 cup ice

1. In a blender, combine plums, blackberries, ginger, coconut milk, and ½ cup ice, and blend until thoroughly combined.

2. While blending, add remaining ice until desired consistency is achieved.

PER 1 CUP SERVING Calories: 278 | Fat: 25 g | Protein: 3 g | Sodium: 15 mg | Fiber: 3 g | Carbohydrates: 17 g

Violet Velocity

With the addition of the carbohydrate-rich oats and omega-rich flaxseed, this vibrantly violet smoothie takes nutrition to a whole new level. Tasting great and packed with complex carbohydrates that provide long-lasting energy, this a delicious way to start your day off on the right foot and keep it moving in the right direction!

YIELDS: 2 CUPS

Ingredients
1 cup blackberries
1 cup blueberry kefir
½ cup rolled oats
⅛ cup ground flaxseed
1 cup water
1 cup ice

1. In a blender, combine the blackberries, kefir, oats, flaxseed, and ½ cup water with ½ cup ice, and blend until thoroughly combined.

2. While blending, add remaining water and ice until desired consistency is achieved.

PER 1 CUP SERVING Calories: 211 | Fat: 4 g | Protein: 12 g | Sodium: 96 mg | Fiber: 8 g | Carbohydrates: 32 g

Excellent Exercise Ender

If you work out, you know that sometimes you need to finish off your workouts with a snack that's brimming with protein. But instead of reaching for an exercise bar, finish up your bout of physical activity in a delicious, nutritious way! Brimming with tons of protein that will help your muscles benefit from your exercise in the best ways possible, this smoothie is the sweetest way to reward your workouts!

YIELDS: 2½ CUPS

Ingredients
1 cup Concord grapes
½ cup Greek-style yogurt
½ teaspoon cinnamon
½ teaspoon ground ginger
½ teaspoon cardamom
½ cup blueberry kefir
1 cup almond milk
1 cup ice

1. In a blender, combine the grapes, yogurt, cinnamon, ginger, cardamom, kefir, and ½ cup almond milk with ½ cup ice, and blend until thoroughly combined.

2. While blending, add remaining almond milk and ice until desired consistency is achieved.

PER 1 CUP SERVING Calories: 115 | Fat: 1 g | Protein: 7 g | Sodium: 71 mg | Fiber: 4 g | Carbohydrates: 25 g

Groovy Grape

Grapes get even greater when they're paired with the zippy addition of fresh, grated ginger. Powerful in taste, vitamin A, and anthocyanins, this delightful duo gets a creamy twist that makes for a pleasant smoothie that will clear your mind and provide everything your body needs for the healthiest of days! With vitamin A for eye health and anthocyanins for improved heart health and immunity, this is a delicious way to boost health with tasty nutrition.

YIELDS: 2 CUPS

Ingredients

1½ cups Concord grapes
1 teaspoon grated ginger
1 cup coconut milk
1 cup ice

1. In a blender, combine the grapes, ginger, and coconut milk with ½ cup ice, and blend until thoroughly combined.

2. While blending, add remaining ice until desired consistency is achieved.

PER 1 CUP SERVING Calories: 301 | Fat: 24 g | Protein: 3 g | Sodium: 17 mg | Fiber: 1 g | Carbohydrates: 24 g

Blended Beet Smoothie

In this simple smoothie, probiotics, vitamin B, and vitamin C join up with powerful antioxidants to create a healthy blend of everything necessary to keep your systems functioning how they're intended. Whipped up in a cool, tasty smoothie, this is a delicious way to get your daily dose of the rainbow!

YIELDS: 2 CUPS

Ingredients

1 cup beets, boiled and peeled
1 cup blueberry kefir
½ cup water
1 cup ice

1. In a blender, combine beets, kefir, and water with ½ cup ice, and blend until thoroughly combined.

2. While blending, add remaining ice until desired consistency is achieved.

PER 1 CUP SERVING Calories: 98 | Fat: 0 g | Protein: 8 g | Sodium: 147 mg | Fiber: 2 g | Carbohydrates: 16 g

Spiced Purple Pain Relief

Just the simple addition of cloves can take a plain old smoothie to a spicy extreme! In this recipe, sweet beets and creamy almond milk pair up with the scrumptious spice to create a delicious concoction of phytochemicals that double as disease-fighters and anti-inflammatory agents that can help take those aches and pains away.

YIELDS: 2 CUPS

Ingredients

1 cup beets, boiled and peeled
1 cup almond milk
½ teaspoon cloves
1 cup ice

1. In a blender, combine the beets, almond milk, and cloves with ½ cup ice, and blend until thoroughly combined.

2. While blending, add remaining ice until desired consistency is achieved.

PER 1 CUP SERVING Calories: 81 | Fat: 1 g | Protein: 2 g | Sodium: 99 mg | Fiber: 2 g | Carbohydrates: 21 g

Burst of Blackberry Energy

If you're looking for an outdoorsy flavor, this smoothie takes you there! As if blackberries weren't tasty enough on their own, this recipe adds in rolled oats and wheat germ to give this smoothie a granola taste that's made even better by the creamy addition of blueberry kefir. Simple, yet powerful, this delicious combo of B vitamins, vitamins A and C, protein, probiotics, and complex carbohydrates gives your body a burst of energy that lasts all day—in an easy-to-drink smoothie that tastes great!

YIELDS: 2 CUPS

Ingredients

1 cup blackberries
½ cup rolled oats
¼ cup wheat germ
½ cup blueberry kefir
1 cup water
1 cup ice

1. In a blender, combine the blackberries, oats, wheat germ, kefir, and ½ cup water with ½ cup ice, and blend until thoroughly combined.

2. While blending, add remaining water and ice until desired consistency is achieved.

PER 1 CUP SERVING Calories: 194 | Fat: 3 g | Protein: 11 g | Sodium: 51 mg | Fiber: 8 g | Carbohydrates: 33 g

Sinful Sweet Smoothie

Benefitting your body from the inside out, grapes have the amazing ability to fight cell damage from free radicals by providing plentiful antioxidants. Skin damage from the sun, pollution, and unhealthy habits can be improved with a smoothie recipe like this one that contains rich grapes, tart lemon juice, and pure maple syrup—all packed with antioxidants that remain untouched by harmful processing that can reduce their potency.

YIELDS: 2 CUPS

Ingredients
1 cup Concord grapes
Juice from ¼ lemon
1 teaspoon organic pure maple syrup
1 cup water
1 cup ice

1. In a blender, combine the grapes, lemon juice, maple syrup, and ½ cup water with ½ cup ice, and blend until thoroughly combined.

2. While blending, add remaining water and ice until desired consistency is achieved.

PER 1 CUP SERVING Calories: 63 | Fat: 0 g | Protein: 1 g | Sodium: 2 mg | Fiber: 1 g | Carbohydrates: 17 g

Sweet and Spicy Beet Treat

In this recipe, sweet beets are all spiced up with the zingy addition of ginger root. Packed with antioxidants like betalain, vitamins C and A, and nitric acid, which all come together to improve the quality of your blood and blood flow, beets and ginger root make for a powerful flavor and nutrition combination!

YIELDS: 2 CUPS

Ingredients
1 cup beets, boiled and peeled
1 banana
1 tablespoon ginger, chopped
1 cup coconut milk
1 cup ice

1. In a blender, combine the beets, banana, ginger, and coconut milk with ½ cup ice, and blend until thoroughly combined.

2. While blending, add remaining ice gradually until desired consistency is achieved.

PER 1 CUP SERVING Calories: 306 | Fat: 24 g | Protein: 4 g | Sodium: 69 mg | Fiber: 3 g | Carbohydrates: 24 g

Spicy Cabbage Concoction

Look out! This savory blend of deep purple cabbage, purple red onion, and spicy garlic makes for a hit of flavors that will liven your senses and get your blood pumping. Packed with vitamins, nutrients, and all of the wonderful antioxidants that make up the purple pigments, this savory smoothie will fit the bill when you're craving something with a kick!

YIELDS: 2 CUPS

Ingredients

1 cup purple cabbage
1 cup red onion (about ¼ of a whole large onion)
2 cloves garlic
1 cup water
1 cup ice

1. In a blender, combine cabbage, onion, garlic, and water with ½ cup ice, and blend until thoroughly combined.

2. While blending, add remaining ice until desired consistency is achieved.

PER 1 CUP SERVING Calories: 45 | Fat: 0 g | Protein: 2 g | Sodium: 10 mg | Fiber: 2 g | Carbohydrates: 10 g

Plentiful Prune Smoothie

Plump up the amazing nutrition of prunes with the added benefits of probiotics and probiotic-rich kefir. When combined, these ingredients work to keep your immune system at its peak performance level and help your body to maintain a healthy balance of good bacteria and bad bacteria. No doubt about it, this is a great smoothie that will keep your body at its toughest at all times!

YIELDS: 2 CUPS

Ingredients

1 cup prunes, pitted
1 serving probiotic supplement (see packaging for exact amount)
1 cup blueberry kefir
1 cup water
1 cup ice

1. In a blender, combine prunes, probiotic, kefir, and ½ cup water with ½ cup ice, and blend until thoroughly combined.

2. While blending, add remaining water and ice until desired consistency is achieved.

PER 1 CUP SERVING Calories: 273 | Fat: 1 g | Protein: 9 g | Sodium: 96 mg | Fiber: 6 g | Carbohydrates: 64 g

Beautiful Blackberry Blend

It's hard to beat the beauty of vibrant berries blended into a nutritious smoothie. In this recipe, the violet combination of sweet and tart blueberries and blackberries with thin rice milk makes for a feast for the eyes as well as for the body. Something this vibrant makes it hard to not want to drink the rainbow!

YIELDS: 3 CUPS

Ingredients
2 cups blackberries
½ cup blueberries
1 cup vanilla rice milk
1 cup ice

1. In a blender, combine the blackberries, blueberries, and vanilla rice milk with ½ cup ice, and blend until thoroughly combined.

2. While blending, add remaining ice until desired consistency is achieved.

PER 1 CUP SERVING Calories: 97 | Fat: 1 g | Protein: 2 g | Sodium: 33 mg | Fiber: 6 g | Carbohydrates: 23 g

Black and Blue Smoothie

Black bananas may not sound too appetizing, and blue bananas may sound just a little too strange, but when you combine the deliciously sweet flavors of blackberries, which offer lung protection, and blueberries (for mood enhancement) with the smooth taste of potassium-packed banana, you end up with a scrumptious, antioxidant-rich, black-and-blue treat you'll be happy to slurp!

YIELDS: 3 CUPS

Ingredients
1 cup blackberries
1 cup blueberries
1 banana, peeled
1 cup vanilla almond milk
1 cup ice

1. In a blender, combine the blackberries, blueberries, banana, and vanilla almond milk with ½ cup ice, and blend until thoroughly combined.

2. While blending, add remaining ice until desired consistency is achieved.

PER 1 CUP SERVING Calories: 135 | Fat: 2 g | Protein: 2 g | Sodium: 35 mg | Fiber: 6 g | Carbohydrates: 32 g

Friendly Figs for All

With the friendly fig packing tons of vitamins A and C, calcium, magnesium, and a host of phytochemicals that protect the nervous system, blood, and brain from dangerous free radical damage, this smoothie is as nutritious as it is delicious. You'll enjoy this sweet smoothie, which combines some very different flavors that end up coming together just beautifully in a sip-by-sip wonder of delicious nutrition.

YIELDS: 4 CUPS

Ingredients
1 cup figs, cored
1 pear, cored
1 banana, peeled
1 cup blueberry kefir
½ cup water
1 cup ice

1. In a blender, combine the figs, pear, banana, kefir, and water with ½ cup ice, and blend until thoroughly combined.

2. While blending, add remaining ice until desired consistency is achieved.

PER 1 CUP SERVING Calories: 110 | Fat: 0 g | Protein: 4 g | Sodium: 48 mg | Fiber: 3 g | Carbohydrates: 24 g

Sweet Berry Swirl

Creamy kefir and rice milk come together in this delightful, rich and creamy blend of beautiful berries. With an assortment of vibrant colors, each contributes its own unique health benefits, which range from respiratory improvement to improved blood cell production. This smoothie packs a health-promoting hit to your system—with the sweetness of creamy berry swirl.

YIELDS: 3 CUPS

Ingredients
1 cup blackberries
½ cup strawberries
½ cup raspberries
1 cup blueberry kefir
½ cup vanilla rice milk
1 cup ice

1. In a blender, combine the blackberries, strawberries, raspberries, kefir, and rice milk with ½ cup ice, and blend until thoroughly combined.

2. While blending, add remaining ice until desired consistency is achieved.

PER 1 CUP SERVING Calories: 91 | Fat: 1 g | Protein: 6 g | Sodium: 79 mg | Fiber: 3 g | Carbohydrates: 17 g

Purple Prunes and Cream

When you combine the delicious tastes of black-berries and prunes with blueberry kefir, you end up creating a sweet, creamy, purple treat that is loaded up with vitamins, minerals, and antioxidants that help you breathe easier, maintain regularity, and create a better balance of good and bad bacteria throughout the body. If you have a hankering for some creamy purple goodness, this smoothie is for you!

YIELDS: 2 CUPS

Ingredients
1 cup blackberries
1 cup prunes, pitted
1 cup blueberry kefir
½ cup water
1 cup ice

1. In a blender, combine the blackberries, prunes, kefir, and water with ½ cup ice, and blend until thoroughly combined.

2. While blending, add remaining ice until desired consistency is achieved.

PER 1 CUP SERVING Calories: 232 | Fat: 1 g | Protein: 9 g | Sodium: 96 mg | Fiber: 8 g | Carbohydrates: 51 g

Purple Pear

As if pears needed anything else to make a smoothie delicious, this purple creation ups the ante with the creative (and beautiful) addition of blackberries. Sweet, creamy, and with a back-ground flavor of delectable coconut milk, this is one smoothie that makes it easy to drink the rainbow!

YIELDS: 2 CUPS

Ingredients
1 cup blackberries
1 pear, cored
1 cup coconut milk
1 cup ice

1. In a blender, combine the blackberries, pear, and coconut milk with ½ cup ice, and blend until thoroughly combined.

2. While blending, add remaining ice until desired consistency is achieved.

PER 1 CUP SERVING Calories: 271 | Fat: 25 g | Protein: 3 g | Sodium: 15 mg | Fiber: 5 g | Carbohydrates: 15 g

Better Beets

In this unique recipe, sweet beets are jazzed up by the intense citrus flavor of a heaping helping of white grapefruit. Grapefruit can be a tart fruit, but puckering up for this smoothie is not necessary; the beautiful blend of these two delightful treats creates a balancing act for your body, mind, and taste buds.

YIELDS: 2 CUPS

Ingredients
1½ cups beets, boiled and peeled
½ grapefruit, peeled and deseeded
1 cup water
1 cup ice

1. In a blender, combine the beets, grapefruit, and water with ½ cup ice, and blend until thoroughly combined.

2. While blending, add remaining ice until desired consistency is achieved.

PER 1 CUP SERVING Calories: 64 | Fat: 0 g | Protein: 2 g | Sodium: 80 mg | Fiber: 4 g | Carbohydrates: 15 g

Blazing Blackberry Beets

Setting deliciously sweet beets afire, this smoothie blend also calls for the intense taste of deep purple blackberries, an aromatic intensity of unique spices, and the calming coconut milk that just makes it perfect! Beaming with beauty and immunity-boosting vitamin C, this is a spicy sweet treat that will blow your mind!

YIELDS: 3 CUPS

Ingredients
1 cup blackberries
1 cup beets, boiled and peeled
1 tablespoon grated ginger
1 teaspoon ground cardamom
1 cup coconut milk
1 cup ice

1. In a blender, combine the blackberries, beets, ginger, cardamom, and coconut milk with ½ cup ice, and blend until thoroughly combined.

2. While blending, add remaining ice until desired consistency is achieved.

PER 1 CUP SERVING Calories: 42 | Fat: 1 g | Protein: 7 g | Sodium: 71 mg | Fiber: 4 g | Carbohydrates: 25 g

Perfect Pear-Apple

Pears and apples in a smoothie; how much simpler can you get? But while this smoothie is straightforward, it's also absolutely delicious and packed with all kinds of great nutrition, including fiber, vitamins A and C, B vitamins, and phytochemicals, which guard against illness and disease. Add all these nutrients together and you get a simple, delicious smoothie that can help everything from breathing to cardiovascular health. Raise your glass and drink up!

YIELDS: 4 CUPS

Ingredients
2 cups blackberries
½ yellow apple, cored
½ pear, cored
1 cup blueberry kefir
½ cup water
1 cup ice

1. In a blender, combine the blackberries, apple, pear, kefir, and water with ½ cup ice, and blend until thoroughly combined.

2. While blending, add remaining ice until desired consistency is achieved.

PER 1 CUP SERVING Calories: 79 | Fat: 1 g | Protein: 5 g | Sodium: 48 mg | Fiber: 4 g | Carbohydrates: 15 g

Exciting Eggplant and Herbs

When you combine the delicious—and unique—taste of eggplant with herbs and garlic, you end up with a savory smoothie blend that makes for a delicious treat any time of day. Easy, convenient, and portable, this smoothie can function as a snack, lunch, or dinner . . . while providing vitamin A, iron, and potassium for better blood health and improved immunity, all in one great-tasting blend of flavors.

YIELDS: 2 CUPS

Ingredients
1 cup purple eggplant
1 clove garlic
1 tablespoon basil
1 tablespoon rosemary
1 cup water
1 cup ice

1. In a blender, combine the eggplant, garlic, basil, rosemary, and water with ½ cup ice, and blend until thoroughly combined.

2. While blending, add remaining ice until desired consistency is achieved.

PER 1 CUP SERVING Calories: 12 | Fat: 1 g | Protein: 1 g | Sodium: 1 mg | Fiber: 1 g | Carbohydrates: 3 g

Grainy Grapes for Great Health

The "graininess" of this smoothie may not sound appetizing, but the amazing taste combination of these three simple ingredients will leave you with a smile. The deep, vibrant Concord grapes in this recipe deliver amazing complex-carbohydrate benefits like longer-lasting energy, improved endurance, and mental clarity, as do the wheat germ and almond milk. Combining the three, you have a jam-packed, delicious smoothie that's designed to make you as healthy as you were hungry.

YIELDS: 2 CUPS

Ingredients
2 cups Concord grapes
¼ cup honey wheat germ
1 cup vanilla almond milk
1 cup ice

1. In a blender, combine the grapes, wheat germ, and almond milk with ½ cup ice, and blend until thoroughly combined.

2. While blending, add remaining ice until desired consistency is achieved.

PER 1 CUP SERVING Calories: 206 | Fat: 3 g | Protein: 5 g | Sodium: 50 mg | Fiber: 3 g | Carbohydrates: 49 g

GrApple Berry

There's probably a "fruit juice" on the market with this same combination, but this version is healthier . . . guaranteed! Packed with all-natural, fresh fruits, and creamy kefir, which contains probiotics and protein, this smoothie has all of the intense flavors of apples, grapes, and berries. Better yet, it contains all of the health benefits, including respiratory relief, blood health, and better brain functioning—and none of the unnecessary additives.

YIELDS: 4 CUPS

Ingredients
1 cup Concord grapes
1 yellow apple, cored
1 cup blackberries
1 cup blueberry kefir
½ cup water
1 cup ice

1. In a blender, combine the grapes, apple, blackberries, kefir, and water with ½ cup ice, and blend until thoroughly combined.

2. While blending, add remaining ice until desired consistency is achieved.

PER 1 CUP SERVING Calories: 95 | Fat: 0 g | Protein: 4 g | Sodium: 48 mg | Fiber: 3 g | Carbohydrates: 20 g

Get Going Grape Smoothie

If you're looking for a great breakfast to kick-start your day, you'll love this smoothie. Simple, sweet, and convenient, this recipe combines the luscious flavor of Concord grapes with added protein powder for a stimulating blend that will give you a long-lasting burst of energy without a crash . . . all whirled into a creamy almond milk blend.

YIELDS: 2 CUPS

Ingredients
2 cups Concord grapes
1 scoop vanilla protein powder
1 cup vanilla almond milk
1 cup ice

1. In a blender, combine the grapes, protein powder, and almond milk with ½ cup ice, and blend until thoroughly combined.

2. While blending, add remaining ice until desired consistency is achieved.

PER 1 CUP SERVING Calories: 209 | Fat: 2 g | Protein: 14 g | Sodium: 48 mg | Fiber: 1 g | Carbohydrates: 42 g

Pruney C Smoothie

This smoothie works to flush your system of excess with delightful prunes. Combine these tasty purple morsels with the citrus zing of orange and white grapefruit, and you have a crazy concoction of flavors that can only be mixed up with sweet, creamy coconut milk for an out-of-this-world taste that'll keep you moving *and* keep you healthy. Packed with vitamin C for improved immunity and antioxidant support, this smoothie tastes great and is the perfect answer if you're feeling "under the weather."

YIELDS: 2 CUPS

Ingredients
1 cup prunes, pitted
½ orange, peeled and deseeded
½ white grapefruit, peeled and deseeded
1 cup coconut milk
1 cup ice

1. In a blender, combine the prunes, orange, grapefruit, and coconut milk with ½ cup ice, and blend until thoroughly combined.

2. While blending, add remaining ice until desired consistency is achieved.

PER 1 CUP SERVING Calories: 391 | Fat: 24 g | Protein: 4 g | Sodium: 16 mg | Fiber: 5 g | Carbohydrates: 47 g

Appendix

At-a-Glance
Produce Chart

If you're looking for a quick and easy way to see what nutrients and benefits you can get from your favorite produce, you're in the right place. Here, you'll find info on all of the beautiful fruits and vegetables that color your delightful smoothie recipes. The fruits and vegetables are listed in alphabetical order for easy searching and you're able to see the color class, serving size, top three nutrients, and benefits of each fruit and vegetable at a glance. This list will help you simplify your smoothie making by choosing recipes that include your favorite fruits and veggies and creating simple grocery lists of those favorites you plan to use, saving time and money by reducing wasted ingredients and limiting trips to the grocery store! Happy smoothie making!

Produce	Serving Size	Color	Main Nutrients	Main Benefits
Acorn Squash	½ cup	Yellow	Vitamin A, vitamin C, potassium	Anti-inflammatory, antibacterial, and insulin-regulating capabilities
Apples	1 medium	White	Vitamin C, fiber, quercitin	Fights infection, satisfies cravings and gives a longer-lasting feeling of fullness, regulates bacteria in the large intestine
Apricots	1 whole/ ¼ cup dried	Orange	Vitamin A, vitamin C, beta-carotene	Protects eyesight by fighting degenerative conditions like cataracts, promotes immunity, and prevents free radical damage in healthy cells
Asparagus	½ cup raw/cooked	Green	Vitamin K, folate, saponins, fiber	Acts as an anti-inflammatory agent and an antioxidant, promotes regularity and colon health
Avocados	1 medium/ ½ cup chopped	Green	Lycopene, beta-carotene, healthy fats	Acts as a strong anti-inflammatory which reduces the symptoms of arthritis and the incidence of heart disease and blood vessel damage
Bananas	1 medium	White	Vitamin B6, vitamin C, potassium	Lowers blood pressure, protects against acid damage in the digestive system, and promotes regularity
Beets	1 large/ ½ cup cut up	Violet	Betalains, folate, manganese	Great detoxifier, prevents cell damage, and promotes immune system and eye health
Blackberries	½ cup	Violet	Vitamin C, calcium, anthocyanins	Fights off infection, promotes digestive health and improves regularity, prevents premature aging and degenerative diseases (for example, macular degeneration)

Produce	Serving Size	Color	Main Nutrients	Main Benefits
Blueberries	½ cup	Blue	Anthocyanins, vitamin C, manganese	Protects against free radical damage to cells and DNA, strengthens memory, and promotes nervous system and optimizes brain functioning
Broccoli	½ cup raw/cooked	Green	Vitamin K, vitamin C, fiber	Helps with iron absorption, promotes regularity, reduces cholesterol
Cantaloupe	½ cup diced	Orange	Vitamin A, vitamin C, beta-carotene	Promotes eye health, protects against free radical damage to cells, promotes immunity
Carrots	1 large/ ½ cup cut up	Orange	Vitamin A, vitamin C, vitamin K	Promotes cardiovascular health, protects eye health from free radical damage, and protects the colon against cancer
Cauliflower	½ cup cooked/raw	White	Vitamin C, vitamin K, folate	Aids in detoxification, protects against free radicals, promotes immunity, helps with iron absorption
Celery	1 stalk/½ cup chopped	Green	Vitamin C, potassium, sodium	Relieves fluid retention, prevents against free radical damage, and promotes immune system functioning
Cherries	½ cup	Red	Anthocyanins, vitamin C, fiber	Fights free radical damage and aids in cell repair, promotes respiratory health, and promotes regularity and optimal digestion
Coconuts	½ cup meat	White	B vitamins, vitamin C, fiber	Enhances immune system, promotes balanced mood, and aids in weight management by providing a lasting feeling of fullness
Corn	½ cup fresh/frozen	Yellow	Folate, thiamin, carotenoids	Protects against cardiovascular conditions, enhances quality mineral absorption, and regulates blood sugar
Cranberries	½ cup	Red	Anthocyanins, pro-anthocyanadins, vitamin C	Prevents UTIs by fighting "bad" bacteria overgrowth in the urinary tract, promotes immunity against illness and disease, and works to prevent gum inflammation and disease
Cucumbers	½ cup cut up/½ medium	Green	Lignans, vitamin C, potassium, silica	Boosts immunity and protects against free radical damage, aids in the prevention of premature aging, helps the body maintain proper hydration and internal fluid balance, strengthens hair and nails
Eggplant	½ medium/½ cup cubed	Violet	Nasunin, potassium, fiber	Protects against free radical damage and contains anti-cancer properties and antibacterial properties that work to fend off an overgrowth of "bad" bacteria

Produce	Serving Size	Color	Main Nutrients	Main Benefits
Figs	½ cup sliced	Violet	Potassium, calcium, fiber	Aids in mineral absorption, contributes to the strength of bones and teeth, and promotes regularity and health of the digestive system
Garlic	1 ounce	White	Allicin, vitamin B6, manganese	Acts as a powerful antibacterial agent, fights inflammation and prevents cardiovascular diseases, fights viral infections
Grapefruit	½ large/½ cup	Red	Lycopene, liminoids, vitamin C	Boosts immune system functioning, prevents free radical damage to healthy cells, and protects cells against various cancers
Grapes	½ cup	Violet	Anthocyanins, vitamin C, manganese	Promotes stable blood sugar levels, prevents insulin spikes, and promotes optimal cognitive functioning
Honeydew Melon	½ cup cubed	Green	Vitamin C, vitamin A, potassium	Promotes eye health, boosts immunity, can relieve respiratory difficulties
Kiwifruit	1 kiwifruit	Green	Vitamin C, potassium, vitamin E	Fights free radical damage of DNA molecules, reduces "bad" cholesterol (LDL) levels, and reduces symptoms resulting from respiratory conditions
Leeks and Scallions	½ cup chopped	Green	Allicin, vitamin C, fiber	Antibacterial, antiviral, aids in clotting and prevents platelets from sticking together
Lemons and Limes	1 medium	Yellow	Limonins, vitamin C, fiber	Fights inflammation; prevents swelling of joints, cardiovascular conditions, blood illnesses, and an overgrowth of "bad" bacteria; and boosts immunity
Mangoes	1 medium/ ½ cup chopped	Yellow	Beta-carotene, B vitamins, vitamin C	Protects eye health, prevents cataracts, enhances mood
Mushrooms	1 cup whole/ ½ cup chopped or sliced	White	Vitamin B, selenium, copper	Prevents free radical damage to healthy cells and may prevent overabundance of estrogen that leads to breast cancer, boosts immune system functioning, may aid in the prevention of diabetes and heart disease
Oranges	1 medium	Orange	Vitamin A, vitamin C, fiber	Promotes health of the respiratory system and relieves discomfort from respiratory conditions, boosts immunity against illness, and improves the regularity and health of the digestive system
Papaya	½ cup cut up	Orange	Vitamin C, folate, vitamin A	Promotes healthy eyesight, optimizes metabolic functions, and boosts immunity

Produce	Serving Size	Color	Main Nutrients	Main Benefits
Peaches and Nectarines	1 medium	Yellow	Vitamin A, vitamin C, fiber	Fights free radical damage, boosts immune system functioning, and protects eye health
Pear	1 medium	White	Vitamin C, copper, fiber	Protects immune system, reverses free radical damage, and helps protect against certain cancers
Peas	½ cup	Green	Vitamin K, vitamin C, manganese	Maintains balanced blood sugar levels, promotes heart health, and boosts immune system functioning
Pineapple	1 cup chopped	Yellow	Bromelain, vitamin C, vitamin B1, manganese	Boosts immunity, assists in the enzymatic activity in digestion, and acts as an anti-inflammatory agent
Plums and Prunes	1 medium	Violet	Vitamin A, vitamin C, fiber	Improves absorption of minerals (especially iron), promotes blood and eye health, and boosts immune system functioning
Pomegranates	½ large	Red	Vitamin C, potassium, anthocyanins	Improves immunity, reduces susceptibility to heart disease, relieves symptoms of Alzheimer's disease, and improves blood quality
Potatoes	1 medium with skin	White	Vitamin C, vitamin B6, copper	Provides energy for cells, aids in enzymatic reactions, and lowers blood pressure
Pumpkin	½ cup fresh/cooked/cubed/puréed	Orange	Beta-carotene, vitamin C, folate, omega-3 fatty acids (ALA)	Supports a healthy immune system, protects cells, acts as an anti-inflammatory agent, and assists in optimal brain functioning
Raspberries	½ cup	Red	Manganese, vitamin C, ellagic acid	Protects against free radical damage, prevents the growth of bacteria, and helps ensure a healthy immune system
Red Cabbage	½ cup chopped	Violet	Anthocyanins, vitamin K, vitamin C	Lowers cholesterol, prevents cancerous changes in cells, and acts as an anti-inflammatory agent
Red Peppers	½ large/½ cup	Red	Vitamin C, vitamin A, vitamin B6	Protects cells from free radical damage, balances blood sugar levels, and protects the eye from degenerative conditions
Romaine Lettuce	1 cup leaves	Green	Vitamin K, vitamin A, vitamin C	Boosts immune system functioning, protects eye health, and promotes heart and blood health

Produce	Serving Size	Color	Main Nutrients	Main Benefits
Spinach	1 cup leaves	Green	Vitamin K, vitamin A, folate	Works as an anti-inflammatory agent to promote cardiovascular health and relieve joint pain, protects against free radical damage, and helps improve bone health
Spirulina	1 serving	Green	Protein, essential and nonessential amino acids, chlorophyll	Improves cognitive functioning, boosts energy levels, helps with digestion and improves regularity, improves cell functioning, provides cancer prevention, and protects cells from free radical damage
Strawberries	1 cup	Red	Anthocyanins, vitamin C, manganese	Protects the body from cancer, promotes heart and blood health, and builds immunity against common illnesses like the common cold and the flu
Tomatoes	1 medium/ ½ cup diced	Red	Lycopene, vitamin C, potassium	Supports healthy functioning of the cardiovascular system, heart, and blood; prevents cancerous changes in healthy cells; and may reduce the incidence of neurological conditions like Alzheimer's Disease
Watermelon	½ cup diced	Red	Vitamin C, vitamin A (beta-carotene), lycopene	Relieves symptoms of respiratory conditions, reduces severity of arthritis, and promotes protein utilization and muscle repair
Wheatgrass	1 serving	Green	Vitamin A, B vitamins, calcium, iron	Improves mineral absorption, optimizes nerve impulses and brain functioning, and improves blood quality
Yams	1 cup cut up	Orange	Vitamin A, vitamin B6, vitamin C	Regulates blood pressure, maintains heart health, and enhances mood
Yellow Onions	1 medium/ ½ cup cut up	White	Quercitin, vitamin C, allicin	Acts as an anti-inflammatory agent, reduces "bad" (LDL) cholesterol levels, and reduces prevalence of cancerous changes in certain areas
Yellow Squash	1 medium/ 1 cup chopped	Yellow	Vitamin C, beta-carotene, zinc	Promotes a strong immune system, stabilizes blood sugar levels, and improves prostate health
Zucchini	1 medium/ 1 cup chopped	Green	Vitamin C, manganese, zinc	Protects cells from the free radical oxidation that can mutate healthy cells, helps the digestive tract fend off unhealthy bacteria, and supports prostate health

Index

About the Author

Britt Brandon, CFNS, CPT is an ISSA-certified Personal Trainer and Fitness Nutrition Specialist, competitive athlete, and award-winning competitive runner. As author of both *The Everything® Green Smoothies Book* and *The Everything® Eating Clean Cookbook*, she uses her education and experience in fitness and nutrition to adhere to a clean, natural diet and share information and tips on the lifestyle with others. She also prepares smoothies daily to promote the health of herself and her family, and attests to the dramatic improvement they can have on pregnancy, athletic performance, children, and even pets. She lives in Jensen Beach, Florida with her husband and three children.

Nicole Cormier, RD, LDN is a registered dietician and owner of the nutrition counseling company Delicious Living Nutrition. She is certified in adult weight management from the Commission of Dietetic Registry. She lives in Middleboro, Massachusetts.